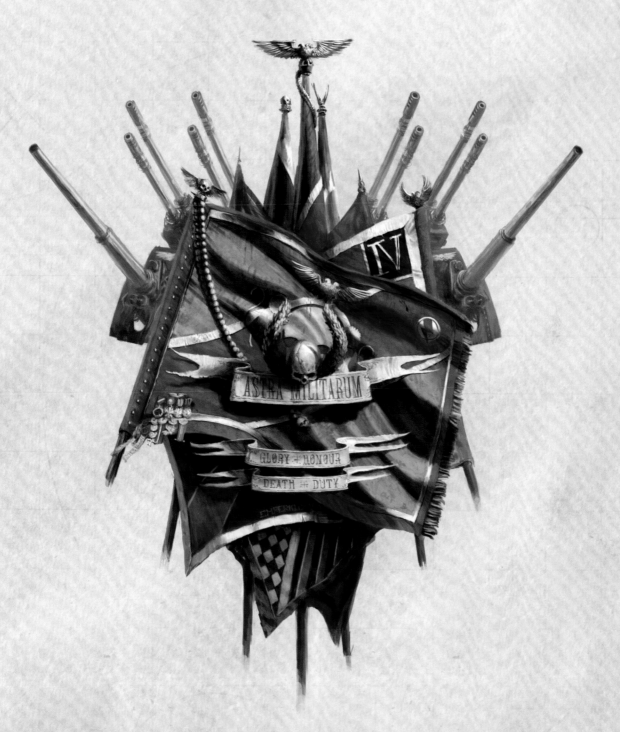

ASTRA MILITARUM

THE IMPERIAL GUARD

CONTENTS

PRODUCED BY GAMES WORKSHOP IN NOTTINGHAM

With thanks to the Mournival for their additional playtesting services

Games Workshop Ltd, Willow Rd, Lenton, Nottingham, NG7 2WS
games-workshop.com

INTRODUCTION

Attention, soldier! You hold in your hands the definitive guide to the battle-hardened regiments of the Astra Militarum. This book will help you to assemble your Citadel Miniatures and muster them into a powerful Imperial army, replete with ranks of dogged troops, bellowing officers and mighty engines of war.

The Astra Militarum is the implacable military arm of the Imperium, and one of the largest armies in the Warhammer 40,000 galaxy. Also known as the Imperial Guard, its ranks are filled with the heaving masses of Humanity who march in unending wars against the enemies of Mankind. Armed with grit, determination and sheer weight of numbers, these mortal soldiers face down the galaxy's greatest horrors, laying low xenos monstrosities and daemonic beasts with massed artillery, rumbling tanks and concentrated las-fire. Bolstered by mighty war engines, attack craft, psykers, priests, preachers and auxiliary abhuman troops, the Astra Militarum is as versatile as it is indomitable. With the Imperium shrouded in darkness, the Guardsmen of the Astra Militarum are called upon as never before to succeed in their grim and thankless duty.

In addition to their destructive capabilities on the battlefield, the forces of the Astra Militarum present a unique and enjoyable opportunity for any modeller and painter. As varied as they are numerous, the regiments of the Astra Militarum are drawn from planets throughout the Imperium, with each regiment's uniform and colours indicative of their native world and culture. Some fight in simple combat fatigues while others march to war in resplendent battle regalia. You can craft your army to be parade-ground ready, every lasgun and helmet polished and every tank and artillery piece immaculate; or you can depict the horrors of war endured by your troops through blood-splattered chainswords, blast-scorched armour plating and boots encrusted with the mud and muck of a dozen battlefields. There are many established regiments to choose from, or you are free to create one of your own.

Within this book you will find all the information you need to collect an Astra Militarum army and field it upon the tabletop.

THE HAMMER OF THE EMPEROR: This section details the storied history of the Astra Militarum and its ongoing wars in service of the Imperium, including accounts of some of its most famous regiments. It also provides an in-depth analysis of how Astra Militarum armies are organised for battle.

REGIMENTAL COLOURS: Here you will find a showcase of beautifully painted miniatures displaying the variegated ranks of the Astra Militarum, along with example armies to inspire your collection.

SOLDIERS OF THE IMPERIUM: This section includes datasheets, wargear lists and weapon rules for every Astra Militarum unit and model for you to use in your games.

BULWARK OF HUMANITY: This section provides additional rules, including Warlord Traits, Stratagems, Relics, psychic powers and matched play points, that allow you to transform your collection of Citadel Miniatures into an Astra Militarum army.

To play games with your army, you will need a copy of the Warhammer 40,000 rules. To find out more about Warhammer 40,000 or download the free core rules, visit games-workshop.com.

The Imperium is faced with manifold horrors. Xenos scum gather in hordes beyond counting, the taint of mutation blights the stars and every day heretics spread their corruption. But Humanity is also mighty, and its warriors many. The soldiers of the Astra Militarum are the Hammer of the Emperor, and by their deeds shall the enemies of Mankind be beaten down.

HAMMER OF THE EMPEROR

The Astra Militarum is the largest coherent fighting force in the galaxy. Billions of human troops, supported by legions of heavy armour and thundering artillery, the Imperial Guard fight a never-ending war for the survival of Mankind.

The origins of the Astra Militarum date back to the Great Crusade, when the Emperor conquered the stars and forged the Imperium of Man. On the front line of this mission of expansion and reclamation were the Space Marine Legions – the Adeptus Astartes – the finest warriors Humanity had ever created, each the equal of a dozen normal men. Despite their formidable battle prowess, the forces of the Space Marines were not limitless, and the relentless demands of building a galactic empire pushed the Legions further apart. Separated by countless thousands of light years, their presence became ever more scattered and dilute. The Emperor required more manpower to ensure the momentum of the Great Crusade did not falter, and so the Imperial Army was created.

The Imperial Army was a vital part of the expedition fleets sent out to claim the stars in the Emperor's name. Gargantuan numbers of brave troops – millions growing to billions of men, ranks of armoured battle tanks and mighty armadas of spaceships – were raised, all subordinate to the Legiones Astartes. At first, the Imperial Army was employed for garrison duties and to mop up resistance in the wake of the Legions, utilised where the back of an enemy was broken and compliance to the Imperium required only a watchful presence. Eventually, certainly by the time the Crusade reached the Eastern Fringe, the Imperial Army was deployed at the forefront of the Crusade, fighting alongside the power-armoured super-soldiers of the Adeptus Astartes. But everything changed when the galaxy was ripped asunder by the treachery of the Warmaster Horus, triggering a cataclysmic civil war that engulfed the newly founded Imperium.

In the aftermath of the Horus Heresy, the organisational structure of the forces of the Imperium were revised significantly. To prevent the possibility of large-scale rebellion occurring again, the titanic armies of the Imperial forces were divided. The Space Marine Legions were split into Chapters. The Imperial Army, as it was, ceased to exist. The link between fleet and army was severed; never again would ground commanders be given direct control over interstellar ships. From its ashes were born the Imperial Navy and

the Imperial Guard – known officially as the Astra Militarum. The Astra Militarum was reorganised into planetary-sized units known as Militarum Regimentos, which in turn were divided into regiments. Commissars of the Officio Prefectus were introduced to ensure loyalty and discipline. The interdependence of the newly formed Imperial Guard ensured that, should a regiment turn against their oaths, they would not be able to spread their treachery beyond a single world, and should a Navy fleet mutiny then they would not have the ability to re-supply or deploy ground troops. The Imperium had learnt a painful lesson from the dark days of the Horus Heresy.

STRATEGIC COMMAND

In theory, the Lord Commander of a Segmentum gives orders to various Sector officers, who in turn relay commands to the individual Militarum Regimentos. In this way the wishes of the High Lords of Terra are enacted by the Departmento Munitorum. In practice, the immense distances and delays in communication between worlds often makes a mockery of such procedures and the sheer scale of the Imperium prevents any meaningful central governance. Operational control of an army group is therefore assumed by a high-ranking Militarum Regimentum officer, such as a general, high marshal or even lord hetman, who assumes responsibility for the completion of their given duties. This might be the initiation of a decade-long conflict to cleanse a star system of savage greenskins, or it could involve the protection of adamantium mines or promethium refineries from pirate raids. Just as common are military recolonisations of planets lost from the Imperium's fold. Whatever the task, the commander of an army group is responsible for the deployment and application of all resources at their disposal – innumerable waves of infantry companies, ranks of battle tanks, batteries of artillery weapons, and a host of other tools of war.

Some commanders are hungry for glory and honour, establishing front-line headquarters and personally leading their men in battle. Banners and pennants proclaiming the officer's many deeds are carried by his entourage, emboldening his troops and filling his enemies with trepidation. Others consider their abilities far too important and valuable to be exposed to front-line conflicts. Surrounded by a host of advisors, data-globes and parchment-bearing servo-skulls, they direct their forces from the relative safety of an orbiting starship, a Proteus-class battle bunker or a lumbering armoured command vehicle.

There are very rare circumstances in which a higher level of command is necessary. In these times, the rank of Warmaster is bestowed upon a mighty and brilliant leader. This rank can only be conferred with the express consent of the High Lords of Terra, and such an individual is said to wield authority second only to the Emperor himself. Several centuries can pass without a Warmaster being appointed and, because of the unrivalled power of the position, there is never more than one in existence at any one time. Due to the stigma associated with the title thanks to the deeds of the Arch-traitor Horus, it is not uncommon for other titles to be used in place of Warmaster, such as Lord Solar.

THE DEPARTMENTO MUNITORUM

The Departmento Munitorum is the military arm of the Administratum and forms the general staff of the Imperial Guard. It is a mammoth bureaucratic organisation responsible for the distribution of all the Astra Militarum's resources. Perhaps its most important function concerns the monitoring of tithes and the raising and transportation of the Astra Militarum between war zones – for which it liaises with the Imperial Navy. Without the adepts and scribes of the Departmento Munitorum, the vast armies of the Imperial Guard would stagnate, and calls for aid would go unanswered. The mighty war-fleets of the Imperial Navy would not intercept enemy invasions, the armies of Mankind would never push back the relentless attacks. Slowly but surely the isolated worlds would fall, and the Imperium would ultimately be lost.

Despite its vital significance, the Departmento Munitorum is at best an unwieldy organisation. A plea for military aid may not be acted upon for months, years or even decades after it has been received. Such requests typically make their way through countless adepts before finally reaching the hands of one who can sanction suitable action, sitting at a dimly lit pulpit-station many hundreds of light years away. A battle group consisting of over a dozen regiments from Mordant and Tremert was raised to eliminate unknown xenos forces on the planet of Hurspraxia, only to arrive over a century too late, finding a lifeless world with no trace of survivors.

Organised at the sector and sub-sector level, every echelon of the Departmento Munitorum has enough autonomy to respond to problems within local star systems. With the vagaries of warp travel and communication, this is essential. Their smaller size allows the individual sub-sectors to respond to emergent threats more quickly and as such, when one comes under attack, an army group is formed from the regiments of all worlds in the local star systems.

When raising an army group, the Departmento Munitorum is responsible for munitions, supplies, recruitment, training, and support both medical and technical. The methods by which forces accumulate are haphazard at best; many thousands of troops from dozens of regiments across several worlds are raised and directed to the appropriate war zone. The unpredictable nature of the warp and the inherent dangers of interstellar travel are such that it is not unusual for entire regiments to be lost or even destroyed in transit. Some may be delayed by the ravages of warp storms or appear from the immaterium many thousands of light years from their destination. That sufficient troops and equipment arrive at a crisis point is only because of the sheer mass of manpower, weapons and vehicles despatched by the Departmento Munitorum in the first place.

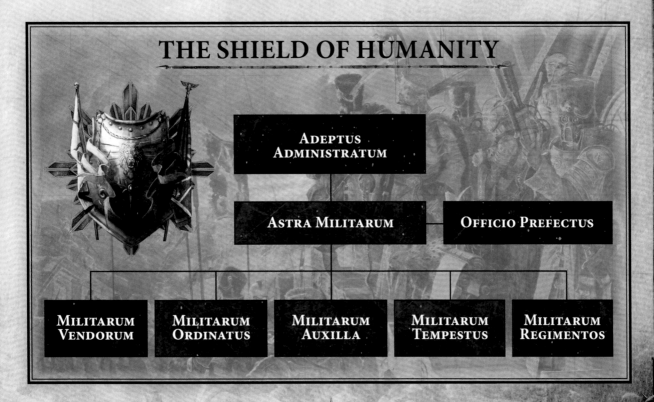

THE SHIELD OF HUMANITY

ADEPTUS ADMINISTRATUM

ASTRA MILITARUM — **OFFICIO PREFECTUS**

MILITARUM VENDORUM | **MILITARUM ORDINATUS** | **MILITARUM AUXILLA** | **MILITARUM TEMPESTUS** | **MILITARUM REGIMENTOS**

RECRUITMENT

Every Imperial Commander in the Imperium, also known as a Planetary Lord or Imperial Governor, is responsible for the defence of their world. This is crucial, as a planet may need to defend itself against the predations of myriad nefarious enemies for many months, or even years, before reinforcements arrive. To this end, they are duty bound to recruit, equip, train and maintain a fighting force. On some planets this may take the form of an official military or a garrison force. On other worlds the duty to defend their world may fall to dozens of separate armies, tribes and hive gangs, some of which may even be warring factions who unite to oppose an invading foe. In any case, these forces are unlikely to ever leave the confines of their home world.

Each of these forces is an individual body within the wider Astra Militarum – a separate Militarum Regimentum. They are free to defend their own world and enforce their own laws as long as these do not conflict with those of the Imperium, and so long as they pay their tithes. A part of the annual tithe that Imperial Governors must fulfil is to send one tenth of their overall fighting force, or more if the Departmento Munitorum deems it necessary, to fight the Emperor's wars throughout the galaxy. It is these tithed regiments that fight in the Astra Militarum's wars. The exact number of regiments that are to be raised for the Astra Militarum will depend upon the individual world's tithe grade and its proximity to hostile war zones. For a hive world such as Armageddon, caught in the throes of an all-consuming war, a draft of at least a hundred million men at arms and several million armoured vehicles is typical – a tiny fraction of the total populace which numbers in the hundreds of billions. A far-flung agri world may have a significantly lower military tribute – perhaps as few as five million men and cavalry – but this may be a significant proportion of the world's population. In any case, should a tithe be of an unacceptable quality, the Imperial Governor's life is forfeit. For this reason, those soldiers selected for the Astra Militarum tend to be drawn from the elite of a planet's troops.

> 'What I cannot crush with words I will crush with the tanks of the Imperial Guard!'
>
> *- Lord Solar Macharius*

Methods of recruiting vary from world to world. On the death world of Catachan, every man, woman and child is expected to serve in the Jungle Fighter regiments and, by extension, the Astra Militarum. On seething hive worlds such as Alcatran, it is common for entire generations to be drafted and sent to fight on distant worlds, the indentured gangs given the choice between volunteering or summary execution. On many planets service in the Imperial Guard is seen as noble and brings much honour to the ruling houses. Many young hopefuls, especially on industrial worlds and factory planets, flock to the world's military forces in the hope of being found worthy of the Imperial Guard – often the only chance of escape from their claustrophobic existence and endless work shifts. It is not unusual for the elite warriors of a planet to compete for promotion to the Astra Militarum. On some of the more savage frontier worlds, these competitions can escalate into affairs that claim as many lives as a small war.

Upon their initial founding, regiments are identified by the name of their home world and a number – for example, the Cadian 144th is the one hundred and forty-fourth regiment to have been raised on the fortress world of Cadia. It is not uncommon for a regiment's number to be recycled following its destruction, a new raising taking the designation of their predecessor. In this way the regiment is re-founded, the new recruits tasked with upholding its honour and traditions. Indeed, the Vintor 823rd serve the Emperor to this day, despite having been wiped out on more than nine different occasions in the span of a single decade. In addition, regiments are often given unofficial names, either inherited and therefore part of tradition, or else earned on the field of battle. For example, the Catachan VII 'Catachan Devils' Regiment take the name of the apex predator from the lethal jungles of their foetid death world, whereas the Cadian 8th 'The Lord Castellan's Own', honour the exploits of their former commanding officer, Lord Castellan Ursarkar Creed.

The uniforms and specific armaments of the different Militarum Regimentos change dramatically from world to world. Upon their raising, each regiment is equipped in the manner of their home world, each newly inducted Imperial Guardsmen issued with the same style of uniform and weapons as those of their fellow soldiers. Troopers may go to war in full battle-dress or little more than primitive armour and tribal tattoos. The only universal piece of equipment common throughout the entirety of the Astra Militarum is the lasgun. This weapon is cheap and easy to manufacture, extremely reliable and simple to maintain. The lasgun is therefore ideally suited to arm the massed armies of the Astra Militarum.

> 'I care not from which worlds my soldiers are drawn, only that they serve with unflinching loyalty. It is their duty to fight and to die so that Humanity may be preserved, and it is mine to see the enemy drowned in the blood of their sacrifice.'
>
> *- Lord Commissar Barron Reed*

REGIMENTAL ORGANISATION

Each Militarum Regimentum comprises multiple regiments, all of which come from the same planet. Because of the shared culture and fighting styles of regiments sourced from a single world, soldiers, officers and even officials of the Departmento Munitorum often interchange the term 'Militarum Regimentum' and 'regiment', referring to all Guardsmen from Cadia as being from the 'Cadian Regiment'. On their home worlds, the forces who serve to defend the planet may have been split into battalions, divisions, cohorts, militia groups, geno-corps and a host of other formations, but in the Astra Militarum these are all different types of regiment.

Although there are many different classes of Astra Militarum regiment, each one is largely uniform in its composition. Infantry regiments, for example, are unlikely to contain much or any heavy artillery, whilst tank regiments contain little or no infantry. Success requires Astra Militarum regiments to work together. Whilst this interdependence may at first seem like an inherent weakness, it is a necessary precaution. Should a regiment rebel against the Emperor, the traitors will not have access to the supporting units needed to prosecute a full-scale war. When the Ocanan 15th declared its allegiance to the Ruinous Powers of Chaos it had little in the way of either heavy armour or artillery support and was unable to compete against the 'combined arms' forces of the Cadian 17th armoured and Elysian 110th drop-troop regiments sent to eliminate them.

Regiments are typically raised with a strength of several thousand soldiers but the precise numbers can vary enormously. The Valhallan 18th 'Tundra Wolves' consists of over one hundred and twenty thousand men whilst the Vostroyan 24th 'Iron Bloods' armoured comprised less than one and a half thousand tank crewmen. Regiments of Baneblades and Shadowswords, each an armoured behemoth capable of laying waste to a small army by itself, rarely consist of more than a dozen super-heavy tanks. The basic principle held by the Departmento Munitorum is that regardless of the number of men at arms or the exact composition of armoured vehicles, the overall fighting strength – and hence combat effectiveness – of one regiment is equivalent to any other. This is clearly a gross oversimplification but a necessary one when organising wars on a galactic scale.

Astra Militarum regiments are divided into several companies according to a complex set of templates detailed in the Tactica Imperium, each placed under the command of a senior officer. The number of companies in a regiment depends upon the type and size of the forces at the commander's disposal, but may consist of as few as three or as many as twenty. Companies are themselves organised into several platoons, typically between three and six. Platoons are typically comprised of a Platoon Command Squad and several ten-man Infantry Squads – the most numerous of the Imperial Guard's forces.

Support units, such as heavy weapons platoons and much-valued specialist units, such as battle tanks, artillery, and abhuman squads, may be attached to a company for a single battle or the entire duration of a campaign. These are rarely permanent additions and are attached as needed by the regimental commanders. It is a common practice, especially amongst armoured and artillery regiments, to break down several companies and second them to infantry forces, granting heavy firepower to the platoons whilst providing troop support for the vehicles. If serving together for extended durations, attached units tend to adopt their foster-

'To see the enemy lines broken is not a victory. To watch them flee in disarray is a false triumph. When they lie crushed beneath our boots, ground into oblivion and unable to ever return, only then has the battle been won.'
- Company Commander Zamalod Chikova

regiment's uniform and unit markings. This not only helps to avoid friendly-fire incidents, but also aids in promoting comradeship with the soldiers they will be fighting and dying alongside.

DEPLOYMENT AND TRAINING

Should an Imperial planet come under attack and the local defences prove insufficient, an Imperial Commander is entitled to request aid from the Departmento Munitorum, whose primary response will be the deployment of the Astra Militarum. As war descends upon neighbouring systems new regiments will be raised and army groups formed, drawn from the resources of all nearby planets. When an army is assembled, regiments are drawn from many different planets, resulting in a conglomeration of uniforms and combat skills rather than a single homogenous force. Bio-screened techno-troopers fight side by side with primitive barbarians and noble-born soldiers rub shoulders with the lowliest gang fighters. When Waaagh! Grax invaded the Ryza System, all planets within ten light years were ordered to recruit and raise at least an additional fifty regiments as a primary reaction to counter the Ork invasion. Should the Imperium's response not prove to be decisive in crushing an enemy then the sphere around the conflict zone is increased in ever-larger increments, as reinforcements are drawn from further away and more regiments are raised to replace the losses. This ponderous process repeats itself until the enemy is ground down and destroyed, the massed forces of the Astra Militarum slowly pounding at the foe until eventually the hammer blow is delivered and all resistance is completely and utterly shattered. In this way, the harder a foe strikes at the Imperium, the greater its response will be.

Many of the newly raised regiments inducted into the Astra Militarum will already have some modicum of fighting experience. This may have taken the form of formal military instruction or simply be the result of the harsh conditions in which they live. Only the strongest survive the gang wars of the hive worlds, the tribal conflicts of medieval feudal worlds or the carnivorous predators that stalk the death worlds. In any case, during the long voyage between their home world and the regiment's destination, the newly inducted Guardsmen will receive intensive training that tempers the natural fighting skills of their many disparate cultures and forges them into soldiers worthy of the Astra Militarum. They are trained in the use of specialised weaponry and vehicles and receive proper indoctrination into the Imperial Cult. Officers are tutored in the broader aspects of the Tactica Imperium, all the while being judged under the vigilant gaze of the Officio Prefectus. The regiment will be drilled for many weeks before their trial by fire in the crucible of war. The training is also intended to adapt and, where necessary, re-educate the new recruits for the inevitable shock of fighting on foreign worlds. It is unlikely that a Guardsman from the monolithic spires of a hive city has ever seen the open sky, whilst those from a backwater agri world will never have seen the towering might of a mountain-sized basilica sanctum or set foot inside the twisting labyrinth of a sprawling factorum-city.

> 'Weep for him, for his faith was not sufficient.
> Rejoice for yourselves, for my faith is bottomless!
> Forward, for the Emperor!'
>
> - Commissar Krieglust

Should a regiment survive a campaign, it is unlikely that it will return to its home world, moving instead from one war zone to another. As casualties reduce the overall strength of fighting forces, regiments are often amalgamated together so that, united, they can continue to wage the Emperor's wars. Where possible, two half-strength regiments from the same Militarum Regimentum will combine, but it is not uncommon for two disparate cultures to find themselves brothers in arms. Many commanders declare that the reduced efficiency of these combined regiments makes them barely worth their rations, infighting and mistrust hampering their battlefield effectiveness. Other commanders are interested only in the number of men-at-arms that can be fielded, their successful integration as fighting units a secondary concern. A handful of particularly canny officers prefer to lead combined regiments, as they can harness the diverse skill sets and ingrained competitiveness of their soldiers.

If a regiment has been so badly mauled that it is considered a waste of time and resources to combine it with other Imperial forces, they may be assigned garrison duties on a nearby world, usually the very same planet they have been fighting over. The safety of the world and its population becomes the duty of the regiment's remnants. The garrisoning of such worlds is vital. After a brutal war in which the local defence forces are inevitably decimated and the government left in tatters, the small Astra Militarum contingent may be the only loyal force left to impose law and maintain control for many decades. In rare circumstances, a regiment may be granted custodianship over a world as a reward. The officers of such forces inevitably become wealthy and powerful figures in the society they maintain watch over, forming the new noble and ruling classes.

THE SCHOLA PROGENIUM

The Schola Progenium nurtures the orphan sons and daughters of Imperial officials from all over the galaxy. They are tutored to love the Emperor and to desire nothing more than to serve him and the Imperium to the best of their abilities. They tolerate no disloyalty and remain ever vigilant for signs of treachery. Many who pass through the hands of the Schola Progenium are initiated into the Adeptus Terra. Some find their way into the Inquisition, and the most studious and zealous are welcomed by the Ecclesiarchy.

For natural warriors, the Militarum Tempestus offers a place in one of the elite Tempestus Scion companies, where the training received is of a brutally high standard. A few individuals, those who are both natural leaders and are fiercely loyal, attract the attentions of the Officio Prefectus. Commissars provide the link between regimental officers and the Departmento Munitorum. They are tough, ruthless individuals whose primary responsibilities are to preserve the courage, discipline and loyalty of the regiment. Commissars have the absolute authority to punish and execute any member of a regiment who fails in their duties. As Commissars are not from the same world as the regiment they serve with, they are not coloured by that world's traditions and culture. Instead, a Commissar can provide an objective and unbiased viewpoint, one seen purely from the Imperium's perspective.

ASTRA MILITARUM COMPANY ORGANISATION

The composition of a company varies from regiment to regiment, even within the same Militarum Regimentum, but all contain a hierarchy of officers to direct the troops in battle. The two most common templates around which companies are formed are the infantry company and the armoured company.

INFANTRY COMPANY

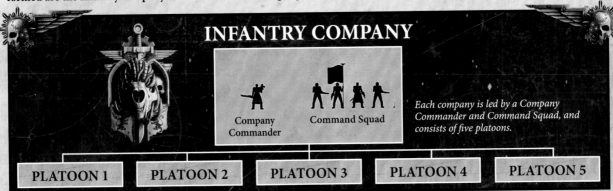

Company Commander

Command Squad

Each company is led by a Company Commander and Command Squad, and consists of five platoons.

| PLATOON 1 | PLATOON 2 | PLATOON 3 | PLATOON 4 | PLATOON 5 |

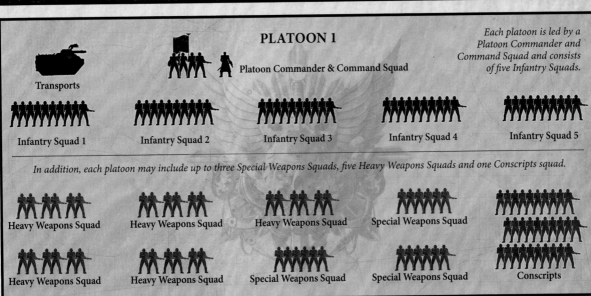

PLATOON 1

Each platoon is led by a Platoon Commander and Command Squad and consists of five Infantry Squads.

Transports

Platoon Commander & Command Squad

Infantry Squad 1

Infantry Squad 2

Infantry Squad 3

Infantry Squad 4

Infantry Squad 5

In addition, each platoon may include up to three Special Weapons Squads, five Heavy Weapons Squads and one Conscripts squad.

Heavy Weapons Squad

Heavy Weapons Squad

Heavy Weapons Squad

Special Weapons Squad

Heavy Weapons Squad

Heavy Weapons Squad

Special Weapons Squad

Special Weapons Squad

Conscripts

ARMOURED COMPANY

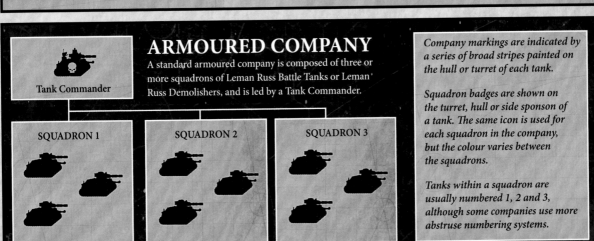

Tank Commander

A standard armoured company is composed of three or more squadrons of Leman Russ Battle Tanks or Leman Russ Demolishers, and is led by a Tank Commander.

Company markings are indicated by a series of broad stripes painted on the hull or turret of each tank.

Squadron badges are shown on the turret, hull or side sponson of a tank. The same icon is used for each squadron in the company, but the colour varies between the squadrons.

Tanks within a squadron are usually numbered 1, 2 and 3, although some companies use more abstruse numbering systems.

SQUADRON 1

SQUADRON 2

SQUADRON 3

THE ADEPTUS MINISTORUM

The essential remit of the great and glorious Adeptus Ministorum, or Ecclesiarchy, is the furtherance of the Emperor's veneration. Nowhere is this mission more important than in ministering to the vast ranks of the Emperor's armies. Many men of faith gravitate toward the Imperial Guard, where their presence is sorely needed both on and off the bloody field of war. Horrors untold bedevil the soldiers of the Astra Militarum, many of whom will barely have made peace with the concept of space flight before they are faced with the unspeakable heresy of the alien or the traitor. Mutation and abomination proliferate while men are slain in graphic and grisly fashion before the eyes of their horrified comrades. Often, the mere spectacle of the battlefields upon which the soldiers of the Astra Militarum must do their duty is so apocalyptic as to shake the reason of the bravest individual. In such circumstances, blind faith can be potent armour for a man's soul.

For this reason, the Ministorum maintains a considerable presence amongst the ranks of the Imperial Guard. Whether orating from the laudhailer-laden pulpit of a shrine-deck, or from atop piled ration crates in a hastily cleared corner of the soldiers' mess, Ministorum clergy have a huge impact upon the confidence and courage of their allotted flock. At the commencement of a campaign, most Guardsmen have been marched amongst thousands into the close-packed hold of a starship, surrounded by strange and often frightening sights and sounds. Their destination a tangle of mystery and rumour, their homes and families never to be seen again, such men find a refuge in the familiarity of Imperial scripture. Many newly founded regiments will cling to their religion like a drowning man clings to driftwood; it is the duty of the Ministorum to shape this fervour into something that high command can use.

If Guardsmen have questions or doubts, the Ministorum must bolster these unfortunates' shield of ignorance before they stray into the wilds of dangerous speculation. Should the slightest sign of warp-taint or heresy present itself – either within the ranks of the Astra Militarum or without – it is the role of the Ministorum to ensure this is swiftly dealt with. Nothing restores a soldier's faith faster than watching accused seditionists or mutants lashed to stakes and set ablaze for their sins. While such measures are doubtless draconian, none can question the Ministorum's flair for grand and faith-affirming spectacles, nor its value to the morale of the Imperial Guardsman.

> '*There are those who raise their voices in anguish and sorrow for the plight of Mankind. Such faithless folk wail of an end to all days, of a final damnation for us all. I say to you, these fools are wrong! Liars, I name them, heretics and sayers of doom. Listen not to such heathens, my brothers, for these are glorious days. Rejoice, for all may stand and fight for a truly righteous cause, and any man – no matter how humble – can earn everlasting glory through martyrdom in the Emperor's sight.*'
>
> *– Confessor Huldwyn before the Black Creek Massacre*

> '*For every unsettling sight the galaxy paraded before my eyes, still some of the strangest came from within our own ranks. Take the Tech-Priests for one. All glowing eyes and waving cables, nests of wires and wasted flesh. To think that any man might choose to do that to himself voluntarily – it fair sets my teeth on edge. And they're secretive too, always removed, always aloof. Dealing with them was tougher than getting a biletick off your boot. Yet for all that, my boys wouldn't have lasted a day in the field without the red-robes. Getting engines running again, fixing up weapons systems, calming angry machine spirits – they'd walk through fire to save one of their precious tanks, those Tech-Priests, even if they couldn't care less about the men inside.*'
>
> *– From the collected memoirs of General Kurtis Hicks, Catachan IV Army Group*

THE MECHANICUS AND THE GUARD

The soldiers of the Astra Militarum are not the only element of the Imperial war machine that requires the ministrations of a priesthood. The Adeptus Mechanicus are masters of arcane automation and technological mysticism, who look to the provision and well-being of the Astra Militarum's countless engines of war. Without these lore-keepers of high technology there would be no ships to carry the Astra Militarum between worlds, and no weapons with which to hold back the countless foes that seek to overwhelm Mankind.

Astra Militarum vehicles and equipment fall into two basic categories. The majority of their materiel is bulk-manufactured on an immense, relentless scale on industrial worlds throughout the Imperium. Some planets specialise in a particular pattern of vehicle or weapon, such as Armageddon, with its vast Chimera manufactories, or Sanctus Valorium, with its renowned las-craft workshops. Others, like Parabellus III or Kogen's Toil, are equipped to turn out the range of tanks, guns and munitions that the Emperor's many wars demand. To supplement this endless tide of ruggedly built basic equipment, Mechanicus forge worlds will, on occasion, provide complements of far rarer war machines to aid their Imperial allies. Such vehicles incorporate the higher mysteries of the Omnissiah. The templates to construct these machines may only exist enshrined upon a single forge world, or may have been lost altogether, making deployment of these relics of war a decision of some weight.

Tech-Priest Enginseers are the members of the Adeptus Mechanicus most commonly seen within the ranks of the Astra Militarum. These cybernetic holy men stand aloof from the Guardsmen that surround them, concerned only with tending to the machine spirits of their foster-regiment's vehicles and weaponry. It is their responsibility to see to it that all the proper rites and rituals are performed before a tank or artillery unit goes to war, as well as to ensure that it comes back in one piece. There are other, rarer, classes of Tech-Priest who aid the Astra Militarum at war. Tacticus Cognosavants sit amid octopoidal tangles of cabling, deep within the bridges of Leviathan Command Crawlers. Logisticus Adepts assist the coordination of Munitorum supply-lines, their servo-scribe harnesses spewing kilometres of parchment every hour. Communication equipment, tactical hololiths, support servitors and countless other vital high command assets are provided by the Mechanicus and continue to function only through the diligence of the mysterious Tech-Priests.

MILITARUM AUXILLA

When Mankind first spread out amongst the stars, they voyaged to the furthest corners of the galaxy. Worlds were settled with diverse and unusual environmental conditions that were to shape and change the peoples that called them home. After the Age of Strife, as the Imperium regained contact with the scattered seeds of Humanity, they discovered human populations who had devolved into entirely separate subspecies. Some of these were freakishly altered or irredeemably hostile, and deserved only swift and total annihilation. A few, most notably the lumbering Ogryns and keen-eyed Ratlings, were accepted into the Imperial fold, albeit with hesitance and distaste. These races are known as abhumans, and their thinly spread populations contribute regiments to the Militarum Auxilla.

The small numbers and specialised abilities of abhuman soldiers mean that Ogryn and Ratling regiments are almost always split for distribution to more conventional Astra Militarum formations. Abhumans evoke revulsion in their genetic cousins, for whom the degenerate inhumanity of their forms is only a step from the heresy of mutation. They must be constantly watched by Commissars and Priests alike for any signs of excess deviancy, and are taught self-disgust and a desire to atone for their failures of birth through honest toil in the Emperor's name. However, these squads have proven their worth time and again. Such units as Magogg's Ratling Rifles in the Damocles Crusade, and the Anark Zeta 88th Bullgryn regiment who carried the breach during the siege of Gregoria, have won great fame.

THE SCHOLASTICA PSYKANA

There are those whose value to the Astra Militarum outweighs the rabid moral repugnance they evoke. Most notable amongst these are the warp-sensitive psykers of the Scholastica Psykana. The untrained psyker is a beacon to the Daemons of the warp, his lack of control and improper absence of self-loathing presenting a deadly danger to all. To counter such hazards, the Black Ships of the Inquisition ply the space lanes of the Imperium, endlessly harvesting nascent psykers and proven witches to take back to Terra for assessment and classification. The fate of many is to feed the infernal mechanisms of the Golden Throne or be yoked to the blazing beacon of the Astronomican. The most stable find a different calling, fighting amongst the ranks of the Astra Militarum as Wyrdvane Psykers, Primaris Psykers and Astropaths.

There are numerous Scholastica Psykana training facilities in remote locations across the Imperium, isolated from populated systems and known warp anomalies. Security at such facilities is nigh impenetrable, intended as much to keep the students in as to ensure outside threats are repulsed. Within the austere surroundings of these psionically shielded scholas, the sanctioned psykers meditate. They gain understanding of their potent abilities, learning how they may control them to better serve the forces of the Imperium. Alongside their mental and spiritual training, those psykers marked for service are taught the basics of close-quarters combat and battlefield survival, but it is the warp-fuelled devastation these individuals can unleash that has won the Astra Militarum so many battles.

The Astra Militarum's might is drawn from the many and varied facets of Humanity. For it to function in serving the will of the Emperor requires unflinching faith, discipline and vigilance.

DEPLOYED FOR WAR

Each Imperial regiment is a powerful combat force, but it is only when the constituent infantry platoons and tank squadrons are fielded together on the battlefield that the deadly potency of the Astra Militarum is truly realised. Lasguns, battle cannons and devastating ordnance fire in coordinated salvoes to eradicate the enemies of Humanity.

The organisational structures of the Astra Militarum are based upon the Tactica Imperium, which groups squads together based on their categorisation. Infantry platoons are pooled together in infantry companies, which then make up infantry regiments, and similarly tank squadrons are grouped into tank regiments comprised of tank companies. However, the many varied demands and challenges of war usually mean that these structural theories cannot be applied on the battlefield. Instead, the various constituent parts of each regiment are often reorganised into much more varied and versatile deployments.

ORDER OF BATTLE

The war zones of the Imperium are as diverse as they are numerous. Some are grinding battles of brute force and attrition, whereas others require guileful feints and swift redeployments. Where one war zone may call for a mechanised advance over a barren planetscape, another will require infiltration into a Heretic-infested hive city. The multifaceted nature of the Astra Militarum allows battle groups to be effectively deployed against all the multifarious enemies of Humanity. The separate components of a Militarum Regimentum are drawn together to form a cohesive fighting force, and if an operational commander can successfully navigate the bureaucracy of the Departmento Munitorum, these battle groups can be tailored to the specific enemies and environments they must face.

A strict hierarchy of officers directs these forces on the battlefield. Terms and naming conventions vary from regiment to regiment, and while the regimental commander is normally a colonel, the military culture from which they are drawn might use an entirely different term. A Militarum Regimentum might be led by a 'Knight Commander' or a 'Chief Hetman', whereas the commander of a company could have the title of 'Taxiarchos' or 'Marzban'.

When an 'all-arms' force is required, units are drafted from the available regiments and placed under the command of a senior officer, such as a colonel or a captain. These battle groups can vary in size, from units of a hundred or so soldiers and five or six vehicles, to a force almost as large as a single regiment. Some are a balanced mix of infantry and vehicles. Many, however, are highly specialised, designed to meet very specific tactical challenges. A battle group might consist of Chimera-mounted infantry and self-propelled artillery assigned to support a lightning-fast armoured breakthrough, or it may be an entire Sentinel company aiding a light infantry force in a jungle fight. Other battle groups are even more specialised, drawing together multiple tank and artillery squadrons to form an entirely armoured force. A 'standard' battle group might comprise multiple infantry companies supplemented by several armoured, artillery and support companies. These can then be fielded in multiple detachments, each of which can have support personnel and materiel seconded from one of the other branches of the Departmento Munitorum, such as the Militarum Auxilla or the Officio Prefectus.

On occasion, a lighter Astra Militarum force may be called for. In such cases, individual detachments are deployed. These small-scale forces adhere to the same hierarchy of command as the larger battle groups, with a Platoon Commander, Tank Commander or possibly even a Lord Commissar operating as the ranking officer. Similarly, these detachments can contain infantry, tanks, artillery or a combination thereof. A single detachment can be outfitted to engage a range of enemies on the battlefield, or it can be equipped to deal with a single, specific set of targets.

Just as battle groups are comprised of several detachments, so too can several battle groups be drawn together into a huge, operational-level force known as an army group. These are led by high-ranking commanders such as generals and high marshals, and will typically contain battle groups from multiple Militarum Regimentos – sometimes as few as two, but on occasion many hundreds.

The method by which forces accumulate at a war zone is haphazard at best, with thousands upon thousands of troops from many dozens of regiments sent upon the alarm being raised. The commanders of the Astra Militarum are more than familiar with the perils of warp travel, which might delay or destroy vast portions of the forces they send to a rally point. As such, where possible, the number of regiments despatched to a war zone will be far in excess of the number needed to achieve victory, increasing the odds that sufficient troops will arrive in time. Meanwhile, the high commander overseeing the battlefield can rarely craft a strategy before knowing which resources they will receive, and will instead have to improvise a battle plan based upon the troops at their disposal. That they are able to do this successfully is partly due to the versatility of Imperial combat doctrine, but more so to the sheer weight of manpower and materiel at their disposal.

With enough perseverance, even the application of an unsuitable tool can reap dividends – particularly if the commander is unconcerned as to how many such tools are destroyed in the process.

> 'What does it matter that our world loses an entire generation in battle, if by not losing it our world has no more generations at all?'
> - Imperial Commander Abrhest Kohlt on the mass conscriptions of Durant III.

Once the army group has been assembled, it operates on the same principle as a battle group, but on a far larger scale. Entire echelons of tanks advance under the thunderous covering fire of a hundred Basilisk self-propelled guns, supported by wave after wave of infantry. While a battle group is capable of securing a single objective, an army group can be used to take and hold an entire planet or even star system, and few enemies of the Imperium are capable of mustering a force able to withstand it.

REGIMENTAL ORGANISATION

Regiments of all types can vary enormously in size and composition. As squads, companies, and entire regiments drop below strength due to battle attrition many undersized formations are merged to create composite groups. In this way the force organisations shown here are more ideal than practical, as few such orderly formations survive the crucible of battle. Shown here are two example regiments from the Cadian defence forces that defended their home world against the thirteenth Black Crusade.

CADIAN 24th ARMOURED REGIMENT
'The Emperor's Thunder'

COMMAND COMPANY
1 Leman Russ,
1 Chimera

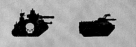

During the Kasr Gehr battles, the Cadian 24th Armoured Regiment was commanded by Colonel Polski. Depending on his needs, Colonel Polski had at his disposal both a command Leman Russ and Chimera.

3rd COMPANY
'The Bunker Busters'
10 Demolishers

2nd COMPANY
'The Steel Avengers'
10 Leman Russ

1st COMPANY
'The Fighting First'
10 Leman Russ

1st HEAVY COMPANY
Steel Faith – Baneblade

The 24th Armoured Regiment had also been assigned the following support units directly under the command of Colonel Polski:

RECON SQUADRON
'Seek & Sneak'

3 Sentinels – The eyes and ears of the armoured columns.

ANTI-AIRCRAFT SQUADRON
'Cloud Shredders'

3 Hydras – The mobile air defence for the entire regiment.

CADIAN 180th INFANTRY REGIMENT

COMMAND COMPANY

The 180th Infantry Regiment was assigned under Colonel Lansted to support the 24th Armoured Regiment. The infantry's role was to ensure territory gained during armoured breakthroughs was cleared and held at all costs.

3rd COMPANY

2nd COMPANY

1st COMPANY

COMPANY COMMAND SQUAD & COMPANY COMMANDER

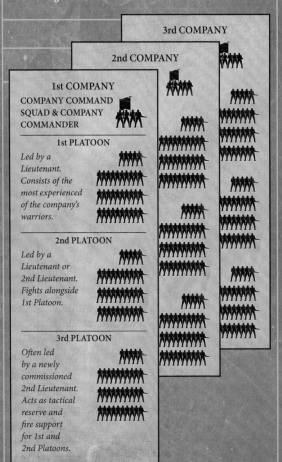

1st PLATOON

Led by a Lieutenant. Consists of the most experienced of the company's warriors.

2nd PLATOON

Led by a Lieutenant or 2nd Lieutenant. Fights alongside 1st Platoon.

3rd PLATOON

Often led by a newly commissioned 2nd Lieutenant. Acts as tactical reserve and fire support for 1st and 2nd Platoons.

OFFICIO PREFECTUS

18 Commissars under Senior Commissar Chaonian

MILITARUM AUXILLA

3 Ogryn squads under Commissar Raven

MINISTORUM

83 Preachers, 101 menials

SCHOLASTICA PSYKANA

9 Wyrdvane Psykers

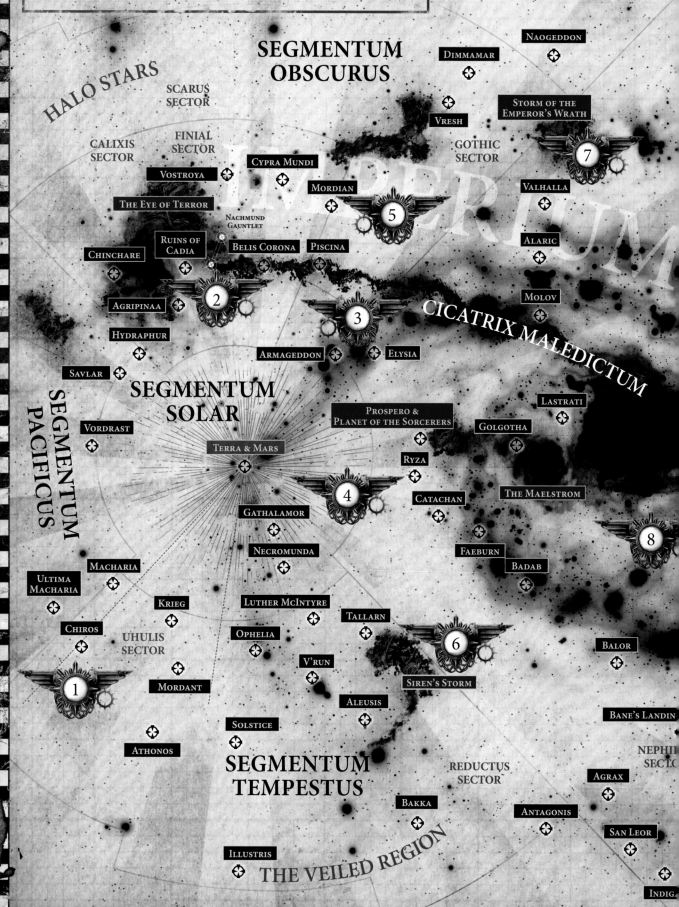

A GALAXY OF WAR

Departmento Munitorum Resource 88 4X/423 – map used by Knight Commander Pask after the fall of Cadia.

SEGMENTUM OBSCURUS

HALO STARS

SCARUS SECTOR

NAOGEDDON

DIMMAMAR

VRESH

STORM OF THE EMPEROR'S WRATH

7

CALIXIS SECTOR

FINIAL SECTOR

GOTHIC SECTOR

CYPRA MUNDI

VOSTROYA

MORDIAN

VALHALLA

THE EYE OF TERROR

5

Nachmund Gauntlet

ALARIC

RUINS OF CADIA

BELIS CORONA

PISCINA

CHINCHARE

MOLOV

2

3

CICATRIX MALEDICTUM

AGRIPINAA

HYDRAPHUR

ARMAGEDDON

ELYSIA

SEGMENTUM SOLAR

SAVLAR

LASTRATI

PROSPERO & PLANET OF THE SORCERERS

SEGMENTUM PACIFICUS

VORDRAST

GOLGOTHA

TERRA & MARS

RYZA

THE MAELSTROM

GATHALAMOR

4

CATACHAN

8

NECROMUNDA

FAEBURN

MACHARIA

BADAB

ULTIMA MACHARIA

KRIEG

LUTHER McINTYRE

CHIROS

TALLARN

BALOR

UHULIS SECTOR

OPHELIA

6

MORDANT

V'RUN

1

SIREN'S STORM

BANE'S LANDIN

ALEUSIS

SOLSTICE

NEPHIL SECTO

ATHONOS

REDUCTUS SECTOR

AGRAX

SEGMENTUM TEMPESTUS

BAKKA

ANTAGONIS

SAN LEOR

ILLUSTRIS

THE VEILED REGION

INDIG.

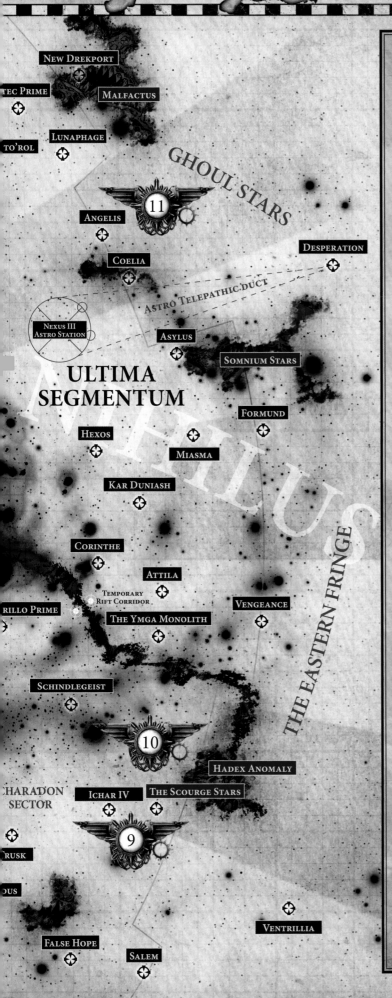

1 **Massed Uprising:** Directed by Inquisitors of the Ordo Hereticus and Ordo Xenos, the Astra Militarum battles to quash the Genestealer Cults emerging across multiple systems in the galactic south-west.

2 **The Cadian Gate:** Even after the fall of Cadia itself, the surrounding systems of Belis Corona and Agripinaa yet stand. Those few regiments who survived Cadia's sundering battle to hold back the tides of Chaos as reinforcements on both sides continue to pour into the war zone.

3 **The Stand at Armageddon:** Already entrenched against invading greenskin hordes, the embattled hive world is now beset by Daemons. Though reinforcements were temporarily halted during the Noctis Aeterna, more and more regiments are now mustering along the hive ramparts and in the choking ash wastes.

4 **The Indomitus Crusade:** The risen Primarch Roboute Guilliman has set out from Holy Terra to purge the Imperium of those who follow the Dark Gods. Upon reaching Catachan, he finds that the regiments of the death world have already scoured their planet of the Chaos taint, and so join Guilliman's expedition.

5 **War Zone Stygius:** Daemons of Tzeentch have invaded Stygius in the wake of the Great Rift's opening. Though the Mordians still fight, entire regiments have been lost, including the Necromundan 44th 'Spirehawks', who were sucked into an empyric vortex.

6 **Outbreak Arcanum:** Daemonic spores from the space hulk *Mother of Miseries* land on dozens of worlds, unleashing the Eater of Lives plague. The Astra Militarum fights to aid the Ordo Sepulturum in containing the outbreak, even as entire regiments are reduced to fleshy, bubbling slime by the sentient pox.

7 **Path to Valhalla:** Ork warbands continue to gather strength. Only through the immense sacrifices of Valhallan-led army groups are they held at bay.

8 **Hungering Tendrils:** Tyranid splinter fleets spew forth from clustered warp storms. Devouring all in their path, they threaten to occlude the passage of fleet-bound army groups en route to the numerous war zones that lie along the Great Rift.

9 **War Zone Ultramar:** Dozens of Astra Militarum army groups are drawn from across the Imperium to fight alongside the Ultramarines and the standing Ultramar Auxilia, as the Death Guard – led by the Daemon Primarch Mortarion – sow hideous plagues across the entire sub-sector.

10 **War Zone Damocles:** The Damocles Gulf burns as the combined forces of the Imperium strive to eradicate the T'au interlopers. Cadian infantry, armoured and artillery regiments fight alongside the Raven Guard, Adeptus Mechanicus and Imperial Knights.

11 **Alone in the Dark:** Thousands of Militarum Regimentos remain cut off from the guiding light of the Astronomican. Entire army groups are lost as they attempt to blindly navigate the roiling warp, devoured by the fell powers of the immaterium or cast light years off course. Others desperately try to defend their systems against encroaching xenos and Chaos forces.

CADIA

For thousands of years, the people of Cadia have known nought but war. Fighting always to hold back the infernal hosts of Chaos that pour from the Eye of Terror, they have evolved into a robust warrior culture. All Cadians – no matter their age, gender or station – must know how to fight, and be capable of facing with unwavering courage all the horrors that proliferate in the 41st Millennium.

> *'Though our tanks and artillery are mighty, it is the vast ranks of Imperial Guardsmen that shall trample the enemy to dust – let them come.'*
> - Lord Castellan Ursarkar E. Creed

The birth and recruitment rates on Cadia were ever synonymous, with each generation undergoing total military indoctrination. By the age of five most Cadians learn to strip and reassemble a lasgun. By six, most are deadly shots, and before their seventh birthdays they receive a no-nonsense introduction to the perils of psyker-taint and mutation. This approach leaves Cadian youths mentally and spiritually fortified, with a grim acceptance of things that would send lesser humans screaming in terror. By the age of sixteen all Cadians are adept in endurance training, weapons handling, hand-to-hand combat, and vehicular and chemical warfare drills, and are raring to prove themselves in the Cadian youth army. These so-called Whiteshields are comparable to the conscripts of many worlds, recognisable by the thick white stripe that runs front-to-back on their helms.

The infantry regiments of Cadia are known as Shock Troops, and are believed by many to be without equal in the entirety of the Imperial Guard. Displaying enviable levels of discipline, excellent marksmanship, and a cynical gallows humour, Cadian foot soldiers hold true to the tenet that to do your best and give your life for the Emperor is the highest form of honour. The same unflinching loyalty and martial prowess are found amongst Cadia's armoured and artillery regiments. The endless load-fire-reload drills the gunners and tank crews of Cadia are taught to master make them nigh unstoppable on the battlefield, their guns capable of pounding even the most monstrous enemies to dust. Whether fielded independently or as mixed-arms battle groups, the regiments of Cadia are famed for their effectiveness and discipline, overlapping fields of precision fire obliterating any foe caught helplessly in their path.

It was on Cadia itself, during the Thirteenth Black Crusade of Abaddon the Despoiler, that the legendary Cadian resolve was put to its most gruelling test. Long foreseen by mystics and strategists alike, the onslaught from the Eye of Terror was like nothing Cadia had ever faced before. As Imperial battlefleets met the dread Chaos warships spewing forth from the immaterium, the planet's already formidable defences were hastily reinforced. Regiments returned in droves from the distant war zones to bolster Cadia's standing garrison. They were joined by the mighty Adeptus Astartes, war engines of the Adeptus Mechanicus and gleaming ranks of the Adepta Sororitas.

Millions perished in the opening assault, and as the first hours of battle turned into days, the slaughter showed no sign of abating. As they had been drilled to do, the Cadian Shock Troops fought to their last dying gasp. Thoughts of despair were quickly drowned out by the bellowed orders of Platoon Commanders, directing those in their charge to hold the line – and hold they did. Every Cadian soldier had been trained from birth to sell their life willingly so that vile Chaos scum might pay for their trespasses in blood.

On uncountable fronts the Cadians meted out as much punishment as they received – obliterating waves of Chaos worshippers with creeping artillery barrages and dogged tank formations, and bringing down colossal daemonic beasts with sheer weight of las-fire. Despite their heroic defiance, Cadia – which for ten millennia had stood as the bulwark against the denizens of the warp – was consumed by a cataclysmic firestorm when Abaddon sent his crippled Blackstone Fortress crashing onto its surface. The planet was beyond saving, its defenders powerless against the hordes of Daemons surging forth to claim the once-defiant world.

Though their home planet was utterly sundered, the resolve of the Cadians has not been not broken. Veteran survivors of the last battle for Cadia, along with regiments of their kinsmen scattered across war zones throughout the galaxy, now fight even more doggedly against the enemies of the Imperium. Whole generations of Shock Troopers are born, raised and trained en route to war zones, and soldiers from other worlds with the mettle to withstand Cadian training are inducted into their ranks. The mantra 'Cadia Stands', which was oft repeated during the planet's final violent days, has gained purchase within the officer corps and amongst the platoons. For Cadia does indeed stand, as long as a single Cadian soldier continues to fight.

Infantry of the Cadian 108th 'Crimson Guard' wear red flak armour over their red and tan fatigues.

The green uniform of the Cadian 717th 'Huntsmen' is supplemented by stark grey armour plates on the upper torso.

Red armaplas on the shoulders and shins offsets the dark camouflage of the Cadian 43rd 'Broken Swords' regiment.

Every regiment has a number of standards that are carried in battle by a Command Squad. Typically, each company will have its own standard, embroidered with the names of their fallen heroes.

Individual platoons may also have their own regimental standard. These banners depict the name and markings of the platoon and are often studded with purity seals.

The short-peak cap with Imperial crest worn Cadian officers makes them easily identifiable upon the battlefield. The triple chevron sleeve marking denotes an Infantry Squad Sergeant.

Cadian squads have unique numbers. A two-digit number with central skull designates command, and Veteran squad numbers begin with one or two zeros.

CATACHAN

Catachan is one of the most notorious death worlds in the Imperium, and its planet-wide jungles are lethal beyond reason. Yet despite the exceptionally perilous nature of the Catachan ecosystem, the servants of the Emperor inhabit this vast world in surprising numbers. Thanks to the brutal environment in which they are raised, Catachans are physically and mentally resilient on a level that much of Humanity simply cannot match. Cunning, resourceful and uncompromising, Catachans must be born survivors simply to reach adulthood. It speaks volumes of the Catachans that they maintain a population capable not only of fighting their own battle for survival, but of sending forces to fight the wider wars of the Imperium as well.

Catachan raises dozens of regiments for the Astra Militarum every year, their skills honed to a knife-edge upon the world of their birth. Viewing daily survival upon Catachan as but a microcosm of Humanity's wider struggle, the death world's warriors proudly answer the Emperor's call to arms. Each regiment raised is exchanged with the Departmento Munitorum for much-needed medical and military supplies. These in turn allow the Catachan settlements to maintain their daily fight for life. This arrangement has stood for thousands of years, and though the Catachans bleed more than most for the Imperium of Man, they would have it no other way.

The very factors that shape the Catachans into such exceptional warriors also leave them proud, aggressive and insular. Individuality is prized amongst the infantry regiments, known as Jungle Fighters, and only a handful of traditions are treated as sacrosanct, such as the wearing of red bandanas that symbolise the blood oath sworn by each newly founded regiment. The Jungle Fighters are notoriously dismissive of the shiny medals and gaudy attire flaunted by other Militarum Regimentos – rank and status are displayed through the inking of specific tattoos, or by the winning of famed Catachan weapons such as a devil's claw. Pragmatism is key to these grizzled warriors, with a favoured tactic being to lay explosive traps before hunkering down in dense cover. Those enemies not outright blown to shreds are quickly finished off by las-fire and torrents of burning promethium.

Catachan's armoured regiments are similarly renowned for the destruction they unleash. With their hulking frames, Catachan crewman are able to heft massive shells and magazines into place with ease, allowing their gunners to lay down a near-unending rain of shots. Bedecked with vines, camo netting or splatters of concealing mud, Catachan tanks may look out of place on the parade ground, but are invaluable on the battlefield.

Catachan leaders typically eschew the privileges of authority, instead suffering through every hardship alongside their troops, a great point of pride among the regiments. Many commanders can claim to have personally saved the lives of half their company. Rather than treat their men as servile underlings, Catachan officers command with crude banter that conceals an underlying mutual respect. Though inarguably effective within Catachan ranks, this style of leadership makes the job of outsiders such as Commissars doubly difficult and often extremely dangerous when they are attached to Catachan regiments.

'As swift as a lash mamba, as sharp as a spineleaf, as stubborn as a wild grox.'
- Colonel Pannent in praise of the Catachan warrior

REGIMENTS OF SAVAGE RENOWN

Catachan XVIII 'Swamprats'
Led by Colonel Gator, the Swamprats fought against a Tyranid horde on Koralkall VIII. Although outnumbered, the regiment suffered remarkably few casualties. The teams of highly experienced Tyranid hunters covered their bodies in xenos ichor to mask their scent from the hunter-beasts, allowing them to launch highly effective surprise attacks.

Catachan XXIV 'Waiting Death'
The Waiting Death are famed for their highly successful employment of traps and ambushes. Most notable of their achievements was the use of Hellmouth Gorge to cripple Warlord Krakskull's Ork horde upon Aranda V.

Catachan XVII 'Screaming Devils'
During the re-pacification of Bad Sanctuary, Captain Thorn and his Screaming Devils 'lost contact' with their assigned Commissar during a treacherous ravine crossing. The regiment's fighting efficiency has markedly increased since that fateful day.

The Catachan MXIV 'Unseen Lurkers' wear dark fatigues and paint their wargear black, allowing them to stalk their prey on night worlds and through underhives.

The mottled green uniform of the Catachan CDVII 'Carnivorous Orchids' matches the lush forests in which they are so often deployed to fight.

Outfitted in grey, the XLVIII 'Spire Hunters' regiment is known for their skill in waging prolonged sieges during cityfights and on dense hive worlds.

The regimental standards of Catachan display company markings in bold colours that are easily identifiable on the battlefield, even through dense forest and plumes of promethium smoke.

Tattoos indicate rank and record a Catachan's valorous deeds. The triple chevron is a Sergeant's mark.

Armoured regiment Tank Commander of the Catachan DXIX 'Savage Jaguars'

The standards borne by individual Catachan platoons display the colours of the company to which they belong, overlaid with additional insignia specific to their platoon.

Catachan officers often wear a peaked cap over their bandana.

A tattoo of a Catachan blade may indicate a particularly heroic melee kill.

ARMAGEDDON

Guardsman Carravos of the 339th Armageddon Steel Legion 'Iron Heads'

The ash wastes of Armageddon are filled with corrosive toxins and industrial pollution. Were a man to breathe the air outside of Armageddon's hives for any extended period his lungs would quickly rot. Despite this, Armageddon has a massive population and is capable of raising a large number of Imperial Guard regiments. Indeed, at the height of the Second War for Armageddon more regiments were being raised each year from the population of Armageddon than from any two other worlds in the entire Segmentum Solar combined. The people of Armageddon are therefore no strangers to warfare. They give no quarter and expect none in return.

Perhaps the most renowned of Armageddon's soldiery are the Steel Legion mechanised infantry regiments. While it is difficult for most Imperial commanders and Planetary Governors to obtain and maintain enough of the vehicles needed for such formations, Armageddon has produced hundreds of these swift-moving regiments. The hive world is one of the chief manufacturing planets for Chimeras, producing countless numbers for use across the Imperium. The extremely industrialised nature of Armageddon means that a far higher proportion of its regiments are mechanised infantry. It is for this reason that these mobile regiments were given their moniker 'Steel Legion'. Fully mobile, the Chimera-mounted infantry squadrons are capable of overrunning enemy positions with large convoys before the infantry dismount to finish them off.

All soldiers within the Steel Legions wear protective clothing such as trench coats, gloves and visors so as to minimise the exposure to their world's polluted atmosphere. Most notably, every trooper carries a rebreather unit capable of filtering out the worst of the airborne poisons. The rebreathers of senior officers are often fashioned in the visage of a grinning skull in an attempt to unnerve the superstitious Orks that have ravaged their war-torn home world in recent years. The warriors of Armageddon reserve a particular hatred for the Orks, who in their lust for war have smashed whole hive cities asunder, and whose presence continues to plague the planet.

Many of the Steel Legion troopers are drafted from amongst the crammed populations of Armageddon's massive hive cities, where only the ruthless survive the ceaseless and brutal gang wars. Many of the Armageddon underhive's most notorious gangs are conscripted directly into the Imperial Guard, without the need for any additional training – their ruthless skills proving more than adequate.

All regiments drawn from Armageddon reap the spoils of the planet's enormous manufactorums, which work ceaselessly to produce the vast quantities of armaments needed to equip so many soldiers. The constant demand for more materiel has transformed Armageddon into an unequalled industrial behemoth. Not only are lasguns, vehicles and war machines produced at an incredible rate, but they are of exemplary quality, honed to perfection after millions of iterations.

> 'We do not wither before the flames of war, for our resolve is like steel and only hardens with heat. Do not let these new foes forget who we are. Show them our strength and our unbending fury!'
>
> – Colonel Makalian during the Third War for Armageddon

In the ongoing Third War for Armageddon, native regiments have been deployed in almost every major battle against the returning greenskin hordes. None have been more gruelling than the siege at Hive Acheron, where Imperial forces, Orks and now Daemons are locked in a maelstrom of bloodshed and destruction as they fight for control of Armageddon's primary hive. Millions from each side crowd the ash wastes around the planet's capital, supported by armoured columns as well as towering Gargants and Titans. An unending rain of explosive shells falls from on high, with the artillery targets shifting as control of the gun emplacements changes hands. Deep within Acheron itself, covert kill teams traverse the vast lattice of promethium pipes that riddles the hive, hoping to circumvent the enemy's defences. Hundreds of Armageddon infantry, armoured and artillery regiments have taken part in this perpetual siege, and their tenacity and expertise at fighting in the ash wastes has seen them fare better than many other Imperial forces. In fact, the mechanised regiments of the Steel Legion have had more Guardsmen survive their first hour of combat at Hive Acheron than any other of Armageddon's regiments.

VOSTROYA

Vostroyan regiments have served the Emperor for countless centuries, fighting to absolve themselves of a terrible shame enacted by their ancestors during the Horus Heresy. At this dark time, Vostroya was ordered to found additional regiments of soldiers. Vostroya was, as it remains today, a factory world providing vital arms and munitions to the Imperium. The Vostroyan government deemed that the sacrifice of manpower in the great smelteries would render their production quotas unattainable. Reasoning that they could better serve by maintaining the work forces and producing the Emperor's weapons of war, Vostroya reluctantly refused the order to raise any extra armies.

In an act of mercy, the Vostroyans were given a chance to atone for their sins and repay their debt to the Emperor. For ten thousand years the Vostroyans have given up the first-born child of every family for service in the Imperial Guard. There are no exceptions to this. Even the greatest noble families must comply. However, to the Vostroyans, it is seen as an honour to serve in the tank crews and Firstborn infantry regiments, for the populace considers the repayment of their debt to be of paramount importance. Their ancient pact drives them onwards, instilling them with a stubbornness, courage and fortitude rarely seen outside the Adeptus Astartes.

Thanks to the inhospitable climate of Vostroya, their regiments are trained in the most adverse of conditions. Within the skeletal remains of collapsed manufactorums, the Firstborn learn the skills of war. Vostroya's governing committee – The Techtriarchy – is composed of Adeptus Mechanicus officials as well as Imperial Commanders, and as a result Vostroyan uniforms tend to incorporate red, the colour of Mars, and cyber-augmentation among the ranks is commonplace. The weapons they carry to war and mount on their vehicles are not mass-produced, but exquisitely hand-crafted by military artisans.

The opening of the Great Rift has not curbed the Vostroyans' steadfast loyalty towards the Imperium. Vostroya itself, along with the majority of its regiments, are cut off from the guiding beacon of the Astronomican by the still-raging Cicatrix Maledictum. However, the Vostroyans have not only defended their own territories, but have also continued sending reinforcements to other war zones – hoping to answer the last cries for help that were heard before the Emperor's light was extinguished and all went silent. Without the Astronomican to guide them, Vostroyan Navigators must fly blind, trusting in esoteric data charts or rote memory to navigate the perilously twisting warp paths. The majority of transports never reach their destination, either emerging far from their target or simply being devoured by the forces of the immaterium. Despite the devastating losses this has caused the Vostroyans, they continue sending their tanks and soldiers outward into the darkness. Never again will they wait when the call to war has been sounded.

Boyar Satomovitch Greisky – Guardsman of the 9th Vostroyan Firstborn 'Old Irascibles'

9th Vostroyan Firstborn 'Old Irascibles'

The Old Irascibles earned their name not through a single battle, but through many hundreds. The regiment served for three and a half centuries during the late 41st Millennium, this being made possible because the Firstborn are one of a very few regiments that ship in reinforcements from their home world in order to stay at fighting strength.

The 9th Vostroyan became one of the most veteran formations in Segmentum Obscurus, before finally meeting their match during the Fall of Karak Prime. The Old Irascibles held the city for eighteen months against a splinter fleet of Hive Fleet Moloch, facing a Tyranid swarm that stretched from the base of the curtain walls to the distant horizon. The defenders knew that the freezing chill of winter would weaken the xenos horde, and that the aliens must feed, by taking the city, before temperatures fell too low. The 9th Vostroyan were running desperately short of ammunition and they knew they would not last that long.

Realising they were doomed, the Old Irascibles opened the city's gates, drawing the ravenous horde within. Only when the bulk of the Tyranid swarm had passed into the city did the 9th Vostroyan detonate its nucleonic stack, incinerating the hive, its defenders and an estimated 85% of the Tyranid swarm. With the coming of midwinter, the few surviving Tyranids starved to death and the splinter fleet was entirely defeated.

VALHALLA

Guardsman Wladislek of the Valhallan Ice Warriors 1212th 'Cold Bloods'

The regiments of Valhalla have a reputation for stoicism and dedication to the Emperor. When attacking, they are renowned for combining massed artillery barrages with infantry assault waves. When defending they show dogged determination, even in the face of defeat.

Valhalla was once a temperate paradise of forests and broad fertile plains. All this changed when a comet of immense size struck the planet. So massive was the comet that it knocked the world from its orbit and raised clouds of dust that blocked out the sun. The temperature plummeted and barely one percent of all life endured; the survivors were forced to build cities deep inside the ice and beneath glaciers, closer to the core of the planet where there was still some modicum of warmth. Valhalla is now nothing more than an inhospitable orb, its landscape a perpetually frozen wasteland. Though the planet is no longer affluent, the Astra Militarum regiments raised there are famous throughout the Imperium of Man.

Not even an Ork invasion shortly after the cataclysmic disaster was able to blunt the Valhallans' spirit, and their grim refusal to surrender despite overwhelming opposition won them a historic – if bloody – victory. After destroying the Ork invaders on their own world, Valhallan regiments, in an act of vengeance, joined with other Imperial Guard armies to cleanse the sector of the hated greenskin menace. Always the Valhallans fought with the same austere determination that was displayed by every man, woman and child in the defence of the ice-cities of their home world. To this day, the courage and tenacity the Valhallans display in battle continues to earn them the respect of other regiments from all over the galaxy.

The Valhallans are a stubborn and stern people who refuse to acknowledge their own hardships, and are rarely deterred by the horrors of the battlefield. They are all but impervious to harsh conditions and have a casual disregard for human life, leading to the superstition amongst other Militarum Regimentos that ice runs through their veins, just as it covers their home world. The notion that 'life is cheap' is heavily espoused in the overcrowded subterranean habitats on Valhalla. Even the most petty crime carries with it the death sentence. Those that do not serve in the Valhallan armoured, artillery or famed Ice Warriors infantry regiments must toil in the dark caverns, cultivating the nutrient slimes that sustain the populace.

Valhallan soldiers are expected to carry each and every item they will need to survive. Without their thermally insulated greatcoats and helmets the Guardsmen's blood would freeze within seconds on the arctic surface of Valhalla. The armoured battle tanks and ordnance units of Valhalla are uniformly camouflaged in a manner suited to this frozen tundra, and each vehicle proudly displays the name of their home world on their hulls.

> 'The Valhallans hate the cold as much as the rest of us, they're just taught that carpin' on about it gets the Commissars all riled…'
>
> – Mosstrooper 'Reiv' Daggat of the Drookian Fenguard 17th after serving alongside Valhallans

The indomitable grit of the Valhallans allowed them to weather the horrors of the Noctis Aeterna, a period when the Astronomican was lost within roiling warp storms. Without it, supply fleets were flung far off course or lost to the warp entirely, and many worlds fell to famine and despair. This created the ideal conditions for the minions of the Dark Gods, and Chaos cults arose amongst crowded and terrified populations across the sector. Not so on Valhalla. The planet had survived calamity before, and it would do so again. The Valhallans kept their vigil and, despite stringent food and heat rations, continued to recruit and train as they had always done.

Valhallans deployed throughout the Imperium Nihilus also fared better than many other Imperial forces. With long-range communications silenced, the lumbering military machine of the Astra Militarum ground to a shuddering halt. Infantry platoons marched hopelessly into war zones without armoured support, and companies scouring planets of xenos were obliterated by the orbital bombardments of allied fleets who were unaware of the ground presence. The Valhallans hunkered down wherever they were stationed, and followed the last orders that had come crackling over comm-links before all had fallen quiet. Their glacial advances continued, driven on in the absence of central command by their inexorable obstinacy.

TALLARN

The regiments drawn from Tallarn consist of mobile guerrilla fighters, evasive as they are opportunistic. They are masters of hit-and-run warfare, striking a killing blow at the heart of an enemy formation before returning to their own lines, prepared to pounce once more. The people of Tallarn are extremely resourceful and pragmatic. They are patient, determined and utterly ferocious in pursuit of their enemies.

The once fertile planet of Tallarn was all but destroyed during the Horus Heresy when the Iron Warriors Traitor Legion launched a surprise attack upon it. Thousands of virus bombs rained down upon the surface of Tallarn, and many of its people died whilst attempting to escape the devastation. When the surviving populace emerged from enviro-shelters hidden deep beneath the surface weeks later, their world was unrecognisable, the deadly attack leaving it a barren, desolate wasteland. The Iron Warriors then launched an invasion onto the planet, but instead of a dead world, the traitors encountered fierce resistance from the remaining Tallarns. Residues of the lethal virus that ravaged Tallarn were still present on the world's surface, making it virtually impossible for infantry to operate outside of protective shelters. The Battle for Tallarn, as this conflict would be later known, was therefore the largest tank engagement in Imperial history. Vast reinforcements were directed to Tallarn by both sides, enormous resources squandered fighting over a devastated world of no notable strategic worth. During the months that followed the Chaos invasion, more than ten million armoured units clashed over the shifting dunes of the planet's blasted surface. The Tallarns rarely met the invaders in open battle, preferring to strike from the flanks and dodging the strongest elements of the Chaos battle line. To this day, the Tallarns have a well-deserved reputation for hit-and-run warfare.

Over the following centuries the final remnants of the virus expired, but Tallarn was irrevocably changed. Deserts of sulphurous sand now stretched from pole to pole, and all water had disappeared except for a thin layer in the atmosphere. No vegetation and few animals remained on the wind-swept surface. The Tallarns lived, as they continue to do, in domed towns or caverns hollowed from the planet's rock where they are protected from the corrosive sandstorms that can strip a man's flesh from his bones. Tall vapour traps were constructed, channelling what water could be extracted into subterranean holding tanks. A complex system of tunnels was eventually excavated to facilitate travel between domes. As a consequence, the Tallarn regiments have adapted to fight in these confines as expertly as they fight on the exposed surface of a planet.

Never has the vaunted mobility of the Tallarns been of more use than now, as growing warp storms continue to claw at the worlds of the Imperium. On battlefields throughout the galaxy the armies of the Imperium are stretched to breaking point. Few Militarum Regimentos share the skill of the Tallarn Desert Raiders infantry regiments at fighting across multiple fronts, or the ability of their armoured regiments at rapidly redeploying their forces to outflank and annihilate their enemies.

Fighting alongside Guilliman's Indomitus Crusade, the Tallarns have also been used as diversionary forces, assaulting lightly fortified moons and orbital platforms within enemy territories. When the foe sends in reinforcements, the Tallarn forces withdraw to strike new targets. These 'Siroccos', as the Tallarns call them, are designed to spread thin the armies of the enemy, but so effective are the guerilla warriors at their charge that often their targets are permanently crippled.

Tallarns have never lost their aptitude for mechanised warfare, and field an abundance armoured regiments. Rather than utilising their vehicles as a slow moving wall of steel – as some Militarum Regimentos do – Tallarn Tank Commanders pride themselves on their ability to coordinate lightning-fast spearhead assaults, their squadrons of swift-moving tanks weaving between allied formations to strike unexpectedly at the unprepared foe.

> 'Be swift and silent as the breeze that crosses the dunes without stirring a grain of sand.'
>
> - Captain Al'rahem

The people of Tallarn are master craftsmen and their wargear is both practical and ceremonial. Indeed, the weapons of many Tallarn officers are inset with precious gems and metals. These officers are usually selected from amongst Tallarn's tribal leaders and a coloured sash tied around every soldier's waist denotes their rank.

Battlegroup 'Desert Fox'

Battlegroup 'Desert Fox' was a composite unit based around the infantry of the Tallarn 95th, the tanks of the Tallarn 668th armoured, and the mobile guns of the Tallarn 212th artillery. The formation was constituted to wage war in the arid sulphur wastes of Lorthax against a large army of separatists, where it would spearhead Operation Umbrage. Due to an administrative error however, the column was issued without any source of fuel and had no choice but to dismount all of its vehicle crews and start the attack as light infantry. Reverting to the desert fighting traditions of Tallarn, Battlegroup Desert Fox infiltrated the enemy lines and launched an entirely unanticipated attack that proved so successful it pushed twelve miles into enemy territory and wiped out the entire separatist high command. Following this great victory, the three regiments were reconstituted as the 1st Tallarn Raiding Regiment, and their vehicles were assigned to other units.

Guardsman Mal'har of the Tallarn 95th 'Jakaros'

REGIMENTS OF DISTINCTION

Countless human worlds provide regiments for the tithe. Although this recruitment base fluctuates with the boundaries of the Imperium itself, there are those planets that have been proudly contributing regiments to the Imperial Guard for thousands of years. Of these, a handful are renowned throughout the Imperium for their exceptional soldiery.

ARMAGEDDON ORK HUNTERS

Soldiers from the Ork Hunter regiments of Armageddon are savage warriors, and in their short history have already earned a fearsome reputation. Based in the Equatorial Jungle of their home planet, they frequently return to the fortified Cerbera Base with grisly trophies taken from the Orks they have slain – teeth necklaces, skulls, stikkbombs and bloodstained armour plates amongst them. In addition to his normal equipment, each Ork Hunter also carries his 'scalper', a huge machete-like weapon that can decapitate a xenos with a single blow. The feral appearance and coarse manner of the Ork Hunters has led to them being regarded as only slightly less savage than the Orks they hunt. This is not far from the truth, and on more than one occasion, the Ork Hunters have actually been forced to ally with the greenskins against the hordes of Daemons that now inhabit the region. Should the abominations of Chaos be defeated, any surviving Humans and Orks invariably turn upon each other once more.

ATHONIAN TUNNEL RATS

Governance of Athonos is in perpetual flux, with leadership positions being constantly vied for by a dozen rival families. The resultant gang warfare – fought in the streets and sewers of the hydroponic gardens – is brutal and unending. Such is the recruiting ground for the Athonian Tunnel Rats. By the time they are drafted for the Imperial tithe, they are already masters of urban combat and amongst the most determined close-quarters fighters of the Imperial Guard.

Due to their expertise in subterranean warfare, the Tunnel Rats are often called upon to quash heretical uprisings in densely packed hive and mining worlds. As such, they have come face to face with a great number of Genestealer Cults. The Athonians tend to eschew the use of mortars and artillery due to their limited effectiveness in the confined caverns in which they fight, instead relying on massed meltaguns, flamers and demolition charges, and utilizing light armour support in the form of Sentinels and Chimeras.

MIASMAN REDCOWLS

The Miasman Redcowls hail from the interlocking space station networks that surround the gas giant Miasma XVI. They are known for the fierce green fire that spouts from their flamers, Hellhounds and incendiary grenades, and though it is more volatile than even promethium, it stinks to high heaven. More than one regiment has objected violently to being stationed alongside the Redcowls. Though the 'Fire Skunks' are issued with rebreathers and heavy robes to escape the sulphurous stench of Miasma XVI's gases, their fellow regiments are usually not so lucky.

The Redcowls are often placed on the front line, where they burn a path through the foe to create room for their allies. They are deployed sparingly in defensive operations, usually on planets that are considered irretrievable, as the firestorms they create are too destructive to be used on densely populated or high-value worlds.

Guardsman Danikka, 3rd Armageddon Ork Hunters 'Pikers'

Guardsman Sevestin, Athonian 18th 'Children of Ganthos'

Guardsman Kymme, Miasman 114th 'Shrouded Ones'

MORDIAN IRON GUARD

The Mordian Iron Guard are superbly drilled and accoutred soldiers from a world bathed in perpetual night and cursed by the attentions of Chaos. In battle, the Iron Guard present a solid wall of brightly uniformed, flawlessly formed troops, cutting down the foe with precisely timed volleys from behind a hedge of polished bayonet points. Many foes have made the fatal error of underestimating the Mordians, mistaking their parade-ground appearance for arrogance. Those who do are soon punished for their presumption.

When the Thousand Sons swept into the Stygius Sector, the invasion was preceded by massive Cultist uprisings, but the Iron Guard used pinpoint shelling and ordered advances to herd the heretics towards the far side of the planet where they burned in the blazing heat of the tidally locked sun. With the worst of the uprisings quashed, the Mordians steeled themselves for the next Chaos wave.

TANITH FIRST AND ONLY

The forest world of Tanith was destroyed shortly after the initial founding of the planet's first three regiments. The only survivors to escape the attack, the Tanith 1st, carry with them the wilderness skills learnt on their home world, making them a superb light infantry regiment. The Guardsmen of the Tanith First and Only wear distinctive camo cloaks and are renowned for their expertise in both scouting and infiltration missions. In addition to their normal equipment, each Guardsman is armed with a straight silver war-knife, unique to the Tanith regiment.

Despite their limited numbers, the First and Only have been instrumental in multiple battles throughout the Sabbat Worlds Crusade. Led by the inspirational Colonel-Commissar Ibram Gaunt, and drawing new recruits from the worlds they fight to liberate and defend, the reputation of 'Gaunt's Ghosts' continues to grow with each passing deployment.

SAVLAR CHEM-DOGS

Scavengers and criminals from the scum-world of Savlar, these dregs of Humanity have been recruited to serve on Armageddon. Motivated by the loot they might be able to recover, they excel in the cramped, noxious battlefields of the hives. Much of their equipment is stolen from other regiments, and much of their courage comes from the use of nitro-chem inhalers, without which they would likely flee in terror from the Daemons that now haunt the ash wastes and underhives.

Chem-Dogs are highly resourceful and surprisingly enterprising. Rather than waiting for battlefield resupplies, they will often re-purpose old equipment. They have been known to strip weapons from vehicles and proceed on foot when fuel is low, or replace broken machine parts with similarly shaped pieces of scrap. Though effective, such practices have seen more than a few Savlar officers executed for heresy by the Adeptus Mechanicus.

Guardsman Gremuelle, Mordian 50th 'Fort Baton Regulars'

Guardsman Markon, Tanith First and Only

Guardsman Pueggis, Savlar 29th 'Lucidites'

Guardsman Quelizaar, Ventrillian 86th
'Carmine Eagles'

Veteran Guardsman Garadux, Indigan 47th
'Lictor Killers'

Guardsman Jaxx, Mordant 12th
'Scarifiers'

VENTRILLIAN NOBLES

On the wealthy jewel world of Ventrillia, those that withstand the subterranean coming-of-age ritual known as the Trial of the Lava Lakes enjoy a wealth that is more than sufficient to buy their way out of the Astra Militarum a dozen times over. But Ventrillia has a proud military culture, with a history of duelling that stretches back to pre-Imperial times, and few Nobles would risk the dishonour of giving up their commissions. Instead, they 'donate' their wealth to Munitorum officials and Rogue Traders in exchange for assignments and passage to war zones rich in adventure and glory, rather than simply being fed to the Imperial meat grinder. When the Nobles go to war they do so armed not only with a lasgun and bayonet, but also an ancestral duelling sword, quickblade or heavy zwei-hander.

Ventrillia's rarest gemstones are of great value to the Adeptus Mechanicus, both for manufacturing and research purposes. To secure a steady supply of these jewels, the Tech-Priests ensure that Ventrillia is supplied with an abundance of super-heavy tanks.

INDIGAN PRAEFECTS

On the former menagerie world of Indiga, the Praefects have the unenviable task of protecting the planet's natives from the megafauna that prowl their verdant realm. The giant predators had once been the pride and joy of the pompous governor, Constantine Principa Argoy, who spent the planet's copious mineral wealth on the purchase of breeding pairs of every dangerous creature he could acquire from planets across the Segmentum. Unfortunately, after a catastrophic earthquake shattered the governor's zoos, the giant animals escaped into the wilds to breed and hybridise.

The Indigan Praefects have become experts at slaying large and dangerous beasts, and their reputation is such they have been requested as reinforcements in multiple war zones assailed by Tyranids. Where these requests have been honoured, the Praefects set about eradicating the xenos fiends with practised efficiency. Veterans who have faced the Tyranid swarms help to drill new recruits, instructing them on how to bring down a Carnifex using lascannon fire and how to bait Mawlocs with tightly packed infantry formations.

MORDANT ACID-DOGS

Mordant Prime is classed by the Adeptus Terra as a night world, its surface a barren wasteland totally unfit for human habitation. The only reason anyone endures on the world is to mine the strains of luminescent bacteria that grow beneath the surface. Once harvested, these bacteria are cultivated in massive farms where they produce vast quantities of acid to be used in Bane Wolf chem cannons. After countless generations of living in mining warrens and working with the potent bio-acids, mutations have begun to plague the populace. Any such mutants discovered on the planet are promptly dissolved in the same acid that helped create them – either at birth, or when their nascent deformity first appears. Few regiments harbour a greater disgust towards abominations of the flesh.

In M38 the Mordant 13th regiment – the 'Lucky Thirteens' – were tasked with putting down the mutant insurgence led by Jihar the Lacerator of the Emperor's Children. Since their resounding success, the Acid-dogs have often been called upon to scour worlds on which signs of mutation have begun to show.

The drilled precision and ardent resolve of Cadia's regiments have been emulated across countless Imperial worlds, with many Militarum Regimentos receiving training from Cadian infantry and tank officers. Cadian-derived tactics and uniforms are therefore seen upon battlefields throughout the galaxy.

ARMOURED REGIMENTS

Almost every Militarum Regimentum has its own armoured, artillery and mechanised infantry regiments, with markings similar to those worn by their foot soldiers.

Chimera driver from the Cadian 1273rd 'Elysion Eagles' mechanised infantry regiment

FAEBURN VANQUISHERS

The Vanquishers hail from the honeycombed caves of Faeburn. Since the opening of the Great Rift, a strange phenomenon has filled Faeburn's skies. The hallucinogenic pattern, known as the Aurora Illuminato, forms shapes and faces, which Faeburn's devout see as signs sent by the Emperor. However, they bring nightmares as often as they bring solace.

TRUSKAN SNOWHOUNDS

The tribes from which the Snowhounds recruit mastered the art of winter warfare long ago. Aside from being an extremely hardy regiment, the Truskans are renowned for their keen vision. Snipers and sharp-shooters are common amongst this regiment, their skills honed hunting the white animals of their home world across snow-drifts and glaciers.

Tank Commander of the Mordian 4th 'Cobalt Lions' Armoured Regiment

VRESH GRENADIERS

The Grenadiers regiments hail from the war-torn tech-slums of Vresh. A strong and violent gang culture pervades this shifting worldscape of rust and metal, and its warriors quickly learn to be cunning in combat and to follow the orders of their leaders. The flak armour they wear is typically fashioned from metal scrap plates, which are beaten into shape to wear during the running slum battles. Once drafted into the Astra Militarum this same armour is given regimental markings, though many of the lurid gang emblems of their former lives are retained on helmets and breastplates.

Basilisk shell loader from the Cadian 781st Artillery Regiment, seconded to the 92nd infantry

HEROES BEYOND NUMBER

The Astra Militarum have fought the Imperium's wars for ten thousand years, and for every warrior immortalised upon a marble plinth, a million more have died unmarked and unmourned. Yet still the soldiers of Humanity muster for war across the galaxy, ready to stand against the most terrible foes it has to offer, for the Emperor and for Holy Terra.

M31–M32 THE AGE OF REBIRTH

The Imperium is rebuilt from the ashes of the Horus Heresy. Doctrines such as the Codex Astartes and Tactica Imperium are drawn up and implemented to ensure that large-scale military rebellion will never again be possible.

The Scouring

A campaign of vengeance is launched in which those traitors who survived the fall of Horus are driven into the Eye of Terror. The nearby planet of Cadia is bolstered until its defences are second only to Holy Terra itself, forming the anchor-point of the Cadian Gate. For a short time the Imperium knows peace from the corrupted followers of the Dark Gods.

Restructuring the Imperial Army

The massive and singular Imperial Army is divided into many autonomous but interrelated parts. Among them is the Astra Militarum, leadership of which is distributed amongst the various Militarum Regimentos.

The First Black Crusade

Abaddon the Despoiler leads the Black Legion out of the Eye of Terror to lay waste to the Imperium. His assault falls upon Cadia. His forces are driven back into the warp by Cadian Shock Troops, the Adeptus Astartes and the Legio Titanicus.

M32–M35 THE FORGING

The Adeptus Terra begins an ambitious project to bring the most important systems in the Imperium under its direct control. At the forefront of this conquest are the Adeptus Astartes and the massive armies of the Astra Militarum. As the advance continues, Astropathic choirs are established on Armageddon, Bakka, Macragge and thousands of others. Long-lost Standard Template Constructs are unearthed amid the ruins of the Cana system, slowing the decline of Imperial technology. The borders of the Imperium expand to a point almost on par with the success of the Great Crusade. Chaos Renegades and xenos are purged from the galaxy in phenomenal numbers, and countless rebel systems are brought to heel.

Shock and Awe

As more and more systems are brought into the Imperial fold, the Shock Troops of Cadia are tasked with imparting their discipline and military doctrine to the leaders of newly colonised worlds. Countless planetary defence forces and Militarum Regimentos are raised based on Cadian principles of warfare.

Limits of Power

In repudiation of the Tactica Imperium, Admiral Usurs forms a powerful military bloc comprising his Imperial fleet as well as armoured and infantry regiments of the Astra Militarum. The High Lords of Terra cannot allow such a concentration of forces, but know that assassinating the Admiral could lead to a costly civil war. Usurs is instead sent on an exploratory mission deep in the intergalactic gulf. For two decades, reports reach Terra detailing the conquering of new systems for the glory of the Emperor, then the communiqués cease. Contact is never attempted with the systems mentioned in Usurs' reports.

The Third Black Crusade

The Despoiler unleashes the Daemon Prince Tallomin in a bloody frontal assault against the Cadian Gate. Millions of Imperial Guardsmen die to the daemonic horde that flows in Tallomin's wake, but the soldiers of Cadia hold out against the onslaught. They give no quarter, and make the invaders pay in blood for every inch of Cadian soil lost. Their defiance buys time for Imperial reinforcements to arrive, and Tallomin is eventually hurled howling back into the warp.

M36–M38 THE AGE OF APOSTASY

Zeal eclipses reason, and misrule reigns supreme. The word of the Emperor is subverted by corrupt ideologues, and the strong prey upon the weak like jackals.

The Reign of Blood

Goge Vandire is made High Lord of the Administratum. He immediately sets about admonishing the massively corrupt Ecclesiarchy, which sparks off a seven-decades-long civil war. Though Vandire's motive to eradicate the rampant corruption within the Imperium appears pure, his own reign brings about nightmarish levels of destruction. By his command entire populations of Imperial worlds are butchered or carpeted with virus bombs. Regiments of the Astra Militarum are put to violent use enforcing his tyranny. Only when loyalist regiments rally under the banner of the preacher Sebastian Thor is the strife ended.

The Great Cull

The High Lords of Terra begin a systematic purging of Imperial command. Every sphere of the Imperium is affected, and many commanders of the Astra Militarum are put to the torch publicly or assassinated in silence.

The Cost of Redemption

The sins of apostasy are purged in blood and tears. Amongst the regiments of the Astra Militarum, as elsewhere, the Imperial Cult grows greatly in power. As billions of heretics are burnt at the pyre, crusade after crusade is launched to re-establish the authority of the Imperium. This rapid outpouring of force leaves many planets all but undefended, their regiments engaged in long and gruelling campaigns across the vast expanse of the galaxy. The Tallarn Desert Raiders earn a fearsome reputation for their ability to rapidly redeploy, conducting simultaneous offensive and defensive manoeuvres that span entire sub-sectors.

M38–M41 THE WANING

The armies of the Imperium are stretched near to breaking point after the Redemption Crusades. Innumerable worlds fall to xenos invasions, Chaos insurgency and internal strife. As entire systems are consumed by anarchy, the Mordian Iron Guard implement stringent and merciless rule throughout their home system, eradicating nine separate uprisings of Tzeentchian cults.

The Ninth Black Crusade
Abaddon leads his Ninth Black Crusade against the hive world of Antecanis. The Black Legionnaires launch a harrowing assault on the Monarchive, slaughtering the planetary defence forces garrisoned in the capital. When reinforcements arrive from Cancephalus to bolster the surviving Guardsmen, Abaddon's forces withdraw and launch dozens of cyclonic warheads from orbit. A seventeen-year war ensues, and despite the tenacity of the Antecanian and Cancephalian regiments, the Despoiler is not brought to heel.

The Macharian Conquests
Lord Commander Solar Macharius musters the greatest Astra Militarum army the galaxy has ever seen. A thousand worlds are conquered on the western fringe of the Imperium, and worlds that had never seen the Emperor's light are brought into the fold. However, upon Macharius' death the territories gained are quickly embroiled in internecine wars.

M41 THE TIME OF ENDING
Darkness continues to consume the Imperium, while the Enemy Without and the Enemy Within grow in strength and number. Imperial tithes are increased and the ranks of the Astra Militarum grow larger than they have been in millennia. Many heroes are forged in the unending crucible of war.

The Gothic War
Abaddon leads his Twelfth Black Crusade against the Gothic Sector of Segmentum Obscurus. Countless Imperial Guardsmen are committed to the war zone alongside three whole Titan Legions and numerous Space Marine battle groups. During the final Imperial victory at Schindlegeist, the Elysian 234th win posthumous commendations for a suicidal boarding action that results in the scuttling of the Hades-class heavy cruiser *Injustice*.

The First War for Armageddon
Angron, blasphemous Daemon Primarch of the World Eaters, descends on Armageddon at the head of a mighty Chaos host. The continent of Armageddon Prime falls swiftly, yet battle lines are held by newly drafted regiments of Steel Legion rallying around the stubborn Space Wolves. Ultimately, Armageddon is saved and Angron banished, but the bloody cost of victory spirals higher as the Inquisition instigates a series of brutal purges – slaughtering the Steel Legion to contain the knowledge of what has transpired.

The Damocles Crusade
The T'au Empire expands into Imperial space. Numerous worlds defect, initiating the protracted Damocles Crusade. Notable victories are won by the Brimlock Dragoons and dauntless Drookian Fenguard, whose sergeants wield huge ceremonial swords as they lead their men screaming into battle. However, after only three years, the encroaching Tyranid threat leads Imperial forces to withdraw, surrendering in weeks the territory paid for in years of blood and toil.

The First Tyrannic War
Hive Fleet Behemoth ploughs headlong into the Realm of Ultramar. Forty-seven regiments of the Ultramar Auxilla join their Ultramarines masters in the defence of their realm.

The Saint Cyllia Aftermath
Nearly a full Titan Legion turns traitor on Saint Cyllia's World, instigating a massacre of unthinkable proportions. Knight Commander Pask rallies elements of the Cadian 423rd and breaks for the safety of Yggdrasil Spaceport, scoring four confirmed engine kills during their escape, including the Reaver Titan *Oblivion's Angel*. Imperial forces finally encircle the traitor Legio upon the Planus Steppes, and the largest armoured offensive since the battle of Tallarn is launched. Over eight thousand tank companies and thirty-five super-heavy detachments are annihilated during the continent-spanning, year-long war that follows. With the support of three full houses of Imperial Knights, Pask's forces corner the surviving Titans and destroy them one by one.

The Second War for Armageddon
The self-proclaimed Ork prophet Ghazghkull Mag Uruk Thraka invades the industrial hive world of Armageddon at the head of an almighty Waaagh!. Billions die as the tide of greenskins sweeps across the

planet, but at Hive Hades the invaders are halted by the defence forces of Commissar Yarrick. Though the hive eventually falls, the Commissar's stoic defiance succeeds in delaying the Orks long enough for Imperial reinforcements to arrive, forcing Ghazghkull to flee the world.

Creed's Triumph
Aeldari forces attack Cadian holdings on Aurent. Ursarkar Creed implements a complex web of contingency plans and sealed, time-delayed orders coupled with psychic obfuscation provided by an entire coven of Primaris Psykers. Creed's tactical genius overcomes even the vaunted Aeldari powers of prescience, securing an overwhelming Cadian victory at the very gates of Aurent's Hive Primus.

The Devourer Rises
As Hive Fleet Leviathan strikes at the underbelly of the Imperium, billions of Imperial Guardsmen are conscripted to face this new threat. Departmento Munitorum tithe-takers report a worrying number of worlds unable to fulfil their demands, leading several dozen planetary governors to face summary execution.

The Third War for Armageddon
Ghazghkull Thraka returns to Armageddon and obliterates Hades Hive from orbit – a clear challenge to his old foe, Commissar Yarrick. The 'Old Man' returns to oppose the Ork Warlord, this time taking command of the entire world's armed forces. As the war degenerates into gruelling battles of attrition, Ghazghkull once again departs. This time Yarrick pursues his nemesis across the stars, determined to make the Warlord pay for the death and destruction visited upon Armageddon.

War Zone Damocles
After the T'au drive the planetary defence forces of Agrellan from their home world, Segmentum Command escalates operations in war zone Damocles. Waves of reinforcements begin a desperate rearguard action to slow the T'au advance. Meanwhile, a mighty armada of Imperial warships departs for Agrellan, bearing over one thousand regiments of Cadian, Catachan, Elysian, Tallarn and Cthonol Guardsmen, several full Battle Companies of Raven Guard and White Scars Space Marines, and the Titans of Legio Absolutium. The hammer of Imperial retribution bears inexorably down upon the attacking T'au, its wielders determined to crush the upstart xenos once and for all.

M41 THE THIRTEENTH BLACK CRUSADE

Abaddon the Despoiler launches his Thirteenth Black Crusade, the most powerful and destructive of his campaigns to sunder the Imperium. Once again, Cadia is his primary target, but more than the fate of this one planet is at stake.

The Storm Gathers

As madness and death spread through the Cadian Gate, the outpouring of horror and zealotry echoes in the immaterium. Warp storm Baphomael expands rapidly into the Cadian System, bringing with it visions of burning worlds overrun by cackling daemonic hosts. The mysterious Cadian pylons begin to resonate at an amplitude similar to that of a Gellar Field, and are found to be developing alarming hairline cracks. Outlying worlds including Dentor, Sarlax and Amistel are left blackened husks by mysterious raiders, and across the system planetary defence forces and Cadian garrisons desperately attempt to quell spreading rebellions.

The Battle of Tyrok Fields

Increasingly concerned by the havoc spreading through neighbouring systems, Cadian High Command orders a general muster on Cadia. Millions of Guardsmen are already assembled outside Kasr Tyrok when the Volscani Cataphracts spring a suicidal trap. Confusion reigns as the traitors open fire upon their former comrades, slaughtering hundreds before any response can be coordinated. The intent of the Volscani's treason is revealed when they swarm aboard the Leviathan command vehicle of the Governor Primus, *Fortress Imperium*. Though they fight hard, Cadian High Command are wiped out in a single stroke. At the darkest moment, Ursarkar Creed rallies the reeling Cadian regiments and orders the counter-attack. Accompanied as always by his trusted Sergeant, Jarran Kell, Creed orders the Cadian 8th to link up with the 7th and advance towards the captured Leviathan. Kell is wounded when he intercepts a las-round intended for Creed, but refuses medical attention and continues onwards. The Leviathan is soon recaptured, the colours of the Cadian 8th flying proudly from its command deck. Shortly after, Ursarkar Creed is appointed Lord Castellan of Cadia and the Cadian 8th are renamed 'The Lord Castellan's Own' in his honour.

Bracing the Gate

Now convinced that an attack on an unprecedented scale will soon fall upon the Cadian Gate, Creed takes what steps he can to prepare the defences. Though heavy with portents of doom, the Emperor's Tarot is consulted time and again in the hope of gleaning insight into the movements of the foe. New fortifications are raised across Cadia and her surrounding worlds. Astropathic choirs begin broadcasting a deafening call for aid. Though it incinerates the minds of countless psykers, Creed orders that Cadia's distress call must ring ceaselessly through the warp.

First Blood

Cadian High Command sends a force of Tempestus Scions out to the very edge of the Eye of Terror in an attempt to gauge where the first blow will fall. Making planetfall upon the benighted world of Urthwart, the expeditionary force finds no sign of life until it breaches the primary planetary shelters. As the vault doors swing open, a billion moaning dead spill from the darkness. Meanwhile, in orbit, a vast traitor armada thunders from the empyrean, its vanguard elements completely annihilating the expedition's transports.

The Great Eye Opens

Abaddon's armada blots out the stars with its sheer volume; mutants and heretics pour from the Eye in numbers beyond count. Despite being overwhelmingly outnumbered, Imperial Navy forces under Admiral Quarren do what they can to stem the tide. Quarren's fleet fights with nobility and distinction, but the heavy toll they exact upon the foe is as drops in the ocean. Forced to disengage, the survivors limp back to Cadia as harbingers of the oncoming storm. Abaddon's forces arrive just hours after Quarren's, the sheer fury of their attack setting the warp aflame. The skies of Cadia fill with fire as twisted landing craft descend like clouds of flies, and invaders in their millions spill onto the surface. Yet a sliver of hope remains, for Cadia's defenders know that Space Marines, Titans, and unnumbered regiments of Guardsmen are rushing to their aid. Creed defends his world with a strategic brilliance not witnessed since the days of Macharius, inspiring every Guardsman to fight to the bitter end with no thought for themselves. If the Cadian Gate should fall then the unbridled fury of the warp will spill forth into the Imperium, sweeping all of Mankind away in a tide of horror and madness.

The Fall of Cadia

The full force Abaddon's Thirteenth Crusade descends upon Cadia. As the servants of Chaos spew from the Eye of Terror, the armies of the Imperium rush to defend the fortress world. Lord Castellan Creed leads the defenders' stand from Kasr Kraf, where millions of Guardsmen die holding back the onslaught of Daemons, Cultists and Heretic Astartes. Morale ebbs at the sight of the atrocities being visited upon the Guardsmen caught outside the walls, but is kept from breaking altogether by Creed's defiant dictum, 'Cadia Stands!' When the Daemon Prince Urkanthos and the Hounds of Abaddon launch an assault on the heart of Kasr Kraf, what little hope remains seems utterly lost – but into the fires of damnation flies Saint Celestine, the hallowed warriors of the Adepta Sororitas following her holy path. Fighting alongside the Cadian defenders, they drive the attackers from the walls. The dead are burned during the brief respite, the Sisters of Our Martyred Lady providing ministrations where they can. Having battled their way through the blockade, Adeptus Astartes and Mechanicus reinforcements also manage to make planetfall. Among their number is Archmagos Dominus Belisarius Cawl, who uses the geometric pylons scattered across Cadia to hold back the warp. As the Despoiler's hordes set about their butchery, Creed is nearly slain by Abaddon himself, but is saved by the last heroic sacrifice of the ever-faithful Colour Sergeant Kell. Then, with agonising finality, the last sliver of hope is shredded – Abaddon sends his orbiting Blackstone Fortress plummeting into Cadia, sundering the pylon network that holds back the immaterium. The number of Imperial soldiers consumed in the cataclysm is unknown, and countless more are slaughtered by the Daemons that pour from the warp tears opening on the planet's surface. Of nearly a billion souls who had stood to defend Cadia, scarcely three million are evacuated. Lord Castellan Ursarkar Creed is not among them.

M41 THE AGE OF THE DARK IMPERIUM

The Imperium Nihilus

The galaxy is torn asunder by a massive wall of warp storms. Tidal waves of unnatural energy rush outwards from the maelstrom, and with a horrific surge the planets of the Imperium are cut off from the guiding light of the Astronomican. For the Astra Militarum soldiers fighting in innumerable war zones, any hope of receiving reinforcement is lost, whilst whole regiments in transit are flung wildly off course or are swallowed outright by the roiling warp. Even when the Astronomican finally blinks back into existence, it cannot pierce the Cicatrix Maledictum – the Great Rift that stretches from the Eye of Terror in the west to the Scourge Stars in the east. Those planets and regiments in the Imperium Nihilus are left to fend for themselves, or be forever consumed by the darkness.

The Warping of Armageddon

The bloody quagmire on Armageddon continues, despite both Ork and Imperial armies being cut off from reinforcements. Whipped up by the maelstrom of the Great Rift, hellstorms ravage the planet's surface, and from them emerge Tzeentchian and Khornate hordes. Titanic Greater Daemons duel for supremacy even as they slaughter the Ork and Imperial armies, and fully half the planet is transformed into a nightmarish landscape resembling a Daemon world. Astra Militarum regiments form uneasy and temporary alliances with the greenskin invaders to fight the daemonic threat. While the Steel Legion and planetary defence forces hold out against hope to secure Armageddon's hives, the Salamanders, along with nine other Chapters of the Adeptus Astartes, succeed in halting the ritual that would bring Angron, the Primarch of the World Eaters, back to the planet that had defied him in ages past.

False Hope

Adrift amongst the stars of the Imperium Nihilus, a fleet-bound Astra Militarum army group believes it has located the Astronomican. They follow the signal through the immaterium, straight into the clutches of a massed Alpha Legion ambush.

Slash and Burn

A battle group en route to war zone Ultramar descend to quell the massive Genestealer Cult uprising on Gretienne's Garden. So rife with mutants are the forests of the verdant world that the Imperial soldiers set the planet's entire western continent ablaze. After months of intense battles, the Genestealer Cults withdraw into the densest woods, and the offensive devolves into a series of seek and destroy missions. The majority of the battle group is called away by order of the Ordo Xenos, leaving only a handful of Catachan armoured regiments and super-heavy vehicles. The departure is fortuitously timed, for days later the system is cut off from all communication – shrouded by the warp shadow emanating from a fast approaching Jormungandr splinter fleet. Undeterred, and with abominations still to kill, the remaining Baneblades blast and bulldoze their way through the lingering hybrids, while Hellhound companies incinerate any living thing that crosses their path. The forest world and every mutant on it is reduced to ash by the time the Tyranid fleet arrives. The armoured Catachans hold out for as long as they can before being devoured by the overwhelming enemy. Finding the once-lush planet stripped of its vital bio-mass, the Jormungandr fleet quickly sets off towards other Imperial worlds.

Call of the Forge

A fragmented message reaches the Astropathic choirs on Vostroya. Though it appears to have been sent by the Adeptus Mechanicus, calling for aid on Canoptis II, the nature of the threat facing the Tech-Priests is unclear. Nevertheless, the Firstborn 22nd 'Riders of Dawn', the 99th 'Only Sons' and the 331st 'True Shots' set out to answer the call, hoping that their Navigators will be able to traverse the now lightless stars.

Wages of War

The Tallarn Desert Raiders, fighting alongside Grey Knights of the Blades of Victory Brotherhood, conduct a series of feinting attacks against the Nurgle Daemons spawned in the wake of Outbreak Arcanum, when the spores of the sentient plague Eater of Lives were unleashed from the drifting space hulk *Mother of Miseries*. Skirmishes flit across barren moons and dead worlds, the Grey Knights instructing the Desert Raiders to never close on their enemy or leave their dead behind. In time, the rotting hordes waste away. The Grey Knights carve the names of the Tallarn Commanders into their armour to honour their service, then put every Guardsmen and officer to death.

Entry to Valhalla

Amidst the darkness of the Imperium Nihilus, fleeing vessels carry word of a greenskin fleet surging towards Valhalla. Planning to intercept the Orks on the nearby hive world of Skovi, the Ice Warriors make a series of short range warp jumps. Upon arrival they learn that the Skovian armouries are severely depleted, having expended their munitions reserves fighting off several Ork waves already. Desperate calls for resupply had been sent, but they were either never received or the Imperial Navy's resupply ships had been lost in the warp. As the main body of the Ork fleet arrives in orbit, the well-equipped Ice Warriors assume command of Skovi's defence, requisitioning what few supplies remain. The Skovians are given knives, hatchets, spears and rocks before being ordered to march alongside the Valhallan infantry towards the greenskin invaders. The Guardsmen in the vanguard are mercilessly butchered by the first Ork charge, but the Ice Warriors hold their ground. From the rear of the Imperial formation, the 888th 'Frostburners' Artillery Regiment begins to shell the front lines. Ordnance blasts send chunks of human and Ork flesh raining across the battlefield, and the creeping barrages continue to cut further and further into the sea of greenskins. By nightfall on the fourth day only a handful of Orks remain. Despite devastating losses and a lack of proper weaponry, the Skovians join the Ice Warriors in hunting them down.

Cadia Stands!

Cadian regiments scattered across war zones throughout the Imperium vow to avenge those who perished when their home world fell. The skill and discipline instilled in each Cadian on their mother planet is imparted to planetary defence forces and newly founded Militarum Regimentos whom they fight alongside, and the Lord Castellan's mantra, 'Cadia Stands' is not forgotten.

The Astra Militarum fight for the Emperor and for the Imperium, and they do not stand alone. Guardsmen are taught to have faith in the implacable strength of Humanity, but also to not rely only on their prayers to bring deliverance. A soldier's darkest hour should not be spent pleading for miracles of salvation – it should be spent facing the issue cast before him, rifle ready to fend off

COMPANY COMMANDERS

Standing proud amid the blood and thunder of the front lines, the Company Commander sets an unfaltering example to the men he leads. The titles held by these officers are as wildly varying as the worlds from whence they hail; an Imperial army on campaign may contain companies led by majors, captains, hetmen, demiconsuls, knights militant, chieftains and dozens more. However their soldiers address them, Company Commanders all bear the same responsibilities. In the face of nightmarish foes, they must provide their men with a bulwark of unwavering courage and decisive leadership. Most are hard-bitten heroes, skilled combatants and pragmatic strategists whose first loyalty is to the Emperor of Mankind. Some rare men of rank may be ineffective fops with commissions awarded through inheritance or politicking, but the hour is too dark for the Munitorum to suffer fools for long. Those who cannot discharge their duties soon discover that being the governor's son means little to a merciless Commissar.

COMMAND SQUADS

Typically, each Company Commander is escorted in battle by a retinue of battle-scarred veterans who support their leader in the field. These squads are often provided with specialist equipment and additional training. Expert voxmen relay the Company Commander's orders to the men on the front lines. Talented field surgeons stand a tense vigil over their comrades, ready to staunch wounds or administer doses of whatever chemical stimulants are required. Should a rank-and-file trooper display exceptional valour and dedication, they may be given the honour of bearing the regimental standard. To earn such a position a man must have performed above and beyond the call of duty, such as gunning down a swathe of rampaging foes in defence of a field hospital or felling a ravening Daemon Engine with a well-placed grenade.

Many Company Command Squads include grizzled special weapons operators or Veteran Heavy Weapons Teams. These soldiers are proven crack-shots to a man, and the presence of such potent weapons close at hand allows Company Commanders personally to oversee the destruction of vital targets, such as lumbering heretic tanks or monstrous xenos beasts. Equally, should the situation deteriorate and the Company Command Squad find themselves threatened by bellowing mobs of greenskins or a looming traitor Helbrute, these same lethal firearms can mean the difference between life and death.

Whether the Company Commander is a cynical career officer, a cold tactician, or a bellowing, barrel-chested Imperial hero, he and his Company Command Squad form the strategic nexus of the Imperial Guard army. The Company Commander's orders crackle across the vox network, bolstering the courage of his men and ensuring that his army functions with precise coordination. By his authority soldiers are instructed to charge to their own deaths so that victory may be achieved, or ordered to hold the line against overwhelming odds. It is the duty of the Company Command Squad to protect their leader in battle, shielding him from incoming enemy assaults so that he may continue to exert his tactical acumen. They also form an offensive core around him, inspiring the rank-and-file troops with their skill and experience. Depending on the battle, they can either lead the charge into the enemy or form the immovable centre of the Astra Militarum line.

'No soldier here has permission to die. Not until you have given these heretic scum a Cadian welcome. First rank, fire! Second rank, fire!'

- Galen Bale, 4th Company Commander of the Cadian 111th, during the last battle of Cadia

TANK COMMANDERS

A Tank Commander rides to battle in the cupola of a mighty Leman Russ battle tank. These grizzled officers are virtually one with their machines, possessing an implicit knowledge of mechanised warfare in all its forms. Granted their pick of the armoured fighting vehicles available to their regiment, they are further entitled to select their crew from the finest veterans. The average Tank Commander is therefore a steely eyed ace, heading up a crew of the very best their regiment has to offer.

To become a Tank Commander, an officer requires a singular and obsessive dedication to the art of tank combat. Each possesses an authority over their crew on par with an infantry commander directing the many squads in a platoon. With a single word, a Tank Commander can coordinate the movement, targeting, firing and reloading of their mechanical steed. A moment's hesitation or a minute lack of clarity could leave their Leman Russ floundering ineffectually on the battlefield. The skill of these 'tread-heads', as they are sometimes called by infantry officers, becomes obvious in combat. A Tank Commander is a veteran of dozens of battles, and knows where and when to direct his attacks to deal maximum damage. The most dangerous heretics and abominations are obliterated before they can reach Imperial lines, while those who lead them are eradicated from afar.

Each Tank Commander is placed at the head of a tank company, where their authority and expertise is put to use directing the actions of multiple squadrons. A skilled Tank Commander is intimately familiar with the vehicles in his company – he understands the strengths and weaknesses of each armament, the limitations of various engine patterns and the idiosyncrasies of every machine spirit. This allows him to wield his squadrons like a rapier or a battering ram depending on the needs of the battle. The Tank Commander knows when to order his battle tanks to launch full-throttle advances, moving to outflank the enemy position or dispersing to dilute incoming fire. Having lived through wars against the Imperium's myriad foes, he can also identify weak spots in the enemy's armour towards which his company's gunners will direct their fire. To compel the might of the Astra Militarum's war machines is an awesome responsibility, for along with the lives of the soldiery a Tank Commander is also charged with responsibility for the regiment's armoured assets – a resource that is far more valuable and difficult to quickly replace.

These veteran armour commanders will often be assigned temporary leadership of infantry or artillery assets. This may see the Tank Commander's squadron line-breaking at the head of an overwhelming infantry offensive, or digging in to provide close cover for thundering batteries of big guns. Whatever the case, the Tank Commander's strategic cunning and deadly armoured war machine can anchor an entire battle line, or smash that of the foe asunder. Infantrymen may grumble when assigned to the command of a tread-head, mistrusting such a man's grasp of the hardships faced by honest footsloggers, yet such complaints soon turn to cheers when the commander's tank squadron rolls into the foe's ranks, all guns blazing and tracks churning enemy bodies to bloody paste. It is a Tank Commander's fusion of combat experience and bellicose leadership that makes them especially deadly, and soldiers from non-armoured regiments serving under them quickly learn to trust in their prowess.

There have been countless Tank Commanders of note in the Astra Militarum's history. Astrov Yemenev of the Vostroyan 24th 'Iron Bloods' Armoured Regiment was noted for taking out the dread Biel-Tan tank ace, Vathwal Heavenlance. The Iron Bloods encountered the Fire Prism pilot on hive world Degis, alone and cut off from his invading army. With a trio of lancing blasts the Aeldari incinerated an entire squadron of Leman Russ Battle Tanks while weaving deftly between the returning Imperial fire. Three more blasts saw another squadron obliterated. With his company below half strength, Yemenev ordered the remaining gunners to lay down a wide blanket of fire on either side of the zigzagging Fire Prism. This left but a narrow channel where Heavenlance could move, through which Yemenev fired the killing blow.

Some Tank Commanders adorn the hull of their vehicle with grim trophies collected by their company in battle. Those of the Armageddon Ork Hunters are renowned for this, and will mount the skull of a defeated Warboss on the prow of their Leman Russ. Other, more pious commanders turn their tanks into battlefield shrines so that the light of the Emperor may ever guide their manoeuvres. Ornate reliquaries are fitted to the turret, the primary weapon is festooned with burning braziers, and from sponson-mounted vox speakers comes the endless cry of incanted hymnals and Imperial prayers.

PLATOON COMMANDERS

The Astra Militarum is a vast fighting formation and even basic troop movements can involve the mobilisation of thousands of men. For these operations to go smoothly the Imperial Guard has a substantial command structure. One of the first links in this chain is the Platoon Commander.

Platoon Commanders are known by a variety of official ranks and titles – lieutenant, marshal and shield-centurion are just a few examples. Their role is to ensure the platoon fulfils the Company Commander's orders and gets the job done. Sadly, for every fresh-faced officer who bravely leads his troops against the enemy there is another who panics and falters in the heat of battle. These incompetent individuals are responsible for wasting countless lives and such ineptitude is quickly punished. Those who survive multiple encounters – both with the enemy and the Commissars attached to their regiment – are given ever greater responsibilities on the battlefield, and those who excel are highly valued. Where almost any lieutenant can be relied upon to simply herd infantry towards the enemy, senior officers turn to their most trusted Platoon Commanders to undertake more nuanced and vital missions – gaining the high ground to outflank the enemy position or knocking out a heavily guarded shield generator so that artillery bombardments can commence.

While the Astra Militarum is vast in its size and reach, its constituent units do not have infinite resources or manpower. A single company may face many threats across multiple fronts, stretching thin the organizational capacity of its commander. In such cases, a Platoon Commander with a proven record of success can be tasked with leading small contingents of soldiers without the supervision of his superior officer. Failure to adhere strictly to the parameters of the mission – as dictated by the Company Commander – is considered an act of insubordination, but otherwise the Platoon Commander is able to direct the soldiers in their charge as they see fit. Those who show exceptional cunning, unfailing determination and the appropriate amount of initiative in fulfilling their charge are often singled out as candidates for promotion.

Like their senior counterparts, Platoon Commanders are often accompanied by a hand-picked Command Squad who help them fulfil their duties. The members of this entourage are typically amongst the most skilled and experienced veterans in the platoon, and provide extra firepower and vox support in battle. In addition, should there be doubts amongst the rank-and-file regarding the competence of a new Platoon Commander, these scar-faced soldiers help to maintain order – if the Commissar doesn't do so first.

INFANTRY SQUADS

Astra Militarum platoons are made up of several ten-man squads, led into battle by a low-ranking commander such as a sergeant. Infantry Squads form the backbone of the Astra Militarum, and countless billions of infantry soldiers fight and die for the Imperium. They are the footsloggers, the dogfaces, the poor bloody infantry. Guardsmen are used for every conceivable action the Imperial Guard may undertake, from holding ground to forlorn charges against enemy positions.

The armies of the Astra Militarum are made from billions of regiments, recruited from every world in the Imperium. There is no universal uniform for these Guardsmen; warriors don the armour and wargear native to their home worlds. The only piece of armament common to all Guardsmen is the lasgun, and even then some regiments from more primitive worlds have been trained with only muskets, crossbows, or even spears. The fighting ability of each regiment reflects the world and society it comes from. Some planets breed cunning gang fighters whilst others raise savage and barbaric warriors.

Guardsmen are disciplined troops indoctrinated to follow orders to the letter. In the face of the enemy the serried ranks of the Astra Militarum are trained to stand firm and respond with a steady aim. When sergeants bellow, the rank-and-file obey; backs stiffen and lasguns level at the foe. Opponents charging at Imperial Guard positions must first survive a blazing hail of las-fire, a fusillade that can stem the tide of all but the most determined assault. The fate of battles is often decided upon the courage and mettle of Infantry Squads – but, they are still only human. On equal terms they are no match for the many alien and tainted horrors they must face.

Should such enemies close the distance the Infantry Squads are, more often than not, slaughtered.

Although some Guardsmen are equipped with a variety of powerful and specialised weaponry, the primary strength of the infantry regiments remains their huge and expendable mass of manpower. The combined firepower of Astra Militarum regiments makes them a deadly opponent, capable of out-shooting almost any enemy. The thundering charge of a thousand Guardsmen can overwhelm the most elite and dangerous of opponents, crushing them underfoot and running them through with a wall of bayonet points.

CONSCRIPTS

In dire situations a world may be required to increase its tithe and raise additional regiments to match some overwhelming threat. A planet may be forced to bring forward its annual conscription, recruiting troops who would otherwise be deemed too young, or have not had the time to complete basic training. These youths are officially designated as probitors. In practice, they are given a variety of nicknames, but the most common moniker is 'Whiteshield'. This name stems from the fact that they show no regimental, company or platoon markings until they have earned the right to do so on the battlefield. The only insignia these recruits display are white helmet stripes. Eager to prove their courage, these reckless cadets enter the fray. Those few that survive might one day be lucky enough to call themselves 'Guardsmen' – far more than a simple promotion, this is a rite of passage amongst the probitors that marks their entry into adulthood.

HEAVY WEAPONS SQUADS

Though much of an infantry regiment is made up of rank-and-file Guardsmen, those soldiers with an affinity for bulky and more complicated weaponry are often gathered together within a dedicated Heavy Weapons Company. This allows an infantry regiment to bring devastating weaponry to bear without relying on the armoured fighting vehicles from other divisions of their Regimentum. Those who serve in a Heavy Weapons Company have but one, straightforward role – to obliterate any enemies who cannot be overwhelmed by massed las-fire.

It is rare that the entirety of the Heavy Weapons Company will be fielded together. Instead, individual Heavy Weapons Squads are assigned to other companies as platoon-support units, where they bolster the battle line and provide close fire support. Placed under the command of an officer, a Heavy Weapons Squad boosts the firepower of the Infantry Platoon to which it is attached, allowing the gunners to engage enemy armoured units or hold off alien hordes that outnumber them many times over. Typically comprising three Heavy Weapons Teams, these squads use concentrated fire to create deadly kill zones. Entire columns of battle tanks can be targeted and exterminated in short order, as can massed waves of oncoming infantry.

Though Heavy Weapons Teams are usually formed up into dedicated squads, they can also be individually attached to Infantry Squads. Due to their size and bulk, each heavy weapon is crewed by a team of two troopers. Generally speaking, one crewman carries and fires the weapon whilst the other hauls and loads the ammunition. Even a single Heavy Weapons Team can unleash a torrent of devastating heavy firepower, reducing the packed ranks of the enemy to nothing but a pile of bleeding corpses in the time it takes to pull a trigger.

Some squads use mortars to rain high-explosive shells upon enemy positions that would otherwise be out of reach, pinning down the enemy whilst fast-moving units move in for the kill. Other Heavy Weapons Squads act as fire support teams – armed with heavy bolters or autocannons, they lay down a curtain of fire that can mow down packed ranks of infantry in a welter of gore whilst tearing apart light vehicles. When equipped with the largest man-portable weapons in the regiment, Heavy Weapons Squads are excellent anti-tank units. Such teams use lascannons and missile launchers to pick out heavy vehicles, large alien creatures and other armoured targets.

SPECIAL WEAPONS SQUADS

Most regiments maintain a separate support company dedicated to providing infantry platoons with troops armed and trained to fulfil a number of specialist roles. These six-man squads may be equipped with sniper rifles, flamers, grenade launchers, meltaguns, or a combination of weapons, each suited to a different style of warfare. Regardless of their configuration, each Special Weapons Squad is deadly on the battlefield. Typically, three lasgun-armed Guardsmen will provide covering fire, allowing three armed with specialist weapons to unload upon the enemy.

VETERANS

Imperial Guard regiments are often called upon to fight gruelling wars of attrition lasting years or even decades. As time passes, each company will shrink in size as casualties take their inevitable toll. Those that survive are the hardiest troopers in the Astra Militarum. Their battlefield training has been honed in the fires of war, forging them into warriors who have learnt how to fight and kill with lethal efficiency. Veterans are the battle-hardened elites of the Astra Militarum, the first squad in an assault and the last in a retreat.

Veterans are natural born survivors. They have escaped ambushes, negotiated mine fields, fought a myriad of foes and lived to tell the tale. Their continued existence, despite the dangers they face, is testament to both their skill at war and their natural survival instinct. In extremely rare cases an entire company may endure the grim wars of a campaign and emerge largely unscathed, their practised skill, peerless cunning and supernatural luck allowing them to avoid heavy casualties. Legendary reputations follow such companies of Veterans, and each new engagement brings them greater renown amongst the rank-and-file troopers. But in the vast majority of cases, only a single squad of combat-hardened Veterans will survive the slaughter of their company. Such squads are attached to larger regiments where it is hoped they will assimilate quickly and their skills may rub off onto less-experienced shoulders. These Veterans may not be from the same regiment or even the same home world, and so may introduce brand new combat-tactics and an entirely different war-ethic to their foster regiment.

Although Veteran squads technically remain part of the same rigid command structure, these grizzled survivors function best when allowed a certain amount of free rein. They provide valuable battlefield experience and may employ unconventional but effective tactics that are not taught by the Tactica Imperium.

Veterans excel in all aspects of warfare, from close-range firefights to heavy demolitions work. Veterans are all inevitably deadeye shots and such warriors are usually kept together to bolster the line, their superior marksmanship making the difference between defeat and victory.

Many Veterans carry weapons and wargear not commonly issued to the massed ranks of the Imperial Guardsmen. An extra plasma blast here or a gout from a heavy flamer there can make the difference between life and death. Veteran squads acquire these non-standard armaments from a variety of sources. Some are 'borrowed' from Munitorum stores, whilst others are battlefield trophies prized out of the cold, dead hands of a fallen enemy. Some squads have in their number a Veteran Heavy Weapons Team. These are the last survivors of Heavy Weapons Squads, who have ample experience in operating their devastating weaponry.

COMBINING REGIMENTS

With few exceptions, new recruits are not added to existing regiments. Under-strength formations are instead simply merged together. Where possible, the formations joined are from the same home world, as was the case when the Cadian 12th and 78th were merged after the Fall of Ice Hive Magnox. Sometimes, however, two very different regiments are combined, such as when the Catachan CLXXXII was merged with the Elysian 90th. As this took place on the Departmento Munitorum world of Prosan, the composite regiment was designated the Prosan 314th. The new regiment became expert in airmobile jungle warfare after being issued Valkyries during the Saikong Justification wars.

CHIMERAS

The Chimera is the Imperial Guard's most commonly used armoured troop carrier. These ubiquitous vehicles are extremely durable and practical, capable of mounting an array of support weapons. From within the armoured confines of a Chimera, an embarked Infantry Squad can utilise the hull-mounted lasgun array to unleash a lethal fusillade of shots into the foe, protected from all but the most destructive of reprisals.

Chimeras are the ubiquitous workhorses of the Astra Militarum and can be fitted with a range of equipment to increase their battlefield effectiveness. All Chimeras are equipped with smoke launchers that can produce an obscuring shroud of chaff at a moment's notice. Some of the transports are also fitted with heavy-duty bulldozer blades to clear a path through ruin and rubble for heavier battle tanks. With auspex arrays and communication voxes, Chimeras also act as mobile bases of operations from which Astra Militarum officers can marshal their forces. In addition, various offensive armaments can be fitted to a Chimera's hull, making it a versatile front-line tank.

Squads of troopers mounted in Chimeras are sometimes referred to as Armoured Fist units. These squads lend speed and tactical flexibility to the often slow and rigid ranks of the Astra Militarum. An infantry regiment does not typically include any mechanised troops, it being difficult for most planetary governors to obtain and maintain the vehicles needed for such formations. Because of this, it is quite common for commanders to attach individual Armoured Fist squads from fully mechanised regiments in order to provide fast-moving armoured transport.

Armoured Fist squads are able to respond quickly to emergent threats or forge ahead of the main advance and seize vital objectives until reinforcements arrive. Enemy positions are quickly overrun, the heavy weaponry of Chimeras spitting a stream of death into the packed ranks of the foe. Infantry Squads then charge down the steel ramps at the vehicles' rear and despatch survivors at point blank range. Armoured Fist squads have a reputation for 'getting the job done' and are in high demand by infantry commanders. The armoured protection of a Chimera is vital for a successful assault, and so they are typically deployed against the most heavily defended of enemy positions. It is therefore no surprise that Armoured Fist squads suffer even higher casualty rates than standard infantry formations.

Over the millennia, the Chimera has been pressed into service in a variety of different forms, proving its reliability and worth time and again. It is a highly versatile vehicle capable of operation in the most hostile environments. Its tracks are capable of traversing almost any surface, and its amphibious design allows it to move through dense swamps, deep marshes and even rivers. Many an enemy army has been destroyed because its general thought his flanks protected by such obstructions, only to find ranks of Imperial Guardsmen – supported by the fearsome anti-personnel weaponry of their Chimera transports – disgorging into the very heart of his forces.

'DO NOT STRIKE UNTIL YOU ARE READY TO CRUSH THE ENEMY UTTERLY, AND THEN ATTACK WITHOUT MERCY, DESTROY EVERY VESTIGE OF RESISTANCE, LEAVE NO ONE TO WORK AGAINST YOU.'

- The Tactica Imperium

TAUROXES

The Taurox APC is designed to hit hard and fast, exploiting gaps in the enemy battle line or plugging any holes torn in the Imperium's own. Though slightly less robust than the Chimera, Tauroxes are the swiftest ground transport vehicle in the Astra Militarum, and as such they are used for rapid redeployment and for vanguard manoeuvres ahead of the main force. There is no better delivery system for small groups of soldiers armed with devastating weaponry, and Veterans, Special Weapons Squads and Command Squads who have shown an aptitude for close-quarters firefights are often assigned a Taurox to carry them into battle. After the Taurox surges through the withering hail of incoming enemy fire, the hatches burst open and the passengers pour out, flamers and meltaguns blazing.

Though lightly armoured, the Taurox still packs a punch. Mounted on its hull are a pair of autocannons that mow down enemy forces as it roars into the breach. Once its infantry payload has disembarked, it can continue to provide a mobile base of heavy fire for them, moving alongside the troops as an assault escort. Alternatively, it may break from its former passengers and head to some other part of the battlefield where it can lay waste to a fleeing enemy unit or pick up and deliver a fresh squad to their target.

The rugged 'Castellan' quad-track unit affords Tauroxes the ability to negotiate even the most tangled terrain with ease. Axial servo-dampeners redistribute the weight of the vehicle across its four tracks as it moves, allowing jagged outcrops and unevenly piled rubble to be traversed at full throttle. The Taurox's mobility is so reliable that Astra Militarum commanders often elect to bring them on long campaigns that range across multiple war fronts. Whether their regiment ends up fighting inside a crumbling hive, through the knotted jungles of a death world or across the open plains of a barren planet, the Taurox will perform its duty.

The Taurox's capacity to punch through seemingly impossible terrain also makes it an ideal counter-attack asset. Astra Militarum commanders will often hold back squads of short ranged, hard-hitting infantry in Taurox APCs, throwing them in to blunt enemy breakthroughs before the foe can build momentum. The twisted wreckage of tanks and piles of corpses that might block other reinforcement efforts are no issue for the Taurox, which will adroitly skirt round such obstacles with ease. For the same reasons, they are also regularly employed as light recon vehicles, or tasked with running escort duties for columns of artillery. The Taurox will swiftly deploy squads of heavy infantry, countering unexpected threats with overwhelming firepower until reinforcements can be brought to bear.

TAUROX PRIMES

A variant of the Taurox built for use by the Militarum Tempestus, the Prime's design is efficient and flexible. The vehicle's chassis incorporates arcane technologies that allow it to sustain Tempestus Scions operating in extremely hostile environments, or even the cold vacuum of space. The vehicle can be internally pressurised, and features a suite of life-support systems. Further, its engines can be compelled – using the proper rituals and prayers – to channel magnetic force into the Prime's tracks. This enables the vehicle to cling to vertical surfaces and operate in zero gravity conditions.

The Taurox Prime's weapon load-out is equally versatile – whether blasting enemy infantry apart with hails of missiles or gatling cannon fire, or bringing down tanks and fortifications with their lightweight battle cannons, these vehicles are the ideal transport for the elite forces of the Militarum Tempestus.

The exceptional versatility of the Taurox Prime was expertly utilized in the Scarus Sector when the Schola Progenium facility came under attack by a Death Guard warband. The 68th Deltic Lions, having battled the worshippers of the Plague God many times before, rushed to defend the world against the emergent corruption. Rather than becoming bogged down in a battle of attrition – a battle that the resilient Plague Marines would probably have won – the Deltic Lions used their many Taurox Primes to move swiftly to wherever the Death Guard lines were weakest. Pitting the entirety of their forces against a single enemy flank forced the lumbering Chaos minions to reposition, but before they could respond, the Tempestus Scions re-embarked and dispersed. Repeated feinting attacks allowed the Deltic Lions to lure their enemy deep into an icy ravine where the snow and cold further hampered the Heretic Astartes' movement. The Taurox Primes, on the other hand, were able to ascend to the cliff-tops on either side of the ravine, from which the Scions rained hell down upon their targets. Hot-shot lasguns incinerated putrid flesh, while Taurox-pattern gatling cannons, battle cannons and missile launchers blasted the enemy's swollen ranks into oblivion.

SENTINELS

The Sentinel is a one-man all-terrain bipedal vehicle, used by the Astra Militarum where mobile patrols must be mounted across rough terrain, or where firepower must be deployed rapidly in response to a threat. Sentinels achieve a perfect balance of robustness and mobility, able to negotiate terrain that would immobilise heavier battle tanks and armoured vehicles whilst still able to face down fire that would shred ranks of infantry.

Employed primarily for reconnaissance and light infantry support, the Scout Sentinel is used by many Astra Militarum regiments to locate and obliterate knots of enemy resistance in daring ambushes and surprise attacks, bursts from multi-lasers and gouts of super-heated promethium eliminating swathes of enemy troops. Scout Sentinels are fitted with sophisticated gyro-stabilisers to assist them as they traverse the rockiest cratered battlefield and the steepest of slopes. Articulated legs enable them to stalk quietly through dense undergrowth or urban ruins whilst permitting an impressive burst of speed over open territory. The scout vehicles' powerplants also incorporate noise-reduction modification so as not to alert the enemy to their presence. The crewmen of these Scout Sentinels often adapt their vehicles further, and all manner of rough terrain innovations are seen across various Militarum Regimentos. The Valhallan Ice Warriors often attach servo-driven claw spikes to the feet of their Scout Sentinels that can grip to glacial planes, whereas the Catachan Jungle Fighters have been known to rig their walkers with giant chainsaws to clear a path through thick jungles.

The Scout Sentinel is not intended for extended front-line combat operations. Its unshielded crew compartment allows the pilot to survey their prey, but at the cost of making them vulnerable to small-arms fire. To maintain mobility, the walker also lacks the armour and ferro-steel plating of a fully-fledged battle tank.

Sentinels become superb battlefront units when they are fitted with extra armour, allowing them to stride through a deluge of weapons fire that would cripple or destroy a lighter walker. The mechanical legs of an Armoured Sentinel are also modified with recoil compensators in place of additional gyro-stabilisers, marginally decreasing their speed but allowing them to fire more powerful weapon systems. Sensor arrays and auspex systems are replaced with additional power cells and cooling systems to allow the Armoured Sentinel to fulfil its role as a mobile heavy weapons platform. Armoured Sentinels are used as roving hunter-killer units, forming search and destroy teams that stalk enemy battle tanks. Once their quarry is located, it is eliminated with practised efficiency, plasma and lascannon fire slicing through the thickest ablative plating.

While Scout Sentinels range ahead of the main force, conducting hit-and-run raids and ambushes, armoured Sentinels march alongside columns of battle tanks or at the fore of Astra Militarum infantry formations, laying waste to the foe without breaking stride. Both Scout Sentinels and Armoured Sentinels are often deployed far from Imperial supply lines, deep within enemy territory. When operating as autonomous units, the pilots of Sentinel squadrons are often forced to use their own initiative – a quality that is not generally fostered in Imperial soldiers. As a result, many Sentinel pilots have acquired a reputation as would-be hotshots, glory seekers or insubordinate mavericks.

'Always endeavour to fight the enemy on your own terms. If you outnumber the foe use reserves to break through when the enemy's overstretched lines collapse. If you are outnumbered then concentrate your forces so that the enemy can fight only your best troops. If you are powerful at close quarters then engage in dense terrain where your advantage will prove greatest. If you are superior at long range then attack along an extended front. Remember always, however, that a commander who puts his faith in heavy weaponry alone will be easily outmanoeuvred and a commander who relies on close combat without adequate support will lose his force to disciplined fire. No one has ever won a battle who failed to take advantage of his enemy's weakness, or take heed of his own.'

- Lord Solar Macharius, prior to the conquest of Kallastin

HELLHOUNDS

Sacrificing the Chimera's transport capacity for larger engines and bulky canisters of volatile promethium, the Hellhound sports a monstrous turret-mounted flame-thrower – aptly named the inferno cannon – that discharges a self-igniting chemical. Typically deployed in dense terrain, the Hellhound excels at flushing dug-in infantry from their bunkers and boltholes. The roar and hiss of chemical flames fill the air as the Hellhound spews out its flaming torrents, melting the armour, clothing and flesh of any unfortunate enough to be caught in the blast. Unspent shell casings explode inside ammunitions belts, blasting shrapnel through muscle and bone. Enemy infantry reel screaming from cover, ablaze from head to toe as the reek of their own burnt flesh fills the air. Any who somehow manage to survive this fiery onslaught fall back in desperate disarray.

The Hellhound's only real disadvantage is the comparatively short range of its primary armament, a limitation that forces it to close with the foe during battle. When coupled with the understanding that a fully fuelled Hellhound is a massive firebomb waiting to happen, it is unsurprising that most Hellhound crews are drawn from punishment details and somewhat unhinged volunteers. These men, however, take a perverse pride in their grim assignment. Many Hellhound crews, treated to the front-row spectacle of heretics and aliens burning in the fires of Imperial justice, begin to see their duties as akin to religious cleansing – such pious pyromania leads to fatalism and risk-taking, but also encourages deadly, enthusiastic efficiency.

> 'We flooded that bunker with fire and watched the heretics burn till they was nothin' but ash on the wind. It was beautiful Sarge, just… beautiful.'
>
> - Gunner 'Scorch' Hennessey, Catachan IX Armoured

DEVIL DOGS

The Devil Dog replaces the Hellhound's primary armament with a snub-nosed melta cannon. Acquiring its name from the high-pitched howl this weapon makes upon firing, the Devil Dog is capable of punching far above its weight in armoured combat. Indeed, many Devil Dog crews style themselves as big game hunters or monster slayers, excelling in the eradication of enemy armour and exceptionally heavy infantry assets. A foe forced to fight protracted campaigns in dense terrain against the Astra Militarum soon learns to dread the hunched silhouette of the Devil Dog – those who don't find their vehicles reduced to molten slag by this aggressive and fast moving tank hunter.

The pairing of Devil Dogs with Hellhounds on the battlefield is commonplace among the battle groups of the Imperial Guard – so much so that an entire page of the Tactica Imperium is dedicated to the deadly synergy achieved by fielding them in mixed 'Desolation Squadrons'. The Hellhound, being vulnerable to heavily armoured enemy tanks, is protected by the liquefying melta blasts of the Devil Dog – conversely, the rivers of flame that pour from the Hellhound's inferno cannon immolate any massed infantry trying to swarm the Devil Dog. Working in concert, these two tanks make short work of the foe.

BANE WOLVES

A deceptively simple adaptation of the Hellhound, the Bane Wolf replaces its promethium with bulky canisters of toxic gas. This incredibly corrosive fume has been certified by the Adeptus Biologis as inimical to almost every life form in the galaxy. Ejected from the tank's chem cannon in hissing jets, the hideous substance chews through ceramite and chitin alike in microseconds. The victim is dissolved by the virulent chemicals; blood boils and organs rupture, skin erupts into bubbling lesions and sloughs from crumbling bone until, eventually, the target is reduced to a slick of organic sludge to be ground beneath the tank's whirring tracks. Commonly, Bane Wolf crews are remote, taciturn individuals who do not mix with other Guardsmen. Their vehicles are as likely to see action quelling the uprisings of traitorous human cults as they are against deadly xenos threats, and to deploy the chem cannon against fellow humans, no matter how debased, can be a harrowing experience. It takes a particular kind of nihilist to crew such a short ranged and grotesque terror weapon.

The sacrosanct formula of gas used in a Bane Wolf's chem cannon is dictated by the Tech-Priests of the Adeptus Mechanicus. Even so, various regiments have been known to employ their own makeshift concoctions. One such mixture, known as 'the penitent's breath', was used to scour a heretical uprising from the scum-pits of Savlar. The iridescent spray proved effective, but the Bane Wolf crews who employed it were themselves swiftly executed for heresy afterwards.

ORDNANCE BATTERIES

When the Astra Militarum marches to war it is accompanied by the thunderous bombardment of artillery fire. Artillery companies comprising dozens of ordnance batteries fire ceaseless barrages from long range, pounding the enemy prior to a general advance. Before the smoke has cleared the infantry emerge, launching their assaults in the wake of the destructive artillery salvoes whilst the enemy is still reeling from the blows.

Many a lengthy siege has been brought to an abrupt conclusion by dedicated artillery regiments, heavy shells breaching walls and flattening fortifications. The Astra Militarum is well equipped to conduct siege warfare, and there are few bulwarks strong enough to withstand the magnitude of firepower unleashed by the Imperium's biggest guns.

BASILISKS

Of all the Astra Militarum's ordnance units, the Basilisk is the most numerous. Like many self-propelled artillery pieces, Basilisks can keep pace with infantry advances, ready to unleash its payload at a moment's notice. Such devastating weapons are not intended to perform the same battlefield role as battle tanks, their lack of ablative amour and exposed crew carriages making them too vulnerable to lead assaults. Instead, Basilisks are fielded in a support role to the front-line regiments.

Basilisks can be redirected, reloaded and fired relatively swiftly. The design of the earthshaker cannon allows the weapon to be elevated to a steep enough angle for it to fire its shells high over the battlefield and onto concealed enemy targets. Basilisks can therefore deploy out of harm's way where the enemy is powerless to retaliate. The powerful shells fired by the earthshaker cannon are capable of smashing apart the enemy lines with ease and are designed to cause catastrophic damage at the impact zone. Targets at the epicentre of such a detonation are immolated immediately, while those in the vicinity are pulverised by the deadly shock wave. The unmistakable shriek of the Basilisks' incoming ordnance is rightly feared by the enemies of the Emperor.

> 'INFANTRY WIN FIREFIGHTS.
> TANKS WIN BATTLES.
> ARTILLERY WIN WARS.'
> - *Old saying amongst Astra Militarum artillery officers*

WYVERNS

The Wyvern suppression tank is armed with a deadly array of stormshard mortars. While it lacks the range and raw power of the Basilisk's earthshaker cannon, this ordnance tank excels in the claustrophobic environment of urban warfare, raining curtains of shells down upon luckless enemy infantry without ever exposing itself to harm.

Using a modified version of the auto-targeting systems found in Hydra flak tanks, the Wyvern runs constant proximity sweeps for concentrations of enemy infantry. The machine spirits of these vehicles are renowned for their malicious streak – they actively seek out the most tightly packed or vulnerable groupings of the foe to target, sometimes even overriding the commands of their own crews.

When a Wyvern does let fly, its stormshard mortars emit a distinctive whooshing roar as they launch clouds of shells high into the air. This is inevitably followed by the howl of those same shells descending, the crackling booms of their detonation and the harrowing screams of victims. The inundation of munitions creates a patchwork of destruction that covers a wide area, making it almost impossible to escape the Wyvern's wrath. Each airbursting shell releases an eviscerating flurry of aquila-shaped flechettes – those not killed outright by the explosions are cut down by the flying shards.

The Wyvern is a highly versatile weapon for an artillery tank. Entire batteries of them can be drawn up to pound a foe into oblivion, but more often they are attached in small numbers to other formations. Even a single Wyvern can provide an infantry platoon with invaluable close-range fire support, fending off waves of enemies that might otherwise overrun the hapless Guardsmen, or routing a dug-in foe from its fox-hole. When deployed in support of tanks, Wyverns prove invaluable at keeping at bay those infantry threats that would attack the vehicles' vulnerable flanks and rear.

HYDRAS

Whether faced by lightning-fast xenos fighters or daemonic, leather-winged monstrosities, the Hydra flak tank is ideally equipped to blow aerial foes out of the sky. The Hydra's predictive logic-spirit singles out and locks onto its targets with the tenacity of a predatory beast. Autoloaders engage with a rising whine as the Hydra's turret traverses, its quad autocannon howling as it fills the air with sawing lines of firepower. Few airborne enemies, no matter how debased or unnatural, can survive for long once they are locked in the Hydra's sights.

Though the Hydra has sufficient armour to weather a fair degree of punishment, it is intended primarily as a support vehicle rather than a main line battle tank. Nonetheless, the Hydra is far from defenceless. Its hull can be fitted with various armaments, and its autocannon can be angled downward to slaughter grounded enemies when necessary. However, the Hydra's machine spirit hungers only for airborne prey, its tracking servos refusing to trace the lumbering paths made by foes that cannot fly, meaning it must be aimed manually and, therefore, less accurately when targeting opponents on the ground. Company Commanders must therefore ensure they have seconded enough infantry or tanks to guard their Hydra batteries from direct attack. With a sufficient escort the Hydras can remain safe from harm while concentrating their efforts on keeping the skies clear.

Even a single Hydra can throw up a storm of flak, swatting enemy aircraft from the skies with an adamantine fist. When several of these vehicles draw up and open fire, the devastation wrought on airborne foes is spectacular. Monstrous xenos wings are reduced to streamers of flesh, the gibbous flight-sacks of daemonic drones burst under the weight of puncturing fire, and even heavily armoured attack craft are reduced to perforated scrap as their fuel tanks and internal magazines explode.

For most Imperial Guardsmen, be they artillery crew, tankers or foot-slogging infantry, the screaming approach of enemy aircraft is a sound that evokes absolute dread. When the black shadow of monstrous wings falls across them, the men of the Guard have little defence besides prayer. So it is that the Hydra has acquired a reputation as an omen of good luck. With nicknames ranging from 'steel saviours' to the more colloquial 'bug-zapper', Hydras are viewed with comradely affection by most soldiers in the Astra Militarum. A common tradition amongst the men of many regiments is to rap their knuckles against the hull of a Hydra before battle; this so-called 'angel's knock' is performed in solemn silence and intended to draw the vigilance of the Hydra's machine spirit in the battle to come. Hydra crews share in their vehicles' popularity, enjoying something approaching folk-hero status amongst their comrades and a place around any squad's camp fire. Some Hydra crewmen revel in the regard of their comrades and the adrenaline rush of their duty, while others find the weight of responsibility uncomfortable, but few are foolish enough to believe the camaraderie of their fellows is untainted by self-interest.

Regardless of their crews' attitudes or affectations, when Hydras roll into battle they can make all the difference to an Astra Militarum army. On Sarentos III, during the battle of the Sandsea, the Cadian 1652nd Armoured were tasked with breaking the Necron line. Roaring across the dunes, the Leman Russ squadrons of the 1652nd directed a withering rain of fire into their deathless foes. Great geysers of crimson sand were blown high into the air as the Necron line disintegrated before the tankers' armoured charge. Then came the Doom Scythes. Screaming over the battlefield on howling repulsor-jets, several wings of the ominous alien craft began to strafe the Imperial tanks with the glowing beams of their death rays. Flames billowed and black smoke gouted forth as first one Leman Russ and then another exploded. Though well prepared and outfitted for ground warfare, the Cadians were fighting without the military support of the aerial formations of the Aeronautica Imperialis, meaning they had no aircraft of their own to intercept this threat in the sky. For a perilous moment it appeared as though the 1652nd would be hurled back in disarray – but their commander had issued his own call for reinforcements. Barrelling over the crest of a nearby dune came three Hydras, tracks churning spumes of sand in their wake. The flak tanks marked their speeding targets and opened fire, filling the sky with fury. One after another, the Necron attack craft were riddled with holes. Driven by eldritch technology, the living metal of the ancient xenos flyers began to writhe, moving to fill in the gaping rents. Yet no matter how fast the puncture wounds were resealed, the Hydras' quad autocannons continued to savage their targets. Flurries of sparks and crackling green lightning wreathed the hulls of the Doom Scythes as they plummeted to the dunes below, tumbling end over end and exploding with enormous force. As the last of the enemy aircraft turned tail and fled, the surviving tanks of the 1652nd pushed forward again, their route to victory now covered by the watchful guns of the Hydras.

MANTICORES

The Manticore Rocket Launcher is an ancient siege engine that dates back to the earliest days of the Imperium. Once, these potent artillery tanks mounted a variety of devastating warheads. Over time, as forge worlds have fallen and technological lore has been lost behind the veil of mythology, the Manticore's versatility has lessened. Though some variants still exist in far flung corners of the Imperium, it is the Munitorum standard for Manticores to go into battle bearing four mighty storm eagle rockets. These munitions are by far the most powerful remaining Manticore armament, and are more than capable of causing unsustainable levels of damage to any foe.

Each storm eagle rocket is a self-contained arsenal. Mounted upon a single-stage booster and fitted with guidance and detonation-augurs, these munitions are capable of extreme range bombardment. The storm eagle warhead contains concentric racks of high explosive bomblets, each soaked in sacred unguents of the Mechanicus and hand-scribed with the One Hundred Canticles of Wrath. Soaring across the battlefield upon a contrail of flame, the storm eagle descends upon its target like an avenging angel. The deafening roar of the rocket's approach causes foes to abase themselves in terror, or flee screaming in a hopeless attempt at self-preservation. Directly above the target zone, the blessed warhead breaks up, unleashing its payload of bomblets across a wide area. Tanks are sent cartwheeling by concussive blasts, or are completely pulverised by the force of multiple detonations. Infantry are atomised or hurled into the air, blackened bodies tumbling down around the impact zone like ash from a hellish conflagration. Each warhead spawns a thunderous carpet of explosions that leave nought but wrath-strewn debris in their wake.

Though its potency is undeniable, the Manticore is an ancient machine and prone to exhibiting considerable technological eccentricities. To reload a Manticore requires several hours of careful, uninterrupted ministration by a crew of Tech-Priests and specialist servitors. This process absolutely cannot be undertaken in the field, rendering the tank's ammunition reserve finite. This is coupled with the fact that the sheer antiquity of the surviving Manticores has rendered their machine spirits truculent and temperamental. If prevailing conditions are not to the tank's liking or its systems are treated without due delicacy, the Manticore has been known to malfunction in a most wilful manner. Storm eagle rockets deviate wildly off course, fall uselessly out of the air, or simply ignore the depression of launch runes with curmudgeonly indifference. A Manticore crew will commonly bow to their machine before and after combat, humbly entreating its permission to discharge its weapons and then thanking it for delivering the Emperor's wrath. During battle they maintain a near-constant mantra of prayer and obeisance with the aim of mollifying their armoured steed, yet operational difficulties are still commonplace.

Despite the Manticore's unpredictable streak, many commanders consider the rewards of their successful employment more than worth the gamble. A single Manticore is adjudged by the Munitorum to be equal in material value to an entire battery of lesser ordnance, and with good reason. When the tanks are attached to Imperial Guard regiments for support, most officers employ them as terror weapons at a pivotal moment, using the might of the Manticore to deliver the decisive killing blow.

DEATHSTRIKES

A rare few weapons within the Astra Militarum arsenal are considered so destructive that to sanction their deployment without due cause and clear purpose is a capital offence. Such weapons are designated 'Ordnance Extremis' by the Munitorum. Chief among these implements of destruction is the Deathstrike missile launcher.

The Deathstrike exhibits huge range and destructive capability, launching a single intercontinental ballistic missile of intimidating size. Each of these colossal rockets is able to visit the wrath of the Emperor upon targets half a world away, allowing the Astra Militarum to stab deep into the heart of enemy-held territory or an encroaching army. Calculating these long-range trajectories takes time, however, and the volatile machine spirit of the missile must be entreated before it is sent hurtling on its martyr's journey. A Deathstrike preparing to fire quickly becomes a priority target for the enemy – the sheer size of its armament allows even the most animalistic xenos races to understand its apocalyptic purpose. As a slow moving asset with only moderate firepower outside of its primary munition, the Deathstrike often requires its own dedicated escort so as not to present the foe with a valuable and relatively soft target. For the Departmento Munitorum, simple logistics has precluded its deployment in all but the most extreme circumstances.

Until recently, the Deathstrike was a weapon in decline. The deployment of a single Deathstrike missile launcher requires a huge investment of resources. The acquisition of these weapons is a process littered with religious and administrative complexities, and can take months. Even the construction of a Deathstrike missile is a procedure whose worth in the Imperium's wars must be carefully weighed before commencement. Each component must be duly sanctified and blessed with hallowed oils, then arrayed as the catechisms of manufacture are intoned in full. A cortège of Tech-Priests then sets about the process of wiring guidance skulls to each of the warhead's actuators. Finally, the mounting ceremony in which the missile is racked on its firing platform is accompanied by its own solemn rites. As Deathstrikes are only requested to fulfil the direst of contingencies, the battles for which they are requested are often long over by the time they arrive at the front.

This is not to say that Deathstrike missile launchers have not seen use, for their formidable value and situational versatility are legendary. Over the past ten millennia they have been used against nearly every enemy of the Imperium. The warhead can be armed with a variety of horrifying payloads, each Deathstrike missile tailored to wreak maximum destruction on its intended target. With a single successful launch, a Deathstrike armed with a godspear warhead can bring down an enemy Titan, punching the towering war engine from its feet amid the false sun of a reactor meltdown. One well-placed missile can deliver virulent pathogens to the core of an army, wipe out the entire command structure of the foe in a holocaust of billowing plasma, or crush the morale of a wavering enemy with its sudden, god-like wrath. Most terrifying of all are the venerated vortex missiles. These warheads are able to sunder reality itself in a roiling wave of warp energy that guarantees the annihilation of anything caught in their blast. Vortex warheads are so rare that the improper launch of one is punishable by immediate summary execution.

It is a mark of how dark the days of the Imperium have become that a brutal new tactic has appeared, one that has seen the Deathstrike experience a renaissance. Held behind Imperial lines, Deathstrikes lurk out of sight, remaining undetected while they await their moment. When enemy forces threaten catastrophic breakthrough, or a suitably valuable target presents itself, waves of infantry are sent to bog the enemy down. Fed short range combat-launch coordinates, the Deathstrikes discharge their terrifying weapons directly into the heart of battle. As the missile descends, friend and foe alike are immolated amid the unleashed blast-wave. Such measures are as inhumane as they are desperate, yet in these times no sacrifice is too great to ensure the survival of Mankind.

Only those rare commanders with an intrinsic understanding of ballistic warfare can fully put to use the true obliterative power of a Deathstrike. One such commander was Zandar At'lan of the Tallarn 115th Armoured Regiment. On Septimius II, his tank companies were engaged with Ork warbands on three fronts spanning several dozen miles. On the verge of being overwhelmed, At'lan ordered all three of his columns to withdraw into the Copper Flats. As the bellicose greenskins gave chase, the armoured companies were instructed to retreat along paths that intersected each other. The launch of the single Deathstrike at At'lan's disposal was timed so that it struck exactly where the pursuing Orks converged. This use of Ordnance Extremis was considered exemplary by an attendant Lord Commissar.

LEMAN RUSS TANKS

Deadly, durable and able to be fielded in large numbers, the Leman Russ is a near-ubiquitous symbol of the Astra Militarum. All but the heaviest enemy fire ricochets harmlessly off the thick armour plating of these battle tanks, allowing them to defend key battlefield locations or surge forward in an implacable offensive.

The Leman Russ battle tank is an ironclad declaration of might made manifest. They are the mainstay of the Astra Militarum's armoured forces, lumbering slabs of armour and intolerance whose inexorable advance has ground a billion foes of the Imperium to bloody ruin.

What the Leman Russ lacks in speed, it more than makes up for in brute force and survivability. Enemy fire patters from its inches-thick armour like dust on the wind. Between its sponsons, hull and turret the Russ carries enough firepower to pound almost any foe into submission. The tank's rugged simplicity and ease of manufacture ensures that the Imperium can field whole companies of Leman Russ with ease, burying the outnumbered foe beneath waves of irresistible armoured fury.

Dedicated Leman Russ tank companies play a key role in Imperial strategy, and the greatest Imperial tank offensives will see armoured formations many miles in breadth sweep all before them in a rumbling tide. However, it is common to see armoured companies broken into squadrons to support infantry and artillery elements in the field. The presence of even one Leman Russ can provide an enormous boost to the fighting strength and morale of Imperial Guard infantry, while a whole squadron of such armoured brutes wields serious destructive power. Leman Russ squadrons can be deployed to spearhead an all-out offensive, reduce an enemy breakthrough to a tangle of blood-soaked wreckage, or safeguard the thundering guns of an artillery company from attack. With its many common variants, the Leman Russ is a versatile and deadly tool in the arsenal of any Imperial Guard commander.

LEMAN RUSS BATTLE TANKS

The standard Leman Russ is the most common battle tank in the Astra Militarum. Its tried and tested design has held up over the millennia better than any other pattern, making it the one most often requested by officers.

With a versatile weapon-fit and hefty battle cannon, the Leman Russ Battle Tank is capable of facing down almost any battlefield target. A single squadron can provide a decisive presence during both offensive and defensive deployments.

Elysion Dawn,
**Cadian 78th
Armoured Regiment,
2nd Company**

LEMAN RUSS EXTERMINATORS

The Leman Russ Exterminator is a common variant of the standard design, capable of laying down a withering hail of fire. The exterminator autocannon's shells can tear through lightly armoured chassis as easily as they rip through flesh and bone.

Though lacking the long range of some other tank variants, the Leman Russ Exterminator is capable of devastating whole ranks of enemy infantry before they have reached the Astra Militarum lines.

Iron Cyclone,
**Cadian 346th
Armoured Regiment,
3rd Company**

LEMAN RUSS VANQUISHERS

The Leman Russ Vanquisher is becoming increasingly rare, as the skills and technology required for the construction of the Vanquisher-pattern battle cannon were lost when the forge world of Tigrus was overrun. However, no other battle tank possesses more raw stopping power, and so the Vanquisher is still deployed whenever possible against heavily armoured enemies. The long range and high first-hit kill ratio of its main armament make it the anti-tank weapon of choice for most commanders.

Maxima Dread,
Cadian 185th Armoured Regiment, 2nd Company

LEMAN RUSS ERADICATORS

The Eradicator's nova cannon fires shells containing a sub-atomic core. Upon detonation they produce a powerful shock wave capable of pulverising both enemy barricades and the infantry sheltering behind them.

The Eradicator's design has been replicated on dozens of forge worlds and is utilised throughout the Imperium. Its main role is to support troop formations fighting in densely packed urban arenas.

Devil's Ire,
Cadian 212th Armoured Regiment, 1st Company

LEMAN RUSS DEMOLISHERS

The Leman Russ Demolisher was devised for but one task – line breaking. It carries the short ranged but highly destructive demolisher cannon, the utter lethality of which makes this pattern of battle tank the undisputed king of the close-range firefight.

With additional armour plating fitted on its front, the Demolisher is capable of pushing through devastating fire to close the gap between Imperial and enemy lines.

Avalanche of Steel,
Valhallan 1013th Armoured Regiment, 3rd Company

LEMAN RUSS PUNISHERS

The Leman Russ Punisher eschews anti-tank effectiveness for the ability to mow down infantry in vast quantities. Its turret-mounted gatling cannon is an unsubtle bullet-hose that applies the simple principle of overwhelming firepower to slaughter its targets.

There are few other tanks in the Astra Militarum capable of such high rates of fire, and Leman Russ Punisher crews have reputations for being both trigger-happy and gung-ho.

Raging Scorpion,
Cadian 12th Armoured Regiment, 3rd Company

LEMAN RUSS EXECUTIONERS

The Executioner is one of the oldest variants of the Leman Russ, and during the Great Crusade entire regiments of this tank were fielded. Gradually, over the millennia, knowledge of plasma technology has been lost, and the Executioner is now a rare relic.

When deployed in battle, the Executioner's plasma cannon fires with the fury of a miniature sun, incinerating tightly packed infantry and burning through vehicle armour with ease.

Sire of Violence,
Catachan DXIX Armoured Regiment, 2nd Company

SUPER-HEAVY TANKS

Each super-heavy tank is a monument to the destructive power of the Astra Militarum. They are the Emperor's undying wrath cast in steel, holy weapons with the power to obliterate anything in their path. Few commanders have earned the honour to field one of these glorious relics in battle, and fewer enemies can withstand their destructive power.

The largest and most destructive weapons of the Astra Militarum are its super-heavy tanks. Powered by enormous multi-fuel engines and driven by ferociously bellicose machine spirits, they are remnants of the Dark Age of Technology that continue to exemplify the implacability of Mankind. The hull of a super-heavy tank is layered with plates of adamantine steel armour, and bristling from this near-impenetrable casing are a multitude of armaments. Each of these monstrous machines boasts enough firepower to eradicate entire enemy formations single-handedly, and certain patterns have even greater offensive potential, with added sponson- and hull-mounted weaponry. Ubiquitous to all variants is a colossal main gun protruding from the turret. Some of these fire ultra-explosive shells, whereas others emit beams of immolating energy or a superabundance of mass-reactive bolts. Regardless of their payload, these weapons are capable of bringing utter ruination to the most fearsome enemies of the Imperium.

During the Great Crusade, entire regiments of super-heavy tanks were fielded in battle. The rumbling of engines rolled like thunder so that the enemies of the Imperium felt their advance long before the armoured wave broke over the horizon. Now, only a handful of forge worlds possess the sacred STCs required for their construction and maintenance. As such, they cannot be deployed on every one of the Astra Militarum's many war fronts. Only in the most crucial theatres, where failure is absolutely unacceptable and sheer weight of Guardsmen corpses has not yet won victory, are these steel behemoths unleashed upon the enemy.

A single super-heavy tank is a dominant presence in an Astra Militarum battle line. As it ploughs inexorably forward it lays down a wide path of destruction. Enemy ranks shatter long before it reaches their position, and those unlucky few who are able to maintain their defensive formations are ground to paste under the slab-like plates of its tracks. To witness such merciless punishment meted out against their foes provides a huge boost of morale to nearby Astra Militarum forces. Though

they face unimaginable horrors, they are given hope by the vessel of incarnate devastation that fights alongside them.

The Baneblade is the most common variant of super-heavy tank. Its primary weapon – the fearsome Baneblade cannon – is capable of delivering apocalyptic bombardments at a terrifying range. At close range, armoured vehicles are blasted to scrap by its hull-mounted demolisher cannon, and infantry and xenos beasts are blown to pieces by its autocannon and twin heavy bolters.

Each other pattern of super-heavy tank has armaments that make it dominant in specific battlefield roles. The Banehammer is the ultimate equalizer when facing a highly mobile enemy force. The massive shells of its tremor cannon are primed to explode only once they have been embedded below ground. The sundering effect of their detonations makes rapid redeployment impossible. The Hellhammer and Stormsword are both designed for use in siege and urban warfare, their respective cannons making a mockery of defensive barricades. The Hellhammer also mounts a demolisher cannon, whereas the Stormsword's siege cannon alone provides reliable devastation. Similarly, the Banesword's quake cannon can pulverise enemy armour and reduce fortifications to rubble. The Shadowsword is equipped with one of the most fearsome primary weapons – the dreaded volcano cannon – and is capable of taking down Titans at extreme ranges. Nothing short of the most powerful energy fields can hope to stop a direct hit from its blasts. The magma cannon of the Doomhammer is a smaller version of the volcano cannon. Though it has a reduced range of fire, its compact size allows for troop transport space within the hull. The Stormlord, on the other hand, is almost entirely dedicated to troop transport, its cavernous bay capable of carrying forty Guardsmen, while its vulcan mega-bolter makes it particularly potent against enemy infantry.

THE BELLY OF THE BEAST

The interior of a Baneblade has more in common with a fortified command bunker than it does with the insides of other, smaller armoured vehicles. Its weapons interfaces, operations points and data relays sprawl across several intermeshed layers of decks, which are connected by a warren of corridors and companionways. Yet despite its enormous bulk there is precious little space for the numerous crew. Every surface is encrusted with sancti-wired servo-skulls, draped with purity seals or pocked with munitions sconces, all of which are devoted to the steering of the Baneblade's raging machine spirit. Before this ancient spirit can be awakened, each control panel and catechetical dial must be daubed with sanctified oils. When the engines do roar to fiery life, these oils quickly vaporise into an acrid fume. Many crews believe this represents the tank sharing its breath with those it has deemed worthy.

The clangour inside a fully active Baneblade rivals that of all but the most apocalyptic of conflicts. Thunderous blasts reverberate throughout the hull every time the primary weapon is fired. A high-pitched clatter fills the stifling air as an unending cascade of spent shell casings rains down through grills into collection receptacles. Even the scratching of quill on parchment is deafening as reams of cogitative data are hastily recorded by batteries of auto-scribes. This is to say nothing of the mighty engine itself, the living heart of the Baneblade that thrums with fury as the mechanical beast drives into battle. Those crew manning the lower decks may hear the sound of lesser vehicles breaking beneath the Baneblade's adamantium tracks. The metallic crunch echoes up through the base plates, as does the splintering of bones from any warriors unlucky enough to be caught in the beast's path. So constant is this deafening sound that many Baneblade crew members begin to loose their sanity when exposed to the relative silence outside of their mechanical cocoon for too long.

The hull of a Baneblade is composed of the most durable steel alloys known to the Tech-Priests of the Adeptus Mechanicus. Even so, it is not completely impervious to damage. Baneblades are sent into battle against the most terrifying abominations in the galaxy – gargantuan machines of eldritch design, towering xenos creatures and heinous Daemons spewed forth from the warp. These profane war machines and apex monstrosities can deliver enough force to breach a Baneblade's hull. When they do, destructive shock waves are sent rippling throughout the interior chambers. The pressure surge is enough to pulverise those inside, caving in the skulls of those closest to the impact and liquefying their organs. But the Baneblade is not dead. Hatches clamp down to contain burning plasma or daemonic bile, and the tank's neuro-couplings are quickly rerouted to the surviving crew members. Though scarred and scorched, the Baneblade can take an inordinate amount of damage without losing any of its destructive potential.

BANEBLADES

Bristling with armaments, a Baneblade is less of a tank and more of a rolling fortress. An unmistakable icon of the Imperium's armoured supremacy, a single one of these super-heavy war engines can serve as the mailed fist of an Astra Militarum offensive, or as the unassailable lynchpin of even the most desperate of defences.

Possessed of overwhelming and versatile firepower, exceptionally thick armour and a near indefatigable power plant, the Baneblade has been deployed in many varied war zones throughout the Imperium. Wherever a Baneblade sees battle it quickly becomes the centre of the battle line. Guardsmen and smaller tanks shelter in its colossal shadow, even as the ranks of the enemy flee from it in abject terror.

Yarrick IV, **Baneblade of the 70th Armageddon Super-heavy Armoured Regiment**

BANESWORDS

The Banesword excels at utterly obliterating both vehicles and fortifications. Walled strongpoints and arrayed enemy armour can prove insurmountable to an Astra Militarum offensive, regardless of how many foot-slogging troops are marched against them. But a single Banesword can level such obstructions with ease.

With a handful of shots, a Banesword's quake cannon tears gaping rents in the most redoubtable defensive lines. Infantry and close-quarters attack vehicles are then free to pour into the breach and eradicate what enemies are left alive. Furthermore, the extreme range of the Banesword's armament allows it to perform this function before the opposing forces can even return fire.

Night Father, **Banesword of the Mordian 519th Super-heavy Armoured Regiment**

BANEHAMMERS

Like all super-heavy tanks, the Banehammer is capable of surging forward and crushing the opposing lines. However, where this metal behemoth truly excels is as a defensive anchor in the Astra Militarum formation. Those enemies not blasted apart by its lobed tremor cannon shells are brought to a crawl as the earth splits beneath their feet. The hobbled foe is then faced with a grim decision – either fall back or push slowly forward against the punishing wall of Astra Militarum fire.

Banehammers are also fitted with an armoured transport hold. Often, this will be used to protect elite infantry units from artillery and tank fire. The infantry are then unleashed once the battered enemy has moved within their range. Alternately, the Banehammer can plough forward and unload its troops in the face of the enemy.

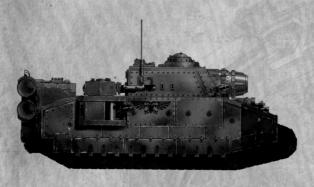

Bringer of Cataclysms, **Banehammer of the Vostroyan 41st Super-heavy Armoured Regiment**

DOOMHAMMERS

The Doomerhammer is part mobile fortress and part close-range Titan killer. Housed within its enormous hull is a sizeable troop bay, allowing it to transport a number of battle-ready Astra Militarum soldiers. Upon reaching the front line, these troops are deployed to gun down opposing enemy infantry and level focused fire at light vehicles, leaving the Doomhammer free to fulfil its primary function.

With a single devastating blast the Doomhammer's magma cannon tears through thick ceramite plating, monstrous chitin scales and adamantium. At extremely close range, the intensity of the blast is even more destructive, unleashing the raging energy of a small star upon its target.

Breath of the Emperor, **Doomhammer of the Tallarn 652nd Super-heavy Armoured Regiment**

SHADOWSWORDS

Where many super-heavy vehicles excel in protracted battles, their thick armour allowing them to outlast endless waves of enemies, the Shadowsword is designed to bring a swift and crushing end to the opposing army. Equipped with a hull-mounted volcano cannon, among the largest weapons ever fitted to a tank, the mere appearance of a Shadowsword on the battlefield spells doom for the enemies of the Imperium.

As a Shadowsword speeds forward, the roar of massive engines is drowned out by the whir of its volcano cannon powering up. The ruby beam of light that it fires pierces the thick smog of battle, blasting through infantry, armour and xenos monstrosities with ease. Even Wraithknights, Bio-titans and Ork Gargants can be toppled by a direct hit from a Shadowsword.

Winter's End, Shadowsword of the Valhallan 409th Super-heavy Armoured Regiment

STORMSWORDS

The Stormsword pattern of super-heavy tank was originally a retro-fit of Shadowswords wrecked during the battle of Coldarkh Hive. Since the resounding success of that battle, Stormswords continue to be crafted and put to use as urban siege engines.

A Stormsword excels at clearing enemy choke points. The shells fired by its Stormsword siege cannon release a concentrated concussive wave upon detonating. Those not outright pulverised by the initial blast are torn apart by the very cover they thought would protect them. Metal barricades are reduced to clouds of shrapnel, and chunks of ferrocrete bunkers are sent hurtling through the air to crush those they once housed.

Eye of Judgement, Stormsword of the Cadian 8th Super-heavy Armoured Regiment

HELLHAMMERS

Hellhammers are perfectly optimized for close-quarters warfare. Driving through a besieged hive or manufactorum, the crew ignore the ineffective shots fired by enemy infantry hidden amongst the rubble, and answer with their own hail of explosive shells. With a fearsome blast radius, the turret-mounted Hellhammer cannon is capable of clearing whole squads of heretic and xenos scum from the holes in which they cower.

A Hellhammer is often used as a vanguard vehicle when making an infantry surge into enemy territory. The massive tank can be fitted with sponsons bearing las, bolt and flamer weaponry, making it nearly impervious to covert flanking manoeuvres. Foot-bound troops can march freely in its wake, safe in the knowledge that the Hellhammer will lay before them a carpet of enemy corpses.

Jungle Reaper, Hellhammer of the Catachan XXXV Super-heavy Armoured Regiment

STORMLORDS

No vehicle in the armouries of the Astra Militarum boasts a greater transport capacity than the Stormlord, and none is more capable of mowing through massed ranks of enemy infantry. The Stormlord is the ultimate assault vehicle, capable of transporting almost an entire platoon single-handedly. On the approach, these troops can level waves of fire at the enemy, softening the opposing lines before disembarking and charging into the fray.

However, the embarked troops are often left with no foe to assault, as the Stormlord itself can wipe all but the most heavily armoured targets off the battlefield. Its front-facing vulcan mega-bolter sends sheets of mass-reactive rounds hurtling towards the enemy lines, reducing whole squads of infantry to clouds of vaporised blood.

Mother of Bolts, Stormlord of the Cadian 1378th Super-heavy Armoured Regiment

LORD CASTELLAN CREED

COMMANDER OF THE CADIAN 8TH

Lord Castellan Ursarkar E. Creed was found, an orphan child, in the war-torn ruins of Kasr Gallan. Clutching a service pistol and a tattered copy of 'De Gloria Macharius', this hard eyed boy was adopted by the Guardsmen of the Cadian 8th who had found him. From a young age, Creed excelled as both soldier and tactician, rising swiftly through the Cadian Whiteshields to earn a command of his own. This stocky and intense young warrior possessed an intuitive grasp of strategy and was a natural leader. From squad-level decisions to exercises with vast regiments of military might, Creed displayed a genius that

some whispered echoed that of Macharius himself. Blistering assaults, devious traps and impenetrable defences were Creed's trademarks, and within three decades the ragged orphan boy had earned acclaim as Cadia's greatest living commander. Only the strict structure of rank and privilege that governs the militarised society of Cadia now held Creed's meteoric career in check.

This was to change when an insidious Chaos plot saw the Cadian Governor Primus treacherously slain. Into the vacuum stepped Creed, who in the wake

of his valiant counter-offensive at Tyrok Fields was publicly named Lord Castellan and Commander-in-Chief of the Cadian Militarum Regimentum. The Lord Castellan rose immediately to this new challenge, beginning his tireless work to strengthen the defences of the Cadian Gate. His efforts came not a moment too early, for soon the Thirteenth Black Crusade of Abaddon the Despoiler was launched from the Eye of Terror.

COLOUR SERGEANT KELL

Wherever Creed went, so too walked the bullish figure of Colour Sergeant Jarran Kell. Friends for decades, Kell risked his life to preserve that of his oldest comrade on numerous occasions. His vox-amplified voice rolled along the Imperial lines, ensuring the Lord Castellan's orders were followed to the letter.

Where Creed was silent and calculating, Kell was roaring and scathing, as only a colour sergeant can be. He was a fearsome fighter and Creed's right hand – a trusted companion who long ago recognised that Cadia's best hope for survival was to follow the word of Creed. As such, keeping Creed alive became Kell's life work.

Kell fought to the end on Cadia, and made his last stand on the Elysion Fields before Abaddon himself. The Great Traitor, determined to crush Cadia's last resistance, led the Chaos Terminators of the Bringers of Despair against Creed's command formation. As the Black Legion warriors tore the Imperial defenders to shreds, Kell pushed the Lord Castellan aboard a Valkyrie and bade it take off. Abaddon raised the bolt-riddled sergeant up by the throat. Knowing he had saved his friend and master for the last time, Kell used the last of his strength to hawk a gobbet of bloody phlegm at his captor before hissing Creed's now-famous mantra – 'Cadia stands'. With a clawed hand, the Despoiler crushed Kell's spine, and the sergeant breathed his last.

Whether Kell's final act of defiance was in vain or not is uncertain. Creed continued to lead the Cadian defence until the planet was destroyed. Cadia fell that day, but as to the fate of the Lord Castellan, none can say.

KNIGHT COMMANDER PASK
CADIA'S ARMOURED BLADE

Knight Commander Pask is Cadia's best-known tank ace, and his grizzled visage has graced propaganda bills across the Cadian Gate for decades. Yet it is on the field of battle, amid the fires of war and the snarl of engines, that Pask is truly at home. Possessing an instinctive nous for armoured combat on any scale, Pask claims to feel the tank he commands as an extension of his own body, and has left the wreckage of foes uncounted blazing in his wake.

The Knight Commander began his rise to fame as gunnery seneschal aboard the Leman Russ *Hand of Steel*, serving as part of the Cadian 423rd Armoured Regiment. Deployed onto the planet Cyris, the regiment formed part of a battle group tasked with halting the relentless advance of Waaagh! Gutcutta. At the battle of Genna's Rift the 423rd found themselves directly in the path of Gutcutta's final, massive armoured push. As the two lines of war machines crashed together, a lumbering Ork Battle Fortress ground its way over the *Hand of Steel*, crushing the tank's turret and commanding officer in the process.

Swiftly taking command of the battered vehicle, Pask had the driver swing around and, drawing a bead on the Ork war engine still grinding through the Cadian lines, executed it with a single pinpoint blast of lascannon fire. The Battle Fortress went up like the Saint Vanus Day fireworks and, as its flaming wreckage rained from the sky, Pask went on to rally the Cadian counter-attack, claiming a further fourteen confirmed armour-kills before the battle's end.

On the planet of Haytor's Hole, the *Hand of Steel* was wrecked by the last survivor of a squadron of Eldar Fire Prisms, though not before Pask's Leman Russ had cut its killer in half with its last, dying salvo. Declining the honour of commanding one of his regiment's mighty Baneblades, Pask instead chose to demonstrate his solidarity with the tankers of the 423rd. Claiming another Leman Russ as his new steed, Pask renamed her the *Hand of Steel*.

> 'THE VICTOR LIVES IN HONOUR; THE VANQUISHED DIES
> IN SHAME.'
>
> *- Departmento Munitorum Strategic Parables 27:2*

This ritual has been repeated on a dozen occasions in the decades since. Whether felling heretic Titans on Saint Cyllia's World or battling bio-monstrosities amongst the Tyranid swarms in the Batran Traverse, it is a brave or foolish foe indeed that strays into the gun sights of Knight Commander Pask and his *Hand of Steel*.

Pask was not present on Cadia when it fell. The 423rd were travelling back from the Damocles Gulf, the Imperium having dealt the T'au invaders of Agrellan a decisive blow, when the Chaos forces launched their attack. Though grieved by the loss of his home world, Pask comports himself as he ever did, and his armoured company has achieved many victories since that darkest of days. The shame he feels at not having fought and died alongside his compatriots is tempered by a cold resolve to bring ruin to the armies of Abaddon the Despoiler.

THE STEEL TITHE

Since the fall of their home world, the armoured regiments of Cadia have had to absorb depleted regiments from other planets in order to maintain their fighting strength. Having trained various Militarum Regimentos across the Imperium, the Cadians are no strangers to drilling troops from other planets to fight in the style of the Shock Troops. Still, these 'foreign' tank crews are not true Cadians, and there is often resentment among these proud warriors at having to formally admit lesser soldiers into their ranks. Amongst the 423rd, Pask himself quashes such imprudent notions. Those Cadians he fights with are made to understand that Imperial victory is more important than insularity and nostalgic pride. Furthermore, the tank crews who come to serve in the 423rd are without fail amongst the most skilled in the galaxy. Rather than petitioning new recruits from the Departmento Munitorum, Pask evaluates the skills of the crewmen from other regiments he fights alongside. If a crew of Valhallan or Athonian tankers exhibits exceptional prowess in combat, they will be requisitioned by Pask himself for service in the 423rd. The tankers of various regiments vie for these summons, for to fight alongside the Imperium's greatest Tank Commander is an honour without equal. Regardless of their experience or accolades, all recruited in Pask's Steel Tithe are drilled as new recruits until they have become as tempered as any true Cadian.

COLONEL 'IRON HAND' STRAKEN
CATACHAN'S MAN OF ADAMANTIUM

Colonel 'Iron Hand' Straken is Catachan's most notorious and storied commanding officer. A veteran of decades of constant warfare, Straken has fought at the forefront of more battles and survived more wounds than most Imperial Guardsmen have eaten hot meals. Irascible and gutsy in the extreme, Colonel Straken leads from the front with a vigour that belies his years. Having worked his way up from footslogging grunt to colonel of the entire Catachan II 'Green Vipers', Straken continues to share every hardship of the common soldier. Larger than life and twice as violent, Straken can always be found where the fighting is thickest. Bellowing a constant stream of orders and invective, the Colonel stands shoulder to shoulder with his fellow Catachans. Straken's lack of tolerance for any display of incompetence or cowardice is legendary, and his men redouble their efforts in their determination to live up to Straken's exacting standards.

Straken's personal code of 'getting stuck in' is matched by a determination never to waste good Catachan lives for ephemeral gains. The Colonel has nothing but scorn for officers who fritter away lives to further their own careers. This fact has caused endless friction with the commanders of other regiments, yet Straken displays the same contempt for upper-echelon politics as he does for the foe. Straken's men all but deify their gung-ho commander, and have carried his battered body to safety almost as often as he has dragged theirs.

Regardless of the top brass' opinion, none can argue with Straken's breathtaking service record. Fighting initially under his mentor, the infamous Colonel Greiss, Straken has distinguished himself at the Battle of Moden's Ridge, the Dulma'lin Cleansing, the Ulani Aftermath and the evacuation of Vartol City to name but a few. On Ulani IV Straken dragged a wounded comrade to safety across half a continent. On Vendal's Landing he repulsed a phalanx of Daemon Engines with only twenty-two men, ten lasguns and a case of short-fused mining charges. At the battle of the Red Rain Straken personally defeated the notorious Drukhari Archon Yrekh Drash in single combat, crushing the degenerate xenos' head in his whirring bionic fist.

> **'Medic! Stop whining, Brook, you've got another damned leg!'**
> - *Colonel 'Iron Hand' Straken, Battle of Moden's Ridge*

During his years of service the Colonel has suffered dozens of wounds in the line of duty, amongst the most serious being the arm he lost to a Miral land shark. Ever willing to turn a weakness into a strength, Straken replaced his missing hand with the deadly 'devil's claw', an augmented appendage capable of punching through a ferrocrete wall. Though this and a plethora of other grave injuries should, by rights, have killed the indomitable Catachan several times over, Straken fights on with undiminished determination. His ravaged body is riddled with an ever-increasing number of gleaming bionics, and his orders punctuated by yells of 'Do I have to do everything myself?!'.

Like any leader worth their salt, Straken never orders the troops in his command to do something he would be unwilling to do himself. When making a near-hopeless assault against a fortified position, it is Straken who leads the charge. In turn, the grizzled Colonel demands that his soldiers emulate the grit and determination he always displays on the battlefield. Between campaigns, the training drills run by Straken are universally brutal, and it is not uncommon for half a platoon to vomit until unconscious after completing a 'light constitutional'.

When necessary, Straken himself administers discipline to the Guardsmen in his company. His punishments are only fatal when a grievous crime has been committed, or if he perceives a soldier to be fundamentally unfit for martial service, and if possible he will eschew the involvement of a Commissar. The Officio Prefectus see this as a usurpation of their officer's duties – they know full well the legendary disregard that Catachans display towards their authority, and there is no better example of Catachan belligerence than Colonel 'Iron Hand' Straken. They begrudgingly accept Straken and his men as exemplary soldiers of the Imperium, but always keep a distrustful eye on the Green Vipers.

GUNNERY SERGEANT HARKER

THE STONETOOTH DEVIL

All Catachans have a reputation for being tough, but 'Stonetooth' Harker is perhaps the hardest of the bunch. It is said that instead of tobacco he chews glass and that he can endure pain like no other man. He can place his hands in searing flames without flinching, and shrug off knife cuts and gun wounds without a grimace. As far as 'Stonetooth' is concerned, pain, and even bleeding, are concepts for weedier soldiers. Harker is a giant of a man, his large frame covered with slabs of muscle and sinew. His strength is such that he carries his heavy bolter, 'Payback', as easily as a normal man might carry a rifle, without even breaking a sweat.

Harker is uncomplaining in the completion of his duties. A tough and grizzled sergeant with guts for brains, he shows an enthusiasm for war that is somewhere between arrogance and bravado. It would be inaccurate to say he possesses no tactical acumen, for when it comes to war, 'Stonetooth' is an expert. But when given the choice between fighting and thinking his way out of tight spot, Harker reaches for Payback every time.

Harker has survived the most gruelling campaigns and has yet to find an enemy that won't die to the bark of his heavy bolter or the sharpened edge of his combat blade. There isn't an aspect of war he has not mastered. From rescue missions to assassinations, reconnaissance to demolitions – Harker will get the job done. He leads a squad of Catachan Devils, exceptional warriors even by the exacting standards of their birth world. The nickname is a reference to the voracious predators of their world. Comprised of the regiment's bravest veterans, Harker's team take the fight directly to the enemy. They are formed to make long-range penetration raids deep behind enemy lines and when the enemy is engaged they bear the brunt of the bloody combat.

> 'Back home, I once fancied me a pair of Catachan Devil boots. Killed me half a dozen of the great ugly critters but never found a single one that wore any!'
> - 'Stonetooth' Harker, to a doubtful Munitorum staffer.

Whilst fighting the tendrils of Tyranid Hive Fleet Leviathan on the twilight world of Jorn V, Harker's squad was ambushed by a pack of Raveners, monstrous organisms that had burrowed beneath the planet's black surface. Harker's own ammunition loader was torn apart in a flurry of claws before a scream had a chance to leave his lips, and the remaining squad members were engaged in a grim fight for their lives. Harker leapt upon the closest beast without pause and wrapped his massive biceps around the alien's throat. The Ravener writhed and tried to buck him off but Harker's grip would not slacken. Harker squeezed until, with an audible crack, the creature's neck was shattered and its serpentine body finally lay still. Harker then hefted his heavy bolter from its tripod stand and opened fire on the remaining Tyranids. Each organism burst apart as the explosive bolts did their work. His dead comrades avenged, Harker dusted himself off, slung a belt of ammunition over each shoulder and stalked off to find the rest of his company, Payback tracking back and forth like a hound searching for prey.

Exaggerated stories of inhuman heroics circulate constantly amongst the soldiers of the Astra Militarum. While dug into fox-holes waiting to face inevitable horrors, these braggadocios tales help to keep fear at bay. Though few such stories can be substantiated, those told about Gunnery Sergeant Harker are generally believed. One of the most famous is of how the gargantuan trooper came to possess the heavy bolter he carries into battle, and of how it earned its name.

When he was a new recruit – so the story goes – Harker's platoon was sent to eradicate a roving greenskin warband in the tangle-barrens of Orriah Ossetti. Only a handful of Orks had been spotted on the death world, so reconnaissance and aerial support were deemed an unnecessary expenditure. What Harker's platoon encountered was not a rag-tag band of savages, but a hardened cadre of Blood Axe warriors. The ambush launched by the Orks was as brutal as it was unexpected, and soon Harker was the only Guardsman remaining. His lasgun's energy cells were fried from overuse, so he reached into the flames where a Heavy Weapons Team had been immolated and retrieved his fallen comrades' heavy bolter. The towering Catachan then trained the massive gun on the remaining greenskins and unleashed vengeful retribution. Since that day, Payback has been massacring Harker's enemies throughout the galaxy.

WARRIORS OF THE FAITH

The mortal men and women of the Astra Militarum are faced daily with gruesome death, their lives insignificant in the grand scale of the Imperium. But their fear is assuaged by righteous zeal, fuelled by the pious frenzy of Ministorum Priests who preach the wrathful dictums of the Ecclesiarchy, and the dauntless Crusaders who prosecute the Emperor's holy wars.

MINISTORUM PRIESTS

The Priests of the Ecclesiarchy play a vital role in the Imperial Guard, imparting the holy teachings of the Emperor and providing spiritual succour to the troops both on and off the battlefield. To these Priests there is no calling higher than tending the Emperor's armies. They lead by example and gladly martyr themselves on blood-soaked fields, the highest sacrifice that is expected of them. Some Ministorum Priests are particularly noted for their fiery zeal in the execution of both their duties and of the heretics they abhor.

More than one Astra Militarum Commander has been grateful for the powerful oratory of a Ministorum Priest. Their fiery speeches can stir a populace to rebel against a heretic lord or persuade an army to lay down its arms and surrender to the mercy of the Emperor – which is inevitably quick and bloody.

Ministorum Priests ensure that the troops are sufficiently motivated to do their duty without fear, as well as fighting fanatically themselves. In battle they harness the faith of the troops to smite the Emperor's foes – chanting litanies of devotion and mantras of hate, they stir the hearts and souls of nearby Guardsmen to righteous anger. Together they charge down the heretical forces that dare oppose the Emperor, determined to purge such filth from the battlefield. During the Second Tyrannic War, the Miasman 15th 'Brimstones' found themselves out of ammunition and cut off from reinforcements on the shrine world of Dystra Angelicus. Roused by the righteous fervour of a trio of Ministorum Priests, the Miasmans sallied forth, butchering half a dozen broods with their knives before they were eventually cut down.

All members of the Ecclesiarchy carry with them a rosarius – a symbol of faith as potent as the holy aquila. The more bloodthirsty of Ministorum Priests, including those that have ties to the redemption cults, often preach in the swirling melee of combat, and so supplement their faith with snarling chainblades and bulky pistols. Few liturgies are more rousing to the soldiery of the Astra Militarum than those accompanied by sprays of traitor blood and the wet thud of carved enemy flesh hitting the ground.

Though a Ministorum Priest may serve within an Astra Militarum regiment – sometimes for an extended period – he is still formally part of the Ecclesiarchy, the religious body of the Imperium. In a practical sense this has little bearing on his place in a battle, for a Priest will follow the orders given to the regiment he has been seconded to, and will fight and die alongside the soldiers he shepherds.

> 'NO ARMY IS BIG ENOUGH TO CONQUER THE GALAXY. BUT FAITH ALONE CAN OVERTURN THE UNIVERSE.'
>
> *- Ecclesiarch Deacis IX*

CRUSADERS

Imperial Guard commanders who show exceptional zeal, unflinching faith and appropriate deference towards the Adeptus Ministorum are sometimes afforded a retinue of Crusaders. These warrior ascetics hail from the most mysterious of all the Ecclesiarchy's many orders – the Cardinals Crimson – and it is said that nowhere in the Imperium can more devout warriors be found, save perhaps for in the ranks of the Adepta Sororitas. Armed with formidable shields, shrouded in robes and wielding heavy longswords wreathed in crackling power fields, Crusaders form a dauntless honour guard that is nigh impenetrable in both body and spirit.

On the battlefield, Crusaders will often form a halo around their commander, allowing them to move freely wherever the Emperor guides. Xenos, heretics and traitors who would approach this holy officer are slaughtered by the Crusaders, while incoming fire ricochets harmlessly off their ornamented storm shields. Blessed are the soldiers serving under such a commander, for to fight in the presence of Crusaders is to be assured that the war being waged is truly righteous.

SERVANTS OF THE OMNISSIAH

With binharic prayers and mystic rites, Tech-Priest Enginseers soothe the machine spirits of their tracked congregation, and daub their metallic hulls with oils and blessed unguents. These cyber-augmented warrior monks serve at the behest of the Adeptus Mechanicus, and their devotion to the vehicles of the Astra Militarum is without bounds.

TECH-PRIEST ENGINSEERS

Tech-Priest Enginseers are representatives of the Cult Mechanicus who serve as custodians for the vehicles of the Astra Militarum. Without their diligent maintenance, the armoured regiments of the Astra Militarum would soon find themselves without heavy vehicles.

The logic-driven Tech-Priests are utterly focused on their task and willingly wade into the fray when a valuable piece of technology is threatened. Clad in power armour and wielding cog-toothed power axes, they shrug off light arms fire, and have faith that the machines they steward will obliterate enemy tanks and monstrous creatures before they can get too close. They are able to effect battlefield repairs on damaged vehicles, and can even rouse the spirits of Imperial tanks to wrath, causing weapons to track and fire even after the crew inside have been killed or injured.

The longer a Tech-Priest spends in the service of the Omnissiah, the more of his flesh-body will have been replaced with blessed augmetics. The most ancient members of the Cult of Mars are more cold steel and hydraulic oil than skin and blood.

SERVITORS

Many Tech-Priest Enginseers are accompanied on the battlefield by retinues of mindless servitors. These lobotomised slaves are often vat-grown, though many were vicious criminals or heretics prior to their enforced conversion. Regardless of their origins, most servitors will boast industrial cybernetics allowing them to aid their master in his work. Others are fitted with hefty heavy weapons whose chattering volleys drive back the foe and permit the Enginseer to make his repairs without interruption.

Servitors make effective battle-line troops, but only when shepherded by a Tech-Priest who can engage the raw circuitry of their minds to direct their unthinking aggression. Without such guidance servitors do little but fire wildly, and may even wander off without warning in pursuit of some erroneous protocol.

TOOLS OF THE CULT MECHANICUS

The servo-arm is the most iconic tool of the Tech-Priest Enginseers serving within the Astra Militarum. Powered by whirring servos, these large robotic limbs are articulated such that they can reach every point within several feet of the Tech-Priest, and have enough strength to lift a tank chassis while track repairs are made. With an industrious machine spirit, a servo-arm is endlessly driven to repair and maintain its fellow mechanical creations, though should a Tech-Priest desire, it can also visit ruin upon those who would interfere with his work. Its powerful claw, designed to clamp shut rents in the hulls of tanks, is equally effective at severing limbs and crushing skulls. With a single swipe, the servo-arm can send a Chaos Space Marine flailing, or punch through the ensorcelled plating of a taint-ridden Daemon Engine.

MILITARUM TEMPESTUS

Militarum Tempestus Scions are cold, proficient killers whose deadly firepower reduces foes to smouldering heaps of corpses. Trained in the Schola Progenium, these men commit to a rigorous program of physical and mental indoctrination that raises them to the peak of human conditioning. Loyal to the Emperor above all else, Tempestus Scions provide High Command with a core of flexible, nigh-incorruptible soldiers. Deployed sparingly, they can be depended upon to complete any mission, no matter how deadly. Racing into battle aboard armoured transports or plummeting down on grav-chutes, the Scions are the sharp edge of the Imperial Guard war machine.

TEMPESTUS SCIONS

Each squad of Tempestus Scions consists of veteran warriors, trained and equipped to the highest standard. Protected by rigid armaplas and reinforced ceramite plates, Scions wield a sophisticated range of high-powered weapons that perfectly complement their shock assault role, and their discipline is such that they can direct their deadly firepower to absolute optimum effect. Unlike the Guardsmen of the Astra Militarum, Scions endure a brutally uncompromising training regime, ensuring that only the most skilled and resolute amongst them ever see battle.

The standard-issue weapon for Tempestus Scions is the hot-shot lasgun. Each of these rifles is fitted with an potent external power cell, allowing them to penetrate thicker armour than the mass-produced lasguns used by rank-and-file Guardsmen. When deployed against armoured enemy infantry, Tempestus Scions wield hot-shot volley guns. With a more powerful blast and extreme rate of fire, they are perfect for bringing down traitor Space Marines and xenos beasts.

Militarum Tempestus Scions are often viewed with fear or resentment by the regular troops – nicknames such as 'glory boys' and 'big toy soldiers' are common. Yet this rancour is nothing to the Scions themselves. Trained in covert operations and rapid insertion strike-tactics, they go to battle confident that their every deed is for the good of the Imperium, carrying out their orders with merciless and uncompromising pragmatism.

TEMPESTOR PRIMES

Each Militarum Tempestus platoon is led into battle by a grizzled officer known as a Tempestor Prime. Such men are promoted on battlefield record alone, their accolades earned through courage and unshakeable discipline in the line of fire. The tactics they employ as a commander are the product of the countless missions they have undertaken as a Scion, and as such they have an intrinsic understanding of the capabilities of their soldiers. Able to operate on their own initiative in a way entirely alien to the majority of the Astra Militarum, these men lead their Progenium brethren into battle with merciless efficiency.

TEMPESTUS COMMAND SQUADS

Each Tempestus Command Squad is comprised of the very best Scions in the regiment. A Tempestus Command Squad will often shadow a Tempestor Prime on an operation, shielding him against incoming fire while answering with salvoes of their own. Vox operators relay the Tempestor Prime's commands across the vox-net while medics patch up and inject stimulant concoctions into downed soldiers so that they can continue to fight. Some Tempestus Command Squads also carry their platoon's banner into battle, waving its colours in proud defiance as they lead the charge against the enemy.

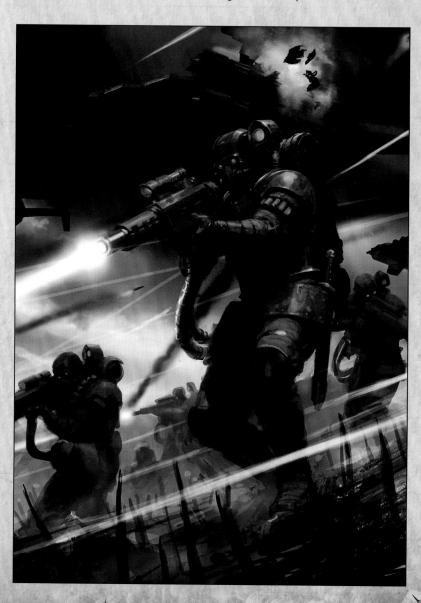

VALKYRIES

The Valkyrie assault carrier is a manoeuvrable, well-armed, twin-engine attack craft. The durable armour and versatile payload of the Valkyrie chassis combined with the aircraft's powerful engines and stable handling make it a popular choice for a broad spectrum of battlefield roles. These attack craft use atmospherically sealed cockpits and omni-combustable promethium in their vector-turbojets, allowing them to be deployed against enemy flyers in the upper atmosphere and against ground forces on even the most hostile worlds.

Sporting a troop transport capacity on par with the ubiquitous Chimera, the Valkyrie is often used to swiftly redeploy squads of infantry. Strikes at key targets by cadres of Tempestus Scions, reinforcement of buckling battle lines by grim-faced bands of Veterans, even hasty transportation for ranking officers – all of these and more are the duty of the Valkyrie.

With a few notable exceptions, most Astra Militarum formations will have small numbers of Valkyries attached to them on a temporary basis; such craft are, first and foremost, the property of the Aeronautica Imperialis. During extended ground operations, however, they are usually repainted to match their assigned regiment, and their pilots report directly to that regiment's senior officer.

With vectored engines permitting vertical take-off and landing, these versatile aircraft can twist and turn through the rigours of low-altitude dogfights, or hover while troops rappel from their holds. In addition, every Valkyrie is equipped with sufficient grav-chutes for all passengers, allowing expedient, if hazardous, high-speed deployment into the thick of combat.

To burst from the steel cocoon of a Valkyrie's transport bay into the icy air above packed ranks of enemies can be jarring, even by the standards of the Astra Militarum. As the chuted infantry descend towards the seething mass of foes they are peppered with fire. Those grav-troopers who manage to touch down may find themselves within feeding range of some mutated xenos monstrosity, or set alight by gouts of daemonic flame. But for all this, the shock of a Valkyrie drop is even more terrifying to the enemy, who find themselves fighting on new and unexpected fronts with no warning, other than the roar of an overflying Valkyrie. Carefully orchestrated offensives are thrown into utter disarray as lasgun-wielding infantry are disgorged to assail the flanks and rear of the assaulting army. Artillery and psykers unleashing their destruction far from the front lines are surrounded and brought down by the massed fire of the descending troopers.

Airborne assaults play a crucial role in the battle plans of many Imperial commanders. Due to the high risk of such manoeuvres, and the high reward of eliminating key enemy assets, it is common for Valkyries to be loaded with the best troops available – Veterans or Tempestus Scions. However, certain pragmatic officers have achieved decisive victories by using Valkyries to distribute rank-and-file soldiers across large swathes of the battlefield. One such Company Commander – Jetta Bacchi of the Athonian 992nd 'Vagrant Blades' – has used Valkyries in multiple city fights across the Imperium to seed the battlefield with his Tunnel Rats before engaging the enemy. Once deployed, each Infantry Squad sets up

choke points and ambushes across the zone of battle. The foe then faces an unenviable decision – either move at a crawl trying not to stumble into the infantry's traps, or barrel ahead full pace to outrun the deadly rain of aerial fire unleashed by the Valkyries.

Even when troop transport is not required, or when the battlefield conditions make such actions impossible, Valkyries are still an invaluable aerial asset. Their armaments allow them to carry out hit-and-run strikes and strafing runs on ground forces whilst swatting enemy flyers from the sky. Though certain xenos attack craft are faster, few boast the balance of offensive and defensive capabilities that make the Valkyrie so resilient and versatile.

Valkyries have a storied history of service alongside Imperial infantry and armour regiments, and are sometimes referred to by Imperial Guardsmen as the Wings of the Emperor. Certainly those Guardsmen who have seen a ravening Carnifex blasted apart from on high by a Valkyrie's hellstrike missiles, or been lifted from the path of an onrushing Ork horde in the tight confines of the transport bay, have nothing but respect for these exceptional aircraft.

'FIRE. DROP. FIRE. RETRIEVE. REPEAT AS NEEDED.'
- *Mantra of Aeronautica Imperialis Valkyrie pilots*

COMMISSARS

Every Imperial citizen recognises the distinctive cap and greatcoat of the Commissar, whether from hab-block propaganda frescoes or grainy Munitorum recruitment picts. To the masses of Humanity, these men are symbols of Imperial authority whose sole remit is to ensure that all do their duty in the Emperor's name. Yet the truth of these high-ranking officers is rather more complex.

Commissars are recruited from amongst the students of the widespread Schola Progenium. While the majority of the Schola's wards go on to become Adepts or join the Militarum Tempestus, only the best of the best will be recommended for service in the Officio Prefectus. Inductees must have absolute faith in the Imperium. They must display the proper levels of sincere totalitarian idealism. They must be able to fight as well as any hive-spire duellist while fulfilling the conflicting roles of merciless taskmaster and inspiring hero with equal ease. It is further the duty of a Commissar to learn the culture and customs of the regiment to which he is attached. He must command equal respect whether assigned to dutiful Vostroyans or hard-bitten, insular Catachans. Should discipline or morale falter, it is the task of the Commissar to take whatever steps are necessary to restore order, and to do so in the absolute knowledge that his actions are just. Under the steely gaze of such a man, Imperial Guardsmen are inspired to deeds they never believed possible. In extremis, a Commissar must be prepared to execute wavering soldiers or incompetent officers without a moment's remorse; few things enforce discipline better than a malcontent or coward being shot dead for their failings, and this message is all the stronger when a mass-reactive bolt shell sprays a Guardsman's brains across his horrified comrades in a shower of gore. Such an unflinching display of a Commissar's authority ensures that the first soldier who tries to flee from battle is invariably the last.

LORD COMMISSARS

Amongst the ranks of the Officio Prefectus there are many heroic individuals who have become legend through their deeds. Some of those paragons may achieve the rank of Lord Commissar. Where a Commissar will be attached as an ancillary officer to a company, fulfilling his charge under the tactical direction of the Company Commander, a Lord Commissar will often lead the soldiers he oversees into battle. In this role he is more than capable – after decades of service within multiple regiments, a Lord Commissar has experienced first-hand the various ways in which the strengths of the Astra Militarum can be put to effective use. A Lord Commissar may be placed in command of soldiers about to enter a particularly nightmarish war zone. At other times, he will assume the position of senior officer after executing the standing Company Commander, whom he has judged and found wanting.

A Lord Commissar is expected to exemplify everything the Imperium strives toward, while still discharging his duties as a grim-faced arbiter of disciplinary retribution. Each is a fearsome warrior whose skill and experience in front-line combat makes them the match of heretical demagogues and xenos warlords on the battlefield. As military leaders, they can appraise the battle lines of the enemy as swiftly as they measure the mettle of their own troops, punishing any weakness they see with merciless expedience.

Plipton's Squad stood motionless on the ridge, the smoke of battle and a wave of Gargoyles drawing ever closer. The Guardsmen had their lasguns at the ready and were formed up into two precise firing rows – five in the front, four in the back. Guardsmen Cortias lay sprawled on the floor, blood and brains oozing from his ruptured skull and soaking steadily into the dirt, with Commissar Gaken standing over his lifeless corpse. Without anger or urgency, the Commissar levelled his still-smoking bolt pistol at the remaining soldiers.

'Does anyone else think we should break for cover?' he asked – his raspy, half-whispered voice devoid of any describable emotion.

The squad remained silent. To a man they could still hear the shot that had killed Cortias ringing in their ears – it almost drowned out the horrific screech of the xenos swarm fast approaching them. Eventually, Sergeant Plipton spoke.

'Sir. If we stay here we'll get cut to shreds by those things.'

Gaken walked over to stand at Plipton's side, then calmly pressed the barrel of his gun to the Sergeant's temple.

'Our orders are to hold this ground. Are you second-guessing your Company Commander's tactics?'

Plipton swallowed. 'No sir,' he replied, his voice shaky.

'Good,' said Gaken, lowering his bolt pistol. 'Then hold this ground we shall.'

COMMISSAR YARRICK
HERO OF HADES HIVE

Commissar Yarrick is a peerless Imperial hero. During the Second War for Armageddon, Yarrick held Hades Hive against the Ork hordes of Warlord Ghazghkull Thraka when the city's fall seemed inevitable. As the legends tell, it was this act of stoic defiance that would save the planet, for in Yarrick the greenskin warlord saw a worthy opponent – a strategist of great cunning against whom he could test his brutal fury. Ghazghkull directed the majority of his forces towards Hades, and joined the battle himself, determined to crush the dauntless Commissar beneath his heel. Yarrick rallied his defenders, and though the casualties were horrific, he managed to hold out until the Blood Angels Chapter of the Adeptus Astartes were able to outflank and destroy Ghazghkull's hordes. Furious at his defeat, the Warlord retreated from the system, ending the Second War for Armageddon. Yarrick's courage and tenacity were an inspiration to his followers, carrying them through hardships untold to eventual victory.

None in the Imperium knew the deranged mind of the Ork Warlord better, and the aged Commissar was able to counter all but the most outlandish assaults devised by the greenskin prophet.

The cataclysmic and ongoing war that ensued stretched the military capacity of the Adeptus Ministorum to near-breaking point. Suffice it to say that, for all of the ferocity and ingenuity of the Ork Warlord, Armageddon did not fall. The Imperial forces withstood the invaders, though the planet was transformed into a brutal, unending war zone.

Eventually, Ghazghkull himself was drawn away by a vision, which he believed was given to him by the greenskin gods themselves. Unwilling to let his nemesis escape only to potentially wreak havoc elsewhere in the galaxy, Yarrick ensured that he was among the Imperial forces who gave chase.

Without the tireless efforts of Commissar Yarrick, Ghazghkull's Waaagh! would have overrun Armageddon long ago and stormed on towards Holy Terra. The Commissar's crusade to slay 'the Beast of Armageddon' continues to this day.

> *'Heroes of Armageddon! You have withstood the evil savagery of the Orks, and they have nothing left for you to fear. So raise high the black banners of vengeance – now is our time!'*
> - *Commissar Yarrick, final address to the defenders of Armageddon*

It was during a brutal hand-to-hand duel with the hulking Warboss Ugulhard in the final battle for Hades Hive that Yarrick lost an arm. He took the Ork's head in return, replacing his severed limb with Ugulhard's own power klaw. When he lost an eye in a vicious fire fight, Yarrick ensured it was replaced with a powerful laser-bionic, playing to the Ork fear of his supposed 'evil eye'. Though his body is a patchwork of scars and bionics, the old Commissar fights on unbowed.

When Ghazghkull's mighty Waaagh! returned once more to the planet, instigating the Third War for Armageddon, Yarrick came out of a well-earned retirement to lead the planet's defence.

OGRYNS

Ogryns are a crude and exceptionally resilient breed of abhuman hailing from a number of high gravity worlds. Ogryns compensate for their stupidity with overwhelming physicality – the brutish creatures stand around ten feet tall and can shrug off wounds that would kill an Imperial Guardsman several times over. These qualities mean that Ogryns make exceptional shock troops, and are often deployed on the front lines of battle.

It is fair to say that Ogryns do have their limitations. Their equipment must be simple and exceptionally rugged, as anything within arm's reach is likely to see brief and violent service as an improvised club. Their heavily built ripper guns must also be fitted with burst limiters to stop the Ogryns from firing ceaselessly – thirty seconds of noisy enjoyment can easily leave these abhumans short of ammunition before a battle has even begun. Ogryns are easily confused, meaning they work best when given simple, straightforward missions, and their lack of personal hygiene borders on the criminal. However, once indoctrinated into the Imperial creed they are doggedly loyal, and their strength and resilience make them a potent weapon.

OGRYN BODYGUARDS

Those Ogryns who show themselves to be particularly capable may be recruited as battlefield bodyguards. In this role they have but one duty – to protect the officer to whom they are assigned. Whether they achieve this by throwing themselves in the line of fire, or by slaughtering all enemies who come near to their charge, they are invaluable retainers in the swirl of combat.

BULLGRYNS

The most obstinate Ogryns, known as Bullgryns, are clad in custom-made armour and carry crude assault weaponry that capitalises on the abhumans' stature and resilience. Some wield power mauls and buckler-like brute shields, while others march to battle carrying simple but effective slab shields, locking together to form a mobile defence line. So deployed, these units provide their comrades with a wall of walking cover as they advance.

Bullgryns take their duties very seriously and will often form a line at the slightest sound of gunfire, which can be most inconvenient in crowded trenches. Yet Guardsmen advancing behind a Bullgryn squad swiftly forget such mishaps as shots whine harmlessly from the Ogryns' shields, leaving those soldiers crouched in their lee unharmed. Needless to say, casualties are high among the abhumans themselves, but the close range bombardments of their grenadier gauntlets exact brutal revenge soon enough. The foe are left reeling and shell-shocked even before the maul-wielding Ogryns charge into their midst and bludgeon the survivors to a red paste.

The Bullgryns of the Anark Zeta 81st 'Immovables' regiment have gained a reputation for holding their position no matter how much punishment they take. This strength is also their greatest weakness, as in lieu of new orders they will remain rooted to the spot, even if an outflanking force has rounded their shield wall. The Immovables are therefore often teamed with squads of Ratling snipers. The diminutive sharpshooters lie in wait behind their giant abhuman cousins, out of sight of the foe. As the enemy approaches the Immovable wall, the Ratlings open fire from their protected positions before quickly redeploying as the tides of battle shift.

NORK DEDDOG

Nork Deddog is an Ogryn bodyguard of legendary repute. Upon his recruitment into the Imperial Guard, Nork displayed an uncommon level of mental aptitude. The surprisingly developed abhuman could sign his own name, count to four, and even speak in short sentences. It was not long before Nork was assigned to special duties as a regimental lifeguard for Colonel Greiss of the Catachan II.

When the regiment was committed to the ongoing war on Balor, it was soon apparent that Nork had found his sizeable niche. While Greiss was as vocally warlike as any good Catachan officer should be, he was old and physically frail. The men of the regiment soon became used to the old Colonel bellowing orders from the shelter of Nork's massive frame, the Ogryn's ripper gun mowing down the foe with shredding bursts as shots intended for his charge rebounded harmlessly from his bulky armour. After the disaster at Hill Gamma Zero, Deddog's reputation was cemented when he carried the badly wounded Greiss to safety through hostile territory, dragging the wreckage of the Colonel's Chimera behind him for cover the entire way.

Since that bloody conflict, Nork's skills as a bodyguard have been in great demand. His loyalty is beyond question, and the hulking Ogryn would rather sustain terrible wounds than permit a single scratch upon his master. When Orks overran the command dugout at the battle of Chabda Bridge, Nork was the only one to stand his ground beside Sub-overlord Ven Vambold. During the ensuing brawl, Deddog bullied his way into the Orks' midst and subjected the xenos Warboss to a headbutt so ferocious that the monstrous Ork was hurled from the dugout to its death in the sizzling acid of the Chabda River far below.

Though unquestioningly loyal, Nork is no leader. Throughout his long career, he has guarded officers with remarkable military acumen, tactical genius and an innate understanding of the Astra Militarum war machine. Unfortunately, none of this has ever rubbed off on the hulking Ogryn. His singular duty demands all of his attention, and has done for the entirety of his illustrious service. In those rare instances when the subject of his protection is grievously wounded and unable to maintain their command, allied soldiers may appeal to Nork for orders – after all, he is typically the most decorated and experienced veteran in a battalion. Such requests, however, are in vain. In Nork's simple mind, he still has but one duty, and he will continue to protect the fallen officer until he is told to do otherwise. Fortunately, having an unconscious officer draped across his shoulder does little to hamper Nork's ability to butcher the enemy.

Nork has saved the lives of well over one hundred officers, earning himself a chest-full of medals in the process. Dozens of war zones that would have descended into anarchy have instead seen the banners of Imperial victory raised high thanks to Nork's constant, selfless heroism. During the brief periods of peace between deployments, Nork experiences chronic discomfort whenever compelled to accompany his latest master to a social function or parade drill. However, such embarrassments only encourage Nork to fight all the harder when he returns to the field of battle, determined to prove his worth and bask in the satisfying glow of being the Imperial Guard's finest bodyguard.

'Nork! Don't let it take me!'

These were the last words screamed by Brigadier Aloysius van Burenvan before he was enveloped by the Mawloc's razor-toothed maw. Charging to defend the screaming officer, Nork Deddog slammed his dense forehead into the serpentine beast's jaw. One of its colossal mandibles cracked under the force of the blow, and the Tyranid let out a jagged, mucosal screech. From within its gullet came the desperate cries of Aloysius, muffled by the slabs of xenos flesh that now surrounded him. Only the monster's head protruded from the hole from which it had burrowed, yet still it towered above Nork. Undaunted, the Ogryn hacked at the Mawloc's feeder flaps again and again with his huge knife. He didn't care that van Burenvan was spoiled and snivelling, even compared to his aristocratic peers; the Ogryn was blind to the fact that his master's selfish cowardice had cost the lives of dozens of Guardsmen who had been left behind to cover his retreat. All that Nork cared about was saving the man he was told to protect, and so he continued to slash. As the beast let out another pained scream, Nork reached into the gaping maw of its mouth and yanked the unconscious van Burenvan free. The Brigadier's lower legs had been partially digested, but he was still alive.

'I got ya, surr,' Nork said with pride. He slung the whimpering officer over his shoulder and set off, his duty done.

RATLINGS

Though less resilient than their human comrades, Ratlings are naturally excellent shots. It is said that Ratling marksmen can take the head off a heretic from over a mile away. Coupled with their knack for staying out of harm's way, this makes Ratlings formidable snipers who can exact a withering toll upon superior enemy forces.

Inevitably, the abhuman Ratlings face prejudice from the men they serve alongside, yet their skill as thieves, fences and black marketeers tends to win them acceptance. Indeed, Guardsmen who give the Ratlings too much grief will often find themselves mysteriously short of ammunition in the heat of battle, while their diminutive tormentors watch gleefully through telescopic sights.

> 'Hit him from here? Are you serious, longshanks? Do I look like a cross-eyed Catachan? I could take his head off from twice this range, just watch this…'
>
> - 'Madeye' McGriffin, Ratling Sniper

Regardless of their small stature, and their questionable status as sanctioned aberrants, Ratlings have proven invaluable to the Imperium's armies time and again. They make exceptional forward scouts, and are able to move covertly into firing positions right under the nose of the enemy army. Only when the opening salvoes of battle have been loosed do they reveal themselves, announcing their presence with hails of precision shots that catch the enemy completely off guard. The effectiveness of Ratling fire can often mislead the enemy into believing they face an entire platoon of Imperial Guardsmen, which in turn can draw large-scale assaults towards the snipers. With no hope of holding their own in close-quarters combat, Ratlings have perfected the art of hastily vacating their redoubts immediately after firing, scurrying away before securing a new vantage point from which to assassinate more of their assailants.

On Crastille, during the War of Weeping, a single squad of Ratlings held the narrow bridge over the tumultuous Widowash River for three full days. Six times the T'au attempted to dislodge Manvolio Grand's Ratling Sharpshooters, and six times they were hurled back by pinpoint fire. Kroot Shapers and Pathfinder Shas'ui tumbled into the river's surging flow, neat holes blown through eye-sockets and throats. When a pack of Kroot Hounds was loosed across the bridge, the Ratlings put each down with a single shot, the last beast skidding to a halt on its face a good three feet short of Manvolio's snipers. Eventually, the T'au were forced to commit several Stealth Teams to the fight – against these near-invisible foes, the Ratlings stood little chance. Most of the abhumans were slaughtered before they could flee, but Manvolio and his closest cronies made it back to Imperial lines alive, there to be hailed as heroes for their efforts.

Though devious, duplicitous and morally dubious, Ratlings possess such unique talents that they will always find a place in the armies of the Imperium. Whether killing off enemy officers or procuring black-market amasec for their own, these adaptable abhumans have certainly found their niche in the ranks of the Astra Militarum.

Driving snow swept down upon Kadyusha City, driven almost horizontal by the howling wind. Even over the screaming gale, the thunder of war was palpable. The roar of archaic bolters mingled with the revving of engines, the hiss of lasguns, and the whoop and boom of artillery shells as the Mordian 10th advanced on the Mausoleum District. Dug in to receive the attack in the Square of Contemplation, a force of Iron Warriors strafed their shots through the tightly packed ranks of Mordians as they struggled up the snowy streets. The Astra Militarum advance was losing momentum with every passing minute, flames dancing amid the blizzard as one Leman Russ after another was disabled by renegade heavy weapons.

Suddenly, the Warsmith commanding the traitors spun on his heel and toppled into the snow, a neat black hole punched front-to-back through his helm. A moment later, several more key Iron Warriors were pitched off their feet, helmet lenses crazed and gorgets punctured by sniper fire. Heavy bolters and lascannons tumbled from their dead hands, and as the traitors' fire slackened, the Mordians surged forward once more. In the mayhem, few noticed the band of short, wiry figures swathed in camo-patched furs. The Ratlings shouldered their sniper rifles and scrambled from the first floor windows of the Chambers Munificent, dropping to the roadway and setting off in search of a new vantage point.

PRIMARIS PSYKERS

Primaris Psykers are rare and extraordinary individuals who wield the destructive power of the warp as a weapon to smite the enemies of the Emperor. With a single thought the psyker conjures forth lightning that leaps from his hands and surrounds his body; with a gesture he hurls these bolts of aether-energy at his opponents, burning the foes' synapses and searing their flesh from their bones.

Mysterious and aloof, Primaris Psykers, also known as primary-psykers, battle-psykers or psyker-lords, are treated with a mixture of awe, fear and suspicion by the superstitious soldiers of the Imperial Guard. Their presence is utterly abhorrent to some commanders and they are at best mistrusted. However, their ability to combat the blasphemous sorceries of aliens and heretics usually outweighs the natural revulsion many feel at their inclusion in the ranks of the Imperial Guard.

A Primaris Psyker is typically attached to a high-ranking Astra Militarum officer who can direct the psyker's powers as the situation necessitates, providing psychic support to the troopers on the front line. The Primaris Psyker marches to war in a uniform daubed with wards and sigils of power, carrying a staff made of rare and precious materials that can channel the psychic energy of the wielder. As part of his indoctrination and training a psyker will learn to focus his prodigious mental strength through this psycho-reactive staff, transforming it into a searing weapon that glows with a barely contained, otherworldly power capable of cutting through reinforced ceramite and ripping the life force from those it strikes.

Of all the psykers judged under the uncompromising gaze of the Inquisition, only those whose mental fortitude is great enough have the merest glimmer of hope of becoming a Primaris Psyker in the Astra Militarum. Battle-psykers are by no means the most powerful of their kind, but even so, they walk a fine line between service to the Emperor and eternal damnation. Every time they unleash their powers they risk predation from the denizens of the warp – daemonic entities swarm to their bright psyker-soul like moths to a flame. Several fail-safes are therefore built into a psyker's wargear. Complex micro-circuitry and neuro-active wiring are connected to psychically attuned crystals embedded in a psyker's hood or collar, designed to bleed away excess warp energy. Such precautions are not limited to the psyker's wargear alone and most have undergone cranial surgeries to implant neural inhibitors that limit the danger of possession – however, such devices tend to blunt the psyker's innate power as well. When combined with a lifetime of training a Primaris Psyker has a reasonable chance of avoiding powerful psychic enemies and resisting daemonic influences. For those who prove to be too weak, however, there is always the final safeguard, in the shape of the smoking muzzle of a

WYRDVANE PSYKERS

Wyrdvane Psykers transform the howling might of the warp into a deadly weapon of Imperial supremacy. They are formed from those Scholastica Psykana inductees not able to control their burgeoning powers without guidance and aid. Some have not yet completed the gruelling training to become a Primaris Psyker. Others will never achieve that goal, introverted beyond rescue by the horrors of their own minds. As individuals, such psykers are unpredictable and unsafe. Yet in concert, these deadly mutants can be a valuable asset.

Eerily attuned to one another, Wyrdvane Psykers draw strength from communion, linking their thoughts to better slaughter the foes of Mankind. Corposant lightning crackles around them as they marshal their powers, moans and wails spill from their lips, tangled amid stringy ropes of vomited ectoplasm. Armoured battle tanks buckle inwards as the psykers focus their power, crumpling upon their horrified crews like a ration-pack in an Ogryn's fist. Heretics are incinerated amid billowing clouds of psychic flame, domes of protective telekinetic force enfold quivering allied Guardsmen, while pervasive many-voiced whispers talk warriors into madness or horrified self-destruction.

Only once a choir of Wyrdvane Psykers have proven their ability to work as a controlled, cohesive whole will they be permitted to take to the field unsupervised. The psykers are formed into potential squads based on the omens of the Emperor's tarot, and must endure numerous inhumane tests before they are declared battle-ready. They must demonstrate their ability to guard one another's minds, to stabilise their companions' more volatile powers and enhance those that flounder or fail. Many will not survive the trials to which they are subjected, and even those that do are still destined to be treated with fear, revulsion and mistrust.

Horror stories abound amongst the Astra Militarum of Wyrdvane Psykers bursting spontaneously into flame in the midst of battle, or else becoming possessed by terrible entities and slaughtering friend and foe alike. However, the Scholastica Psykana's screening stamps out many such potential disasters before they can occur, and for every uncontrolled explosion of warp energy there are a dozen battles where the Wyrdvanes prove their worth.

Insular in the extreme, squads of Wyrdvane Psykers are only too aware of their comrades' superstitious disgust. Yet for all this, they are loyal and dedicated soldiers of the Imperium, risking their very souls to fight in defence of the Emperor's realm. Indeed, while most officers would be loathe to admit it, a squad or two of Wyrdvane Psykers is often worth several times their number of 'proper' Imperial Guardsmen, and as Humanity's psychic potential squirms closer to the surface, Wyrdvane Psykers have become an increasingly common presence in Astra Militarum regiments.

The night was black as pitch. Around the Valhallans' position, unseen things moved in the darkness, drawing slowly, inexorably closer. Wirlen mopped at his bloody nose with a rag and tried to ignore the muttering of the infantrymen around him. He squashed the familiar spike of resentment as he caught the words 'mutant' and 'cursed'. These are not bad men, he told himself, just scared, and ignorant. Yet that might make them dangerous. It was time to remind them that the Wyrdvane Psykers were powerful servants of the Emperor. Closing his eyes and opening his mind, Wirlen reached out and found his brothers. Poor Stocht, gibbering and rocking. Holsul, his mind a placid lake. Eurum, his anger burning as bright as the fires he could conjure with a thought. Like a choir of voices rising in harmony, the Wyrdvanes entwined their thoughts as they had been trained. Gathering power to themselves and shutting out the whispered temptations of the warp, the psykers' spirits quested outward, the gloom no obstacle to their witchsight. There, amongst the ruins, lithe xenos forms crept ever closer to the unsuspecting Valhallans. Rising to their feet, the exhilaration of unity singing through their minds, Wirlen and his brothers focused their powers to a single, furious point. The night lit up with psychic fire as a roaring bolt of energy lashed out, engulfing the screaming Drukhari and turning them to ash. As he returned to his body Wirlen noted the Valhallans were now wide-eyed and silent. Let them think on that, he smiled to himself, before reaching out with his mind in search of fresh xenos to slaughter.

REGIMENTAL ADVISORS

The Adeptus Munitorum can call upon a vast array of esoteric personnel to advise Company Commanders in battle. Be they enigmatic astrosavants, starch-collared aide-de-camps or ancillary military officers, these regimental advisors form an eclectic entourage who lend their diverse skills to whichever command post they are assigned to. While many senior officers resent the peculiar proclivities or bombastic second-guessing of such advisors, none can deny the strategic value of having these specialists present in the heat of battle.

Each type of advisor serves as a representative of a different arm of the Imperial war machine. A Master of Ordnance, for example, serves as a combat attaché despatched from a Militarum Regimentum's artillery companies. They are the eyes on the battlefield, spotting for batteries of long-range weaponry nested far from the front lines. Utilising complex ocular arrays and barometric auguries, they coordinate devastating artillery strikes on the enemy's positions. Wherever the Master of Ordnance directs their gaze, a rain of exploding shells is sure to follow. If mobile artillery is needed closer to the thick of combat, the Master of Ordnance will typically be stationed nearby to coordinate their devastating firepower.

An Officer of the Fleet performs a similar role to the Master of Ordnance, but is responsible for the coordination of aerial support for ground troops. As a junior commander of the Aeronautica Imperialis assigned to an Astra Militarum company, an Officer of the Fleet has the authority to direct the attack craft and personnel transports of the Imperial Navy. Under their guidance, squadrons of Valkyries are ordered to converge on designated targets where they lay down a fiery curtain of las-blasts and missile strikes. If a particularly high-value target cannot be reached by the Valkyries, an Officer of the Fleet can request a precision strike to be delivered by Aeronautica Imperialis vessels stationed in low orbit above the battlefield. With but a few calm words over long-range vox, Marauder bombers descend from the stratosphere to drop their explosive payload on top of the unsuspecting enemy.

Astropaths are registered psykers in the service of the Scholastica Psykana, and are commissioned to the Astra Militarum to aid the soldiers of the Imperium with their prognostications. Their ability to divine the shifting psychic currents amidst the roiling swirl of combat makes them invaluable to a Company Commander. Guided by an Astropath's dread visions, commanders order their Heavy Weapons Teams and tank squadrons to fire into seemingly empty patches of cover – the resultant enemy screams and the wet splatter of shredded flesh quickly silence any doubts as to the psyker's intuition. Astropaths are known to unsettle their comrades with their hollow, eyeless gaze and the susurrus of telepathic murmurs that fogs the air around them. Yet none can deny that their ability to project their thoughts, or to influence the thoughts of others, can make them a potent weapon on the battlefield.

REGIMENTAL COLOURS

An Astra Militarum army presents an exciting challenge for modellers and painters alike. The wide range and broad scope of models available makes for a varied collection, while the ordered ranks of Guardsmen gives them an impressive tabletop presence. Infantry, artillery, aircraft and tanks, the Astra Militarum have it all.

Lord Castellan Ursarkar Creed

Colour Sergeant Jarran Kell

Colonel 'Iron Hand' Straken

Commissar Yarrick

An armoured Cadian column advances towards the ranks of the Thousand Sons, supported by Basilisk fire and the inexorable surge of Leman Russ Battle Tanks. Infantry officers bellow their orders over the thunder of the engines, while from the skies the Valkyries of the Aeronautica Imperialis rain death upon the Heretic Astartes.

Cadian Company Commander and Command Squad

Officer of the Fleet

Master of Ordnance

Lord Commissar

Commissar with power sword and plasma pistol

Astropath

Tech-Priest Enginseer

Primaris Psyker

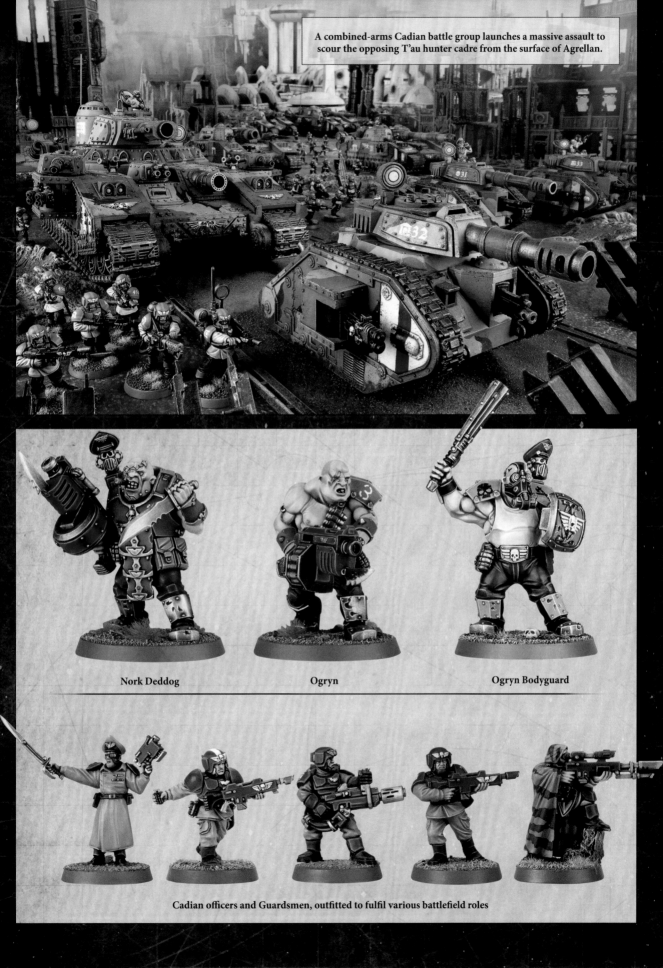

A combined-arms Cadian battle group launches a massive assault to scour the opposing T'au hunter cadre from the surface of Agrellan.

Nork Deddog

Ogryn

Ogryn Bodyguard

Cadian officers and Guardsmen, outfitted to fulfil various battlefield roles

Gunnery Sergeant Harker and his fellow Catachans fight amidst the burning jungles of a besieged death world.

Catachan Company Commander and Command Squad

Catachan Guardsmen with lasguns

Heroic and hard-bitten Catachan Veterans, armed and equipped for a range of combat situations

Catachan Guardsman with sniper rifle

Guardsmen of the Tallarn Desert Raiders take cover behind the massive bulk of a Baneblade, allowing the super-heavy tank and the rear-line Heavy Weapons Squads to soften the enemy before launching their charge.

Heedless of the casualties they sustain and the harsh conditions in which they must fight, the Valhallan Ice Warriors trudge towards the opposing line, pausing only briefly to unleash yet another salvo of withering fire.

Tank Commander Pysell Roderrik steers his Cadian armoured battle group through the overgrown ruins, the tank hulls shielding the crewmen inside from corrosive gales as they hunt their Necron quarry.

After redeploying on the Ork warband's flank, the Kappic Eagles of the Militarum Tempestus lay down a hail of fire to cover a punishing Bullgryn charge.

Tempestor Prime and Militarum Tempestus Command Squad

Company Commander and Command Squad of the Cadian 122nd 'Kasr Kraf Jackals'

The soldiers of the Astra Militarum's many and varied regiments can be created by combining parts from different Citadel Miniatures kits. The conversions below show the Guardsmen and officers of just some of the Imperium's myriad worlds.

Mordian Veteran

Tanith First and Only Guardsman

Miasman Redcowl Guardsman

Savlar Chem-dog Sergeant

Indigan Praefects Veteran

Ventrillian Noble Guardsman

Armageddon Ork Hunter

The Guardsmen below are made using the Cadian Shock Troops range of Citadel Miniatures, with variant colour schemes and iconography specific to each of their home worlds.

Faeburn Vanquisher

Truskan Snowhound

Vresh Grenadier

Adorned in their full war regalia, the Ventrillian Nobles 118th 'Opal Raptors' forms a bristling defence line, arraying their autocannons to fire upon the first wave of Drukhari Raiders to come tearing over the horizon.

Vostroyan Leman Russ Demolisher with heavy bolters

**Vostroyan
Company Commander**

**Vostroyan Command Squad
standard bearer**

**Vostroyan Guardsman
with medi-pack**

**Vostroyan Guardsman
with vox-caster**

Vostroyan Sergeant

Vostroyan Guardsmen

MUSTERING FOR WAR

The Astra Militarum are as powerful as they are diverse. Two quite different starting forces are presented below, the first providing heavy-duty firepower and the second offering on speed and manoeuvrability.

The first starting force is composed of miniatures from the Start Collecting! Astra Militarum set. Leading this force is a Lord Commissar, who is represented by the Officio Prefectus Commissar miniature. A single Infantry Squad is under his command, and they are supported by a Heavy Weapons Squad and a Leman Russ Battle Tank for fire support. With a single HQ choice and Troops choice, as well as two Heavy Support choices, the miniatures in this set can be fielded as a Patrol Detachment,

as described in the *Warhammer 40,000* rulebook.

The second starting force is made using the Start Collecting! Militarum Tempestus set. It is led by a Tempestor Prime, who is flanked by a Commissar and a Militarum Tempestus Command Squad. To the rear of the formation is a unit of Militarum Tempestus Scions and a Taurox Prime to allow for rapid redeployment. With two Elites choices and one choice each of HQ,

Troops and Dedicated Transports, this force also fulfils the requirements of a Patrol Detachment.

As all of their units belong to the same Faction and make up a Detachment, each of the armies below is Battle-forged. Being Battle-forged affords Command Points, which can be spent during a game on various Stratagems that bolster your troops and vehicles. As you add more Detachments to your army, you will gain even more command points to use.

Lord Commissar Marialis leads soldiers of the Cadian 8th, supported by a Leman Russ Battle Tank.

A detachment of Militarum Tempestus 55th Kappic Eagles, led by Tempestor Prime Javier Dollen.

THE CLAW OF CADIA

Below is a larger battle group – the Claw of Cadia – comprising several Detachments drawn from various armoured and infantry regiments, affording a total of between seven and twelve Command Points that can be used in battle.

Knight Commander Pask leads this battle group from the turret of the *Hand of Steel*. To his sides are a Leman Russ Battle Tank and a Leman Russ Demolisher, each taken from his 423rd regiment, and together the trio of tanks forms the armoured core of the Spearhead Detachment. With a range of armaments and Pask directing their fire, few enemies can withstand their onslaught. Arrayed behind the tanks are three Hydras, their quad autocannons ready to clear the skies of enemy fliers. Rounding off the Detachment is a squadron of Fast Attack vehicles comprising a single Devil Dog and two Hellhounds. This 'Desolation Squadron' can outflank an opposing formation to incinerate infantry with burning promethium or blast enemy armour with melta cannons.

Also in Pask's battle group is a Battalion Detachment composed of soldiers from the Cadian 92nd 'Firebrands'. This regiment was nearly wiped out by Shas'vre Dasir's Hunter Cadre during the Damocles Crusade, but their numbers have since been bolstered by recruits inducted from other Militarum Regimentos. At the head of this Detachment is Company Commander Massar Darnell, shadowed by his Command Squad – they carry the regimental standard of the 92nd, and also have a medic and vox-operator among their number. A total of six Infantry Squads from the 92nd march in Massar's Detachment, with a variety of special weapons specialists between them for maximum tactical flexibility. They are overseen by Lord Commissar Gaken, and ride to war in a mix

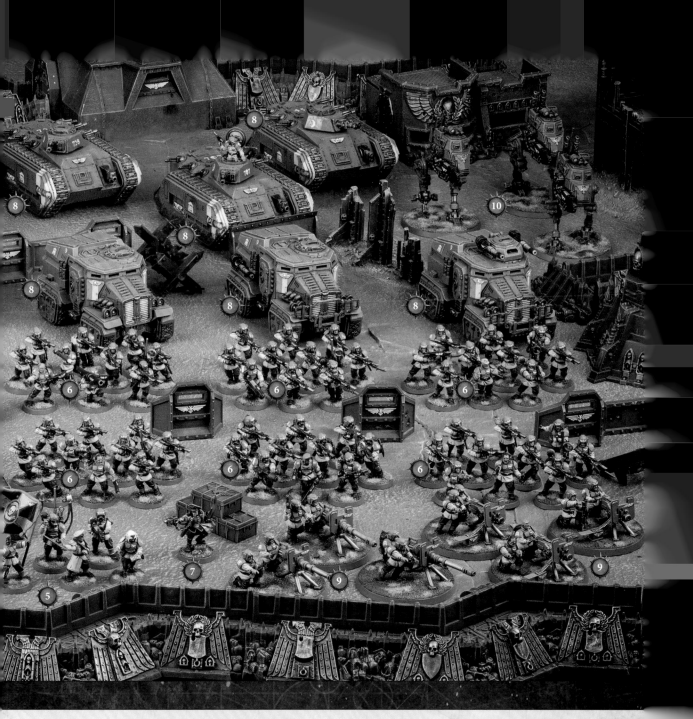

of Tauroxes and Chimeras. Two Heavy Weapons Squads provide raw firepower to the battalion, while a trio of Armoured Sentinels seconded from the 1332nd regiment round out the battle line.

A Patrol Detachment of Kappic Eagles also fights for Pask, headed by Tempestor Prime Mathius Krassus. With his Militarum Tempestus Command Squad, three units of Militarum Tempestus Scions and two Taurox Primes, Krassus' force is an adaptable and highly mobile element of the battle group. A single squad of Bullgryns also fight in this Detachment, where they are deployed in defence of valuable battlefield assets, such as the Hydra battery or Pask himself.

When required, the separate elements of this army can be merged into a single Brigade Detachment. This restricts the operational autonomy of the Militarum Tempestus Detachment, but in return affords even greater tactical command over the battle group, granting twelve Command Points to be spent on Stratagems.

1. **Knight Commander Pask**

2. **Tanks of the Cadian 423rd Armoured Regiment**

3. **Hydra battery**

4. **Hellhounds and Devil Dogs 'Desolation Squadron'**

5. **Company Commander Darnell and Command Squad**

6. **Infantry Squads of the Cadian 92nd 'Firebrands'**

7. **Lord Commissar Gaken**

8. **Chimera and Taurox troop transports**

9. **Heavy Weapons Squads**

10. **Armoured Sentinels of the Cadian 1332nd**

11. **Tempestor Prime Mathius Krassus and Tempestus Command Squad**

12. **Kappic Eagles Tempestus Scions**

13. **Taurox Prime troop transports**

14. **Bullgryns of the Anark Zeta 81st 'Immovables'**

SOLDIERS OF THE IMPERIUM

This section contains all of the datasheets that you will need to fight battles with your Astra Militarum miniatures, and the rules for all of the weapons they can wield in battle. Each datasheet includes the characteristics profiles of the unit it describes, as well as any wargear and special abilities it may have. Any abilities that are common to several units are described below and referenced on the datasheets themselves.

KEYWORDS

Throughout this section you will come across a keyword that is within angular brackets, specifically <Regiment>. This is shorthand for a keyword of your own choosing, as described below.

<Regiment>

Most Astra Militarum units are drawn from a regiment. Some datasheets specify which regiment the unit is drawn from (e.g. Sergeant Harker has the Catachan keyword, so is drawn from the Catachan Regiment). If an Astra Militarum datasheet does not specify which regiment it is drawn from, it will have the <Regiment> keyword. When you include such a unit in your army, you must nominate which regiment that unit is from. You then simply replace the <Regiment> keyword in every instance on that unit's datasheet with the name of your chosen regiment. Units with the Militarum Tempestus keyword treat this as their <Regiment> keyword in all respects, but the Militarum Tempestus keyword cannot be used to replace the <Regiment> keyword on any other datasheet.

For example, if you included a Command Squad in your army and wanted them to be from Vostroya, their <Regiment> Faction keyword is changed to Vostroyan and their Regimental Standard ability would say: 'All friendly Vostroyan units add 1 to their Leadership whilst they are within 6" of any Vostroyan Veteran with a regimental standard.'

'When a man has known the cold of Valhalla, the galaxy offers no other hardship to compare. Alien monsters, unnatural diseases, mud, blood and blades; all of these are kindly gifts by comparison.'

- Sergeant Voshnek,
Valhallan 97th 'Icehearts'

ABILITIES

The following abilities are common to several **Astra Militarum** units.

VOICE OF COMMAND

This unit may issue one order per turn to the soldiers under their command at the start of their Shooting phase. Orders may only be issued to **Infantry** units within 6" of this unit that have the same <**Regiment**> keyword as this unit. To issue an order, pick a target unit and choose which order you wish to issue from the table below. A unit may only be affected by one order per turn.

ASTRA MILITARUM ORDERS

ORDER	
Take Aim!	*Even amid the clangorous din of battle, the bellowed instructions of an officer recall the countless days each soldier spent conducting targeted fire drills.* Re-roll hit rolls of 1 for all the models in the ordered unit until the end of the phase.
First Rank, Fire! Second Rank, Fire!	*By sheer weight of fire, the mortal soldiers of the Astra Militarum can annihilate whole armies of enemies. A good officer is quick to take advantage of this.* All lasguns and all hot-shot lasguns in the ordered unit change their Type to Rapid Fire 2 until the end of the phase.
Bring it Down!	*Guided by the experienced eye of their leader, a squad is able to pinpoint an enemy's weakest point, and in doing so fell the most terrifying enemies of the Imperium.* Re-roll wound rolls of 1 for all the models in the ordered unit until the end of the phase.
Forwards, for the Emperor!	*With the correct motivation, Astra Militarum soldiers can march at full pace without eschewing their duty to fire upon their enemy.* The ordered unit can shoot this phase even if it Advanced in its Movement phase.
Get Back in the Fight!	*To retreat is not always to concede defeat, and a tactical withdrawal can open up new opportunities for troops to showcase their firing skills.* The ordered unit can shoot this phase even if it Fell Back in its Movement phase.
Move! Move! Move!	*When the needs of the battle dictate, soldiers can be ordered to march double-time, moving quickly to close range with the enemy or to secure an open flank.* Instead of shooting this phase the ordered unit immediately moves as if it were the Movement phase. It must Advance as part of this move, and cannot declare a charge during this turn.
Fix Bayonets!	*With a bellicose cry, troops can be ordered to descend upon their foe with close-quarter weaponry, stabbing, slashing and bludgeoning until they have secured victory for the Emperor.* This order can only be issued to units that are within 1" of an enemy unit. The ordered unit immediately fights as if it were the Fight phase.

ASTRA MILITARUM WARGEAR LISTS

Many of the units you will find on the following pages reference one or more of the wargear lists below. When this is the case, the unit may take any item from the appropriate list. The profiles for the items in these lists can be found in the Armoury of the Imperium section (pg 126-129).

RANGED WEAPONS

- Bolt pistol
- Boltgun
- Plasma pistol

MELEE WEAPONS

- Power sword
- Power fist

SPECIAL WEAPONS

- Sniper rifle
- Flamer
- Grenade launcher
- Meltagun
- Plasma gun

HEAVY WEAPONS

- Mortar
- Autocannon
- Heavy bolter
- Missile launcher
- Lascannon

VEHICLE EQUIPMENT

- Augur array
- Dozer blade
- Heavy stubber *
- Hunter-killer missile
- Storm bolter *
- Track guards

A vehicle cannot have both a heavy stubber and a storm bolter.

REGIMENTAL ORDERS

Many Astra Militarum regiments maintain specialised training regimes, tactics and even entire battlefield languages to direct their troops. The table below contains additional orders for use with the Voice of Command ability which may be used by officers with the appropriate regiment keyword. For example, CATACHAN officers may issue the Catachan 'Burn them out!' order in addition to any of the standard orders from the list on the previous page. Some of the orders below are noted as being Tank Orders. These may only be issued by a TANK COMMANDER with the appropriate <REGIMENT> keyword, in addition to those listed on their datasheet and using the rules for Tank Orders as described on their datasheet.

GRINDING ADVANCE

The Leman Russ tank's sturdy frame allows it to keep up a fearsome rate of fire even as it advances on the foe. If this model moves under half speed in its Movement phase (i.e. it moves a distance in inches less than half of its current Move characteristic) it can shoot its turret weapon twice in the following Shooting phase (the turret weapon must target the same unit both times). Furthermore, hit rolls for this model's turret weapon do not suffer the penalty for moving and shooting a Heavy weapon. The following weapons are turret weapons: battle cannon, eradicator nova cannon, exterminator autocannon, vanquisher battle cannon, demolisher cannon, executioner plasma cannon and punisher gatling cannon.

REGIMENT	ADDITIONAL ORDER
Cadian (Tank Order)	**Pound Them to Dust!:** *After endless drilling, Cadian tank gunners are sure to make every shot count on the battlefield.* For the duration of this phase, you can re-roll the dice when determining the number of attacks the ordered model can make with turret weapons (as described in the Grinding Advance ability above) that use a randomly determined number (e.g. Heavy D6).
Catachan	**Burn Them Out!:** *Hacking their way through countless tangled death worlds has made the Jungle Fighters experts at flushing out foes with burning promethium.* You can re-roll the dice when determining the number of attacks the ordered unit can make with flamers and heavy flamers until the end of the phase. In addition, units targeted by models from the ordered unit with these weapons do not gain any bonus to their saving throws for being in cover this phase.
Valhallan	**Fire on My Command!:** *Life is cheap on Valhalla, and the officers of the Ice Warriors regiments will not sacrifice victory to reduce casualties.* The ordered unit can shoot at enemy units that are within 1" of friendly units until the end of the phase, but each time you roll a hit roll of 1 for such an attack, resolve that attack against a friendly unit within 1" of the target unit instead. You may choose which friendly unit is hit. This order may not be issued to a unit which is within 1" of an enemy unit.
Vostroyan	**Repel the Enemy!:** *The Firstborn regiments are drawn from those who have learned to fight in the cramped ruins and alleys of their home world.* Until the end of the phase, the ordered unit can fire any of its weapons while it is within 1" of the enemy, regardless of the weapon's type. If they do so, they must target enemy units within 1", even if friendly units are within 1" of these units.
Armageddon	**Mount Up!:** *Rapid mechanised redeployments are paramount to success in the choking ash wastes of Armageddon.* Until the end of the phase, the ordered unit can shoot and then immediately embark within a friendly ARMAGEDDON TRANSPORT VEHICLE, as long as all models in the unit are within 3" of the vehicle. This order may not be issued to a unit which disembarked in the preceding Movement phase.
Tallarn (Tank Order)	**Get Around Behind Them!:** *The Tallarns use their tanks not as simple hammers, but as rapiers – darting swiftly into combat to deliver the killing blow.* The ordered model can move up to 6" in this phase, either before or after it shoots, as if it were the Movement phase. This does not affect how far the vehicle has moved for the purposes of determining how many times it can fire its turret weapon (as described in the Grinding Advance ability above).
Militarum Tempestus	**Elimination Protocol Sanctioned!:** *In the Schola Progenium, the shock troopers of the Militarum Tempestus are trained to eradicate even the most fearsome enemies of the Imperium.* You can re-roll failed wound rolls for models from the ordered unit when attacking any enemy VEHICLES or MONSTERS this phase.
Mordian	**Form Firing Squad!:** *With but a word from their commanding officer, the Mordian infantry take on the role of executioners.* Until the end of the phase, the ordered unit can target CHARACTERS with their Rapid Fire weapons, even if they are not the closest enemy unit.

LORD CASTELLAN CREED

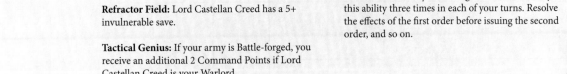

NAME	M	WS	BS	S	T	W	A	Ld	Sv
Lord Castellan Creed	6"	3+	3+	3	3	4	3	9	4+

Lord Castellan Creed is a single model armed with two hot-shot laspistols and a power sword. Only one of this model may be included in your army.

WEAPON	RANGE	TYPE	S	AP	D	ABILITIES
Hot-shot laspistol	6"	Pistol 1	3	-2	1	-
Power sword	Melee	Melee	User	-3	1	-

ABILITIES	**Voice of Command** (pg 85)	**Supreme Commander:** Lord Castellan Creed's Voice of Command ability has a range of 12", and he may use this ability three times in each of your turns. Resolve the effects of the first order before issuing the second order, and so on.
	Refractor Field: Lord Castellan Creed has a 5+ invulnerable save.	
	Tactical Genius: If your army is Battle-forged, you receive an additional 2 Command Points if Lord Castellan Creed is your Warlord.	
FACTION KEYWORDS	IMPERIUM, ASTRA MILITARUM, CADIAN	
KEYWORDS	CHARACTER, INFANTRY, OFFICER, LORD CASTELLAN CREED	

COMPANY COMMANDER

NAME	M	WS	BS	S	T	W	A	Ld	Sv
Company Commander	6"	3+	3+	3	3	4	3	8	5+

A Company Commander is a single model armed with a laspistol and frag grenades.

WEAPON	RANGE	TYPE	S	AP	D	ABILITIES
Laspistol	12"	Pistol 1	3	0	1	-
Chainsword	Melee	Melee	User	0	1	Each time the bearer fights, it can make 1 additional attack with this weapon.
Frag grenade	6"	Grenade D6	3	0	1	-

WARGEAR OPTIONS	• This model may take a chainsword or an item from the *Melee Weapons* list. • This model may replace its laspistol with an item from the *Ranged Weapons* list.	
ABILITIES	**Voice of Command** (pg 85)	**Senior Officer:** This model may use the Voice of Command ability twice in each of your turns. Resolve the effects of the first order before issuing the second order.
	Refractor Field: This model has a 5+ invulnerable save.	
FACTION KEYWORDS	IMPERIUM, ASTRA MILITARUM, <REGIMENT>	
KEYWORDS	CHARACTER, INFANTRY, OFFICER, COMPANY COMMANDER	

TANK COMMANDER

NAME	M	WS	BS	S	T	W	A	Ld	Sv
Tank Commander	*	6+	*	7	8	12	*	7	3+

DAMAGE
Some of this model's characteristics change as it suffers damage, as shown below:

REMAINING W	M	BS	A
7-12+	10"	3+	3
4-6	7"	4+	D3
1-3	4"	5+	1

A Tank Commander is a single model. He rides to battle from the cupola of a Leman Russ battle tank, which is equipped with a battle cannon and a heavy bolter.

WEAPON	RANGE	TYPE	S	AP	D	ABILITIES
Battle cannon	72"	Heavy D6	8	-2	D3	-
Demolisher cannon	24"	Heavy D3	10	-3	D6	When attacking units with 5 or more models, change this weapon's Type to Heavy D6.
Eradicator nova cannon	36"	Heavy D6	6	-2	D3	Units attacked by this weapon do not gain any bonus to their saving throws for being in cover.
Executioner plasma cannon	When attacking with this weapon, choose one of the profiles below.					
- Standard	36"	Heavy D6	7	-3	1	-
- Supercharge	36"	Heavy D6	8	-3	2	For each hit roll of 1, the bearer suffers 1 mortal wound after all of this weapon's shots have been resolved.
Exterminator autocannon	48"	Heavy 4	7	-1	2	
Heavy bolter	36"	Heavy 3	5	-1	1	
Heavy flamer	8"	Heavy D6	5	-1	1	This weapon automatically hits its target.
Lascannon	48"	Heavy 1	9	-3	D6	-
Multi-melta	24"	Heavy 1	8	-4	D6	If the target is within half range of this weapon, roll two dice when inflicting damage with it and discard the lowest result.
Plasma cannon	When attacking with this weapon, choose one of the profiles below.					
- Standard	36"	Heavy D3	7	-3	1	-
- Supercharge	36"	Heavy D3	8	-3	2	On a hit roll of 1, the bearer is slain after all of this weapon's shots have been resolved.
Punisher gatling cannon	24"	Heavy 20	5	0	1	-
Vanquisher battle cannon	72"	Heavy 1	8	-3	D6	Roll two dice when inflicting damage with this weapon and discard the lowest result.

WARGEAR OPTIONS	
	• This model may replace its battle cannon with an exterminator autocannon, vanquisher battle cannon, eradicator nova cannon, demolisher cannon, punisher gatling cannon or executioner plasma cannon.
	• This model may replace its heavy bolter with a heavy flamer or a lascannon.
	• This model may take two heavy bolters, two heavy flamers, two multi-meltas or two plasma cannons.
	• This model may take items from the *Vehicle Equipment* list.

ABILITIES

Grinding Advance (pg 86)

Explodes: If this model is reduced to 0 wounds, roll a D6 before removing it from the battlefield. On a 6 it explodes, and each unit within 6" suffers D3 mortal wounds.

Smoke Launchers: Once per game, instead of shooting any weapons in the Shooting phase, this model can use its smoke launchers; until your next Shooting phase your opponent must subtract 1 from all hit rolls for ranged weapons that target this vehicle.

Tank Orders: This model can issue one order each turn to a friendly <REGIMENT> LEMAN RUSS at the start of your Shooting phase. To issue a tank order, pick a target LEMAN RUSS within 6" of this model and choose which order you wish to issue from the table to the right. Each LEMAN RUSS can only be given a single order each turn.

Emergency Plasma Vents: If this model fires a supercharged plasma cannon, and you roll one or more hit rolls of 1, it is not automatically destroyed. Instead, for each hit roll of 1, the bearer suffers 1 mortal wound after all of this weapon's shots have been resolved.

TANK ORDERS
ORDER

Full Throttle!
Instead of shooting this phase the ordered model immediately moves as if it were the Movement phase. It must Advance as part of this move, and cannot declare a charge during this turn.

Gunners, Kill on Sight!
Re-roll hit rolls of 1 for the ordered model until the end of the phase.

Strike and Shroud!
This order can only be issued to a model that has not yet used its smoke launchers during the battle. The ordered model can shoot its weapons and launch its smoke launchers during this phase.

FACTION KEYWORDS	IMPERIUM, ASTRA MILITARUM, <REGIMENT>
KEYWORDS	CHARACTER, VEHICLE, LEMAN RUSS, OFFICER, TANK COMMANDER

KNIGHT COMMANDER PASK

DAMAGE

Some of this model's characteristics change as it suffers damage, as shown below:

REMAINING W	M	BS	A
7-12+	10"	2+	3
4-6	7"	3+	D3
1-3	4"	4+	1

NAME	M	WS	BS	S	T	W	A	Ld	Sv
Knight Commander Pask	*	6+	*	7	8	12	*	8	3+

Knight Commander Pask is a single model. He rides to battle in the cupola of his trusty Leman Russ battle tank, *Hand of Steel*, which is equipped with a battle cannon and a heavy bolter. Only one of this model may be included in your army.

WEAPON	RANGE	TYPE	S	AP	D	ABILITIES
Battle cannon	72"	Heavy D6	8	-2	D3	-
Demolisher cannon	24"	Heavy D3	10	-3	D6	When attacking units with 5 or more models, change this weapon's Type to Heavy D6.
Eradicator nova cannon	36"	Heavy D6	6	-2	D3	Units attacked by this weapon do not gain any bonus to their saving throws for being in cover.
Executioner plasma cannon	When attacking with this weapon, choose one of the profiles below.					
- Standard	36"	Heavy D6	7	-3	1	-
- Supercharge	36"	Heavy D6	8	-3	2	For each hit roll of 1, the bearer suffers 1 mortal wound after all of this weapon's shots have been resolved.
Exterminator autocannon	48"	Heavy 4	7	-1	2	-
Heavy bolter	36"	Heavy 3	5	-1	1	-
Heavy flamer	8"	Heavy D6	5	-1	1	This weapon automatically hits its target.
Lascannon	48"	Heavy 1	9	-3	D6	-
Multi-melta	24"	Heavy 1	8	-4	D6	If the target is within half range of this weapon, roll two dice when inflicting damage with it and discard the lowest result.
Plasma cannon	When attacking with this weapon, choose one of the profiles below.					
- Standard	36"	Heavy D3	7	-3	1	-
- Supercharge	36"	Heavy D3	8	-3	2	On a hit roll of 1, the bearer is slain after all of this weapon's shots have been resolved.
Punisher gatling cannon	24"	Heavy 20	5	0	1	-
Vanquisher battle cannon	72"	Heavy 1	8	-3	D6	Roll two dice when inflicting damage with this weapon and discard the lowest result.

WARGEAR OPTIONS	• *Hand of Steel*'s battle cannon may be replaced with an exterminator autocannon, vanquisher battle cannon, eradicator nova cannon, demolisher cannon, punisher gatling cannon or executioner plasma cannon. • *Hand of Steel*'s heavy bolter may be replaced with a heavy flamer or a lascannon. • *Hand of Steel* may take two heavy bolters, two heavy flamers, two multi-meltas or two plasma cannons. • *Hand of Steel* may take items from the *Vehicle Equipment* list.

ABILITIES

Grinding Advance (pg 86)

Smoke Launchers: Once per game, instead of shooting any weapons in the Shooting phase, Knight Commander Pask can launch *Hand of Steel*'s smoke launchers; if he does so, until your next Shooting phase your opponent must subtract 1 from any hit rolls that target it.

Tank Orders: Knight Commander Pask can issue orders to a friendly **CADIAN LEMAN RUSS** at the start of your Shooting phase. To issue a tank order, pick a target **LEMAN RUSS** within 6" of Knight Commander Pask and choose which order you wish to issue from the table to the right. Each **LEMAN RUSS** can only be given a single order each turn.

Knight Commander: Knight Commander Pask may use the Tank Orders ability twice in each of your turns. Resolve the effects of the first order before issuing the second order.

Emergency Plasma Vents: If this model fires a supercharged plasma cannon, and you roll one or more hit rolls of 1, it is not automatically destroyed. Instead, for each hit roll of 1, the bearer suffers 1 mortal wound after all of this weapon's shots have been resolved.

Explodes: If this model is reduced to 0 wounds, roll a D6 before removing it from the battlefield. On a 6 it explodes, and each unit within 6" suffers D3 mortal wounds.

TANK ORDERS

ORDER

Full Throttle! Instead of shooting this phase the ordered model immediately moves as if it were the Movement phase. It must Advance as part of this move, and cannot declare a charge during this turn.

Gunners, Kill on Sight! Re-roll hit rolls of 1 for the ordered model until the end of the phase.

Strike and Shroud! This order can only be issued to a model that has not yet used its smoke launchers during the battle. The ordered model can shoot its weapons and launch its smoke launchers during this phase.

FACTION KEYWORDS	IMPERIUM, ASTRA MILITARUM, CADIAN
KEYWORDS	CHARACTER, VEHICLE, LEMAN RUSS, OFFICER, TANK COMMANDER, KNIGHT COMMANDER PASK

COMMISSAR YARRICK

7 POWER

NAME	M	WS	BS	S	T	W	A	Ld	Sv
Commissar Yarrick	6"	2+	2+	3	4	4	3	9	4+

Commissar Yarrick is a single model armed with a bolt pistol, storm bolter, power klaw and the Bale Eye. Only one of this model may be included in your army.

WEAPON	RANGE	TYPE	S	AP	D	ABILITIES
Bale Eye	6"	Pistol 1	3	-2	1	-
Bolt pistol	12"	Pistol 1	4	0	1	-
Storm bolter	24"	Rapid Fire 2	4	0	1	-
Power klaw	Melee	Melee	x2	-3	D3	When attacking with this weapon, you must subtract 1 from the hit roll.

ABILITIES	**Aura of Discipline:** ASTRA MILITARUM units within 6" of a friendly COMMISSAR can use the Commissar's Leadership instead of their own. **Iron Will:** Roll a D6 each time Commissar Yarrick loses his final wound; on a roll of 3+ that wound is not lost. **Power Field:** Commissar Yarrick has a 4+ invulnerable save.	**Hero of Hades Hive:** You can re-roll hit rolls of 1 made for friendly ASTRA MILITARUM units within 6" of Commissar Yarrick. You may re-roll any failed hit rolls for friendly ASTRA MILITARUM units within 6" of Commissar Yarrick when attacking ORK units. **Summary Execution:** ASTRA MILITARUM units within 6" of a friendly COMMISSAR can never lose more than one model as the result of any single failed Morale test.
FACTION KEYWORDS	IMPERIUM, ASTRA MILITARUM, OFFICIO PREFECTUS	
KEYWORDS	CHARACTER, INFANTRY, COMMISSAR, YARRICK	

LORD COMMISSAR

4 POWER

NAME	M	WS	BS	S	T	W	A	Ld	Sv
Lord Commissar	6"	2+	2+	3	3	4	3	9	4+

A Lord Commissar is a single model armed with a bolt pistol and power sword.

WEAPON	RANGE	TYPE	S	AP	D	ABILITIES
Bolt pistol	12"	Pistol 1	4	0	1	-
Power sword	Melee	Melee	User	-3	1	-

WARGEAR OPTIONS	• This model may replace its power sword with up to two items from the *Melee Weapons* list. • This model may replace its bolt pistol with one item from the *Ranged Weapons* list.	
ABILITIES	**Aura of Discipline:** ASTRA MILITARUM units within 6" of a friendly COMMISSAR can use the Commissar's Leadership instead of their own. **Refractor Field:** This model has a 5+ invulnerable save.	**Summary Execution:** ASTRA MILITARUM units within 6" of a friendly COMMISSAR can never lose more than one model as the result of any single failed Morale test.
FACTION KEYWORDS	IMPERIUM, ASTRA MILITARUM, OFFICIO PREFECTUS	
KEYWORDS	CHARACTER, INFANTRY, COMMISSAR, LORD COMMISSAR	

COLONEL 'IRON HAND' STRAKEN

NAME	M	WS	BS	S	T	W	A	Ld	Sv
Colonel 'Iron Hand' Straken	6"	2+	3+	6	4	5	4	9	3+

Colonel 'Iron Hand' Straken is a single model armed with a plasma pistol, shotgun, frag grenades, krak grenades and a bionic arm with devil's claw. Only one of this model may be included in your army.

WEAPON	RANGE	TYPE	S	AP	D	ABILITIES
Plasma pistol	When attacking with this weapon, choose one of the profiles below.					
- Standard	12"	Pistol 1	7	-3	1	-
- Supercharge	12"	Pistol 1	8	-3	2	On a hit roll of 1, the bearer is slain.
Shotgun	12"	Assault 2	3	0	1	If the target is within half range, add 1 to this weapon's Strength.
Bionic arm with devil's claw	Melee	Melee	User	-1	2	-
Frag grenade	6"	Grenade D6	3	0	1	-
Krak grenade	6"	Grenade 1	6	-1	D3	-

ABILITIES	Voice of Command (pg 85) **Been There, Seen It, Killed It:** You can re-roll failed wound rolls made for Colonel 'Iron Hand' Straken in the Fight phase when attacking enemy **MONSTERS**. **Refractor Field:** Colonel 'Iron Hand' Straken has a 5+ invulnerable save.	**Cold Steel and Courage:** All models in friendly **CATACHAN** units within 6" of Colonel 'Iron Hand' Straken at the start of the Fight phase can make 1 additional attack each time they fight during that phase. **Senior Officer:** Colonel 'Iron Hand' Straken may use the Voice of Command ability twice in each of your turns. Resolve the effects of the first order before issuing the second order.

FACTION KEYWORDS	IMPERIUM, ASTRA MILITARUM, CATACHAN
KEYWORDS	CHARACTER, INFANTRY, OFFICER, COLONEL 'IRON HAND' STRAKEN

TEMPESTOR PRIME

NAME	M	WS	BS	S	T	W	A	Ld	Sv
Tempestor Prime	6"	3+	3+	3	3	4	3	8	4+

A Tempestor Prime is a single model armed with a hot-shot laspistol, frag grenades and krak grenades.

WEAPON	RANGE	TYPE	S	AP	D	ABILITIES
Bolt pistol	12"	Pistol 1	4	0	1	-
Hot-shot laspistol	6"	Pistol 1	3	-2	1	-
Plasma pistol	When attacking with this weapon, choose one of the profiles below.					
- Standard	12"	Pistol 1	7	-3	1	-
- Supercharge	12"	Pistol 1	8	-3	2	On a hit roll of 1, the bearer is slain.
Chainsword	Melee	Melee	User	0	1	Each time the bearer fights, it can make 1 additional attack with this weapon.
Frag grenade	6"	Grenade D6	3	0	1	-
Krak grenade	6"	Grenade 1	6	-1	D3	-

WARGEAR OPTIONS	• This model may take a chainsword or one item from the *Melee Weapons* list. • This model may replace its hot-shot laspistol with a Tempestus command rod, a bolt pistol or a plasma pistol.

ABILITIES	Voice of Command (pg 85) **Tempestus Command Rod:** A model with a Tempestus command rod may use the Voice of Command ability twice in each of your turns. Resolve the effects of the first order before issuing the second order.	**Aerial Drop:** During deployment, you can set up this model in a high-altitude transport, ready to deploy via grav-chute, instead of placing it on the battlefield. At the end of any of your Movement phases the model can make an aerial drop – set it up anywhere on the battlefield that is more than 9" away from any enemy models.

FACTION KEYWORDS	IMPERIUM, ASTRA MILITARUM, MILITARUM TEMPESTUS
KEYWORDS	CHARACTER, INFANTRY, OFFICER, TEMPESTOR PRIME

PRIMARIS PSYKER

NAME	M	WS	BS	S	T	W	A	Ld	Sv
Primaris Psyker	6"	3+	3+	3	3	4	3	8	5+

A Primaris Psyker is a single model armed with a laspistol and force stave.

WEAPON	RANGE	TYPE	S	AP	D	ABILITIES
Laspistol	12"	Pistol 1	3	0	1	-
Force stave	Melee	Melee	+2	-1	D3	-

ABILITIES	**It's For Your Own Good:** If this model is slain as a result of Perils of the Warp whilst within 6" of a friendly **Commissar**, they are executed before anything untoward can happen – the power they were attempting still fails, but units within 6" of them do not suffer D3 mortal wounds as normal.
PSYKER	This model can attempt to manifest one psychic power in each friendly Psychic phase, and attempt to deny one psychic power in each enemy Psychic phase. It knows the *Smite* power and two psychic powers from the Psykana discipline (pg 137).
FACTION KEYWORDS	**IMPERIUM, ASTRA MILITARUM, ASTRA TELEPATHICA, SCHOLASTICA PSYKANA**
KEYWORDS	**CHARACTER, INFANTRY, PSYKER, PRIMARIS PSYKER**

A Cadian Infantry Squad shields their battle group's psykers from enemy fire, giving them time to unleash their destructive powers.

INFANTRY SQUAD

3 POWER

NAME	M	WS	BS	S	T	W	A	Ld	Sv
Guardsman	6"	4+	4+	3	3	1	1	6	5+
Sergeant	6"	4+	4+	3	3	1	2	7	5+
Heavy Weapons Team	6"	4+	4+	3	3	2	2	6	5+

This unit contains 1 Sergeant and 9 Guardsmen.
• Each Guardsman is armed with a lasgun and frag grenades.
• The Sergeant is armed with a laspistol and frag grenades.

WEAPON	RANGE	TYPE	S	AP	D	ABILITIES
Lasgun	24"	Rapid Fire 1	3	0	1	-
Laspistol	12"	Pistol 1	3	0	1	-
Chainsword	Melee	Melee	User	0	1	Each time the bearer fights, it can make 1 additional attack with this weapon.
Power sword	Melee	Melee	User	-3	1	-
Frag grenade	6"	Grenade D6	3	0	1	-

WARGEAR OPTIONS	• One Guardsman may take a vox-caster. • Two other Guardsmen may form a Heavy Weapons Team who must take an item from the *Heavy Weapons* list. • One other Guardsman may replace his lasgun with an item from the *Special Weapons* list. • The Sergeant may replace their laspistol with an item from the *Ranged Weapons* list. • The Sergeant may take a chainsword or a power sword.
ABILITIES	**Vox-caster:** If a friendly **OFFICER** is within 3" of a unit with a vox-caster when using their Voice of Command ability, you may extend the range of the order to 18" if the target unit also contains a vox-caster.
FACTION KEYWORDS	IMPERIUM, ASTRA MILITARUM, <REGIMENT>
KEYWORDS	INFANTRY, INFANTRY SQUAD

CONSCRIPTS

3 POWER

NAME	M	WS	BS	S	T	W	A	Ld	Sv
Conscript	6"	5+	5+	3	3	1	1	4	5+

This unit contains 20 Conscripts. It can include up to 10 additional Conscripts (**Power Rating +1**). Each Conscript is armed with a lasgun and frag grenades.

WEAPON	RANGE	TYPE	S	AP	D	ABILITIES
Lasgun	24"	Rapid Fire 1	3	0	1	-
Frag grenade	6"	Grenade D6	3	0	1	-

ABILITIES	**Raw Recruits:** Roll a D6 each time an **OFFICER** uses the Voice of Command ability to issue an order to this unit; on a 4+ the order applies as normal, otherwise the order has no effect and no other orders can be issued to this unit for the rest of this turn.
FACTION KEYWORDS	IMPERIUM, ASTRA MILITARUM, <REGIMENT>
KEYWORDS	INFANTRY, CONSCRIPTS

3 POWER

MILITARUM TEMPESTUS
SCIONS

NAME	M	WS	BS	S	T	W	A	Ld	Sv
Tempestus Scion	6"	4+	3+	3	3	1	1	6	4+
Tempestor	6"	3+	3+	3	3	1	2	7	4+

This unit contains 1 Tempestor and 4 Tempestus Scions. It can include up to 5 additional Tempestus Scions (**Power Rating +2**).
- Each Tempestus Scion is armed with a hot-shot lasgun, frag grenades and krak grenades.
- The Tempestor is armed with a hot-shot laspistol, chainsword, frag grenades and krak grenades.

WEAPON	RANGE	TYPE	S	AP	D	ABILITIES
Bolt pistol	12"	Pistol 1	4	0	1	-
Flamer	8"	Assault D6	4	0	1	This weapon automatically hits its target.
Grenade launcher	When attacking with this weapon, choose one of the profiles below.					
- Frag grenade	24"	Assault D6	3	0	1	-
- Krak grenade	24"	Assault 1	6	-1	D3	-
Hot-shot lasgun	18"	Rapid Fire 1	3	-2	1	-
Hot-shot laspistol	6"	Pistol 1	3	-2	1	-
Hot-shot volley gun	24"	Heavy 4	4	-2	1	-
Meltagun	12"	Assault 1	8	-4	D6	If the target is within half range of this weapon, roll two dice when inflicting damage with it and discard the lowest result.
Plasma pistol	When attacking with this weapon, choose one of the profiles below.					
- Standard	12"	Pistol 1	7	-3	1	-
- Supercharge	12"	Pistol 1	8	-3	2	On a hit roll of 1, the bearer is slain.
Plasma gun	When attacking with this weapon, choose one of the profiles below.					
- Standard	24"	Rapid Fire 1	7	-3	1	-
- Supercharge	24"	Rapid Fire 1	8	-3	2	On a hit roll of 1, the bearer is slain after all of this weapon's shots have been resolved.
Chainsword	Melee	Melee	User	0	1	Each time the bearer fights, it can make 1 additional attack with this weapon.
Frag grenade	6"	Grenade D6	3	0	1	-
Krak grenade	6"	Grenade 1	6	-1	D3	-

WARGEAR OPTIONS	• One Tempestus Scion may replace their hot-shot lasgun with a hot-shot laspistol and a vox-caster. • For every five models in the unit, up to two other Tempestus Scions may replace their hot-shot lasgun with a flamer, meltagun, plasma gun, grenade launcher or hot-shot volley gun. • The Tempestor may replace their chainsword with an item from the *Melee Weapons* list. • The Tempestor may replace their hot-shot laspistol with a bolt pistol or plasma pistol.
ABILITIES	**Aerial Drop:** During deployment, you can set up this unit in a high-altitude transport, ready to deploy via grav-chute, instead of placing it on the battlefield. At the end of any of your Movement phases the unit can make an aerial drop – set it up anywhere on the battlefield that is more than 9" away from any enemy models. **Vox-caster:** If a friendly OFFICER is within 3" of a unit with a vox-caster when using their Voice of Command ability, you may extend the range of the order to 18" if the target unit also contains a vox-caster.
FACTION KEYWORDS	IMPERIUM, ASTRA MILITARUM, MILITARUM TEMPESTUS
KEYWORDS	INFANTRY, TEMPESTUS SCIONS

MASTER OF ORDNANCE

NAME	M	WS	BS	S	T	W	A	Ld	Sv
Master of Ordnance	6"	4+	3+	3	3	3	2	6	5+

A Master of Ordnance is a single model armed with a laspistol and an artillery barrage.

WEAPON	RANGE	TYPE	S	AP	D	ABILITIES
Artillery barrage	100"	Heavy D6	8	-2	D3	This weapon can only be fired once per battle, and cannot be used if the bearer moves. This weapon can target units that are not visible to the bearer (when doing so, subtract 1 from the hit rolls). You may only use one artillery barrage per turn, regardless of how many Masters of Ordnance you have in your army.
Laspistol	12"	Pistol 1	3	0	1	-

ABILITIES	**Master of Ballistics:** You can re-roll any hit rolls of 1 made for friendly <Regiment> Basilisks, Wyverns, Manticores or Deathstrikes when they target enemy units over 36" away in the Shooting phase, if they are within 6" of this model.
FACTION KEYWORDS	Imperium, Astra Militarum, <Regiment>
KEYWORDS	Character, Infantry, Officer, Master of Ordnance

'The meaning of victory is not to defeat your enemy but to destroy him, to eradicate him from living memory, to leave no remnant of his endeavours, to crush utterly his every achievement and remove from all record his every trace of existence. From that defeat no enemy can ever recover. That is the meaning of victory.'

- Lord Solar Macharius

PLATOON COMMANDER

NAME	M	WS	BS	S	T	W	A	Ld	Sv
Platoon Commander	6"	3+	3+	3	3	3	3	7	5+

A Platoon Commander is a single model armed with a laspistol and frag grenades.

WEAPON	RANGE	TYPE	S	AP	D	ABILITIES
Laspistol	12"	Pistol 1	3	0	1	-
Chainsword	Melee	Melee	User	0	1	Each time the bearer fights, it can make 1 additional attack with this weapon.
Frag grenade	6"	Grenade D6	3	0	1	-

WARGEAR OPTIONS	• This model may take a chainsword or an item from the *Melee Weapons* list. • This model may replace its laspistol with an item from the *Ranged Weapons* list.
ABILITIES	**Voice of Command** (pg 85) **Refractor Field:** This model has a 5+ invulnerable save.
FACTION KEYWORDS	Imperium, Astra Militarum, <Regiment>
KEYWORDS	Character, Infantry, Officer, Platoon Commander

COMMAND SQUAD

NAME	M	WS	BS	S	T	W	A	Ld	Sv
Veteran	6"	4+	3+	3	3	1	1	6	5+
Veteran Heavy Weapons Team	6"	4+	3+	3	3	2	2	6	5+

This unit contains 4 Veterans. Each model is armed with a lasgun and frag grenades.

WEAPON	RANGE	TYPE	S	AP	D	ABILITIES
Heavy flamer	8"	Heavy D6	5	-1	1	This weapon automatically hits its target.
Laspistol	12"	Pistol 1	3	0	1	-
Lasgun	24"	Rapid Fire 1	3	0	1	-
Chainsword	Melee	Melee	User	0	1	Each time the bearer fights, it can make 1 additional attack with this weapon.
Frag grenade	6"	Grenade D6	3	0	1	-

WARGEAR OPTIONS	• Any Veteran may replace their lasgun with a laspistol. • Any Veteran with a laspistol may also take a chainsword. • One Veteran may take a vox-caster. • One other Veteran may replace their lasgun with a heavy flamer. • One other Veteran may take a regimental standard. • One other Veteran may take a medi-pack. • Two other Veterans may form a Veteran Heavy Weapons Team which must take an item from the *Heavy Weapons* list. • Any other Veteran may replace their lasgun with an item from the *Special Weapons* list.
ABILITIES	**Medi-pack:** At the end of any of your Movement phases, a model with a medi-pack can attempt to heal a single model. Select a friendly **ASTRA MILITARUM INFANTRY** unit within 3" and roll a D6. On a roll of 4+, one model in the unit recovers a wound it lost earlier in the battle (if the unit has a Wounds characteristic of 1, one model slain earlier in the battle is returned to the unit instead). A unit can only be the target of this ability once in each turn. **Regimental Standard:** All friendly <REGIMENT> units add 1 to their Leadership whilst they are within 6" of any <REGIMENT> Veteran with a regimental standard. **Vox-caster:** If a friendly **OFFICER** is within 3" of a unit with a vox-caster when using their Voice of Command ability, you may extend the range of the order to 18" if the target unit also contains a vox-caster.
FACTION KEYWORDS	IMPERIUM, ASTRA MILITARUM, <REGIMENT>
KEYWORDS	INFANTRY, VETERANS, COMMAND SQUAD

COLOUR SERGEANT KELL

NAME	M	WS	BS	S	T	W	A	Ld	Sv
Colour Sergeant Kell	6"	3+	3+	3	3	4	3	7	4+

Colour Sergeant Kell is a single model armed with a laspistol, power fist and power sword. Only one of this model may be included in your army.

WEAPON	RANGE	TYPE	S	AP	D	ABILITIES
Laspistol	12"	Pistol 1	3	0	1	-
Power fist	Melee	Melee	x2	-3	D3	When attacking with this weapon, you must subtract 1 from the hit roll.
Power sword	Melee	Melee	User	-3	1	-

ABILITIES	**Colours of the Cadian 8th:** Friendly **CADIAN** units within 6" of Colour Sergeant Kell may re-roll failed Morale tests. **Listen Up, Maggots!:** You can make one additional order with a single friendly **CADIAN OFFICER** within 6" of Colour Sergeant Kell in each of your turns.	**Sworn Protector:** Roll a D6 each time Lord Castellan Creed loses a wound whilst he is within 3" of Colour Sergeant Kell; on a 2+ Lord Castellan Creed does not lose a wound but Colour Sergeant Kell suffers a mortal wound.
FACTION KEYWORDS	IMPERIUM, ASTRA MILITARUM, CADIAN	
KEYWORDS	CHARACTER, INFANTRY, COLOUR SERGEANT KELL	

SPECIAL WEAPONS SQUAD

NAME	M	WS	BS	S	T	W	A	Ld	Sv
Guardsman	6"	4+	4+	3	3	1	1	6	5+

This unit contains 6 Guardsmen. Each model is armed with a lasgun and frag grenades.

WEAPON	RANGE	TYPE	S	AP	D	ABILITIES
Lasgun	24"	Rapid Fire 1	3	0	1	-
Frag grenade	6"	Grenade D6	3	0	1	-

WARGEAR OPTIONS	• Three models must replace their lasgun with an item from the *Special Weapons* list.

FACTION KEYWORDS	IMPERIUM, ASTRA MILITARUM, <REGIMENT>

KEYWORDS	INFANTRY, SPECIAL WEAPONS SQUAD

VETERANS

NAME	M	WS	BS	S	T	W	A	Ld	Sv
Veteran	6"	4+	3+	3	3	1	1	6	5+
Veteran Sergeant	6"	4+	3+	3	3	1	2	7	5+
Veteran Heavy Weapons Team	6"	4+	3+	3	3	2	2	6	5+

This unit contains 1 Veteran Sergeant and 9 Veterans.
• Each Veteran is armed with a lasgun and frag grenades.
• The Veteran Sergeant is armed with a laspistol and frag grenades.

WEAPON	RANGE	TYPE	S	AP	D	ABILITIES
Autogun	24"	Rapid Fire 1	3	0	1	-
Lasgun	24"	Rapid Fire 1	3	0	1	-
Laspistol	12"	Pistol 1	3	0	1	-
Heavy flamer	8"	Heavy D6	5	-1	1	This weapon automatically hits its target.
Shotgun	12"	Assault 2	3	0	1	If the target is within half range, add 1 to this weapon's Strength.
Chainsword	Melee	Melee	User	0	1	Each time the bearer fights, it can make 1 additional attack with this weapon.
Frag grenade	6"	Grenade D6	3	0	1	-

WARGEAR OPTIONS	• Any Veteran may replace their lasgun with a shotgun or an autogun. • One Veteran may take a vox-caster. • One other Veteran may replace their lasgun with a heavy flamer. • Two other Veterans may form a Veteran Heavy Weapons Team who must take an item from the *Heavy Weapons* list. • Up to three other Veterans may replace their lasgun with an item from the *Special Weapons* list. • The Veteran Sergeant may take a chainsword or an item from the *Melee Weapons* list. • The Veteran Sergeant may replace their laspistol with an item from the *Ranged Weapons* list.

ABILITIES	**Vox-caster:** If a friendly OFFICER is within 3" of a unit with a vox-caster when using their Voice of Command ability, you may extend the range of the order to 18" if the target unit also contains a vox-caster.

FACTION KEYWORDS	IMPERIUM, ASTRA MILITARUM, <REGIMENT>

KEYWORDS	INFANTRY, VETERANS

SERGEANT HARKER

NAME	M	WS	BS	S	T	W	A	Ld	Sv
Sergeant Harker	6"	3+	3+	4	3	3	4	7	5+

Sergeant Harker is a single model armed with Payback, frag grenades and krak grenades. Only one of this model may be included in your army.

WEAPON	RANGE	TYPE	S	AP	D	ABILITIES
Payback	36"	Assault 3	5	-2	1	-
Frag grenade	6"	Grenade D6	3	0	1	-
Krak grenade	6"	Grenade 1	6	-1	D3	-

ABILITIES	**Harker's Hellraisers:** You can re-roll hit rolls of 1 in the Shooting phase for friendly **CATACHAN** units within 6" of Sergeant Harker.
FACTION KEYWORDS	**IMPERIUM, ASTRA MILITARUM, CATACHAN**
KEYWORDS	**CHARACTER, INFANTRY, SERGEANT HARKER**

MILITARUM TEMPESTUS COMMAND SQUAD

NAME	M	WS	BS	S	T	W	A	Ld	Sv
Tempestus Scion	6"	4+	3+	3	3	1	1	6	4+

This unit contains 4 Tempestus Scions. Each model is armed with a hot-shot lasgun, frag grenades and krak grenades.

WEAPON	RANGE	TYPE	S	AP	D	ABILITIES
Flamer	8"	Assault D6	4	0	1	This weapon automatically hits its target.
Grenade launcher	When attacking with this weapon, choose one of the profiles below.					
- Frag grenade	24"	Assault D6	3	0	1	-
- Krak grenade	24"	Assault 1	6	-1	D3	-
Hot-shot lasgun	18"	Rapid Fire 1	3	-2	1	-
Hot-shot laspistol	6"	Pistol 1	3	-2	1	-
Hot-shot volley gun	24"	Heavy 4	4	-2	1	-
Meltagun	12"	Assault 1	8	-4	D6	If the target is within half range of this weapon, roll two dice when inflicting damage with it and discard the lowest result.
Plasma gun	When attacking with this weapon, choose one of the profiles below.					
- Standard	24"	Rapid Fire 1	7	-3	1	-
- Supercharge	24"	Rapid Fire 1	8	-3	2	On a hit roll of 1, the bearer is slain after all of this weapon's shots have been resolved.
Frag grenade	6"	Grenade D6	3	0	1	-
Krak grenade	6"	Grenade 1	6	-1	D3	-

WARGEAR OPTIONS	• One model may replace its hot-shot lasgun with a hot-shot laspistol and a vox-caster. • One other model may replace its hot-shot lasgun with a hot-shot laspistol and a medi-pack. • One other model may take a platoon standard. • Up to four other models may replace their hot-shot lasgun with a flamer, meltagun, plasma gun, grenade launcher or hot-shot volley gun.
ABILITIES	**Aerial Drop:** During deployment, you can set up this unit in a high-altitude transport, ready to deploy via grav-chute, instead of placing it on the battlefield. At the end of any of your Movement phases the unit can make an aerial drop – set it up anywhere on the battlefield that is more than 9" away from any enemy models. **Platoon Standard:** All **MILITARUM TEMPESTUS** units within 6" of any friendly units with a platoon standard may add 1 to their Leadership when taking Morale tests.	**Medi-pack:** At the end of any of your Movement phases, a model with a medi-pack can attempt to heal a single model. Select a friendly **ASTRA MILITARUM INFANTRY** unit within 3" and roll a D6. On a roll of 4+, one model in the unit recovers a wound it lost earlier in the battle (if the unit has a Wounds characteristic of 1, one model slain earlier in the battle is returned to the unit instead). A unit can only be the target of this ability once in each turn. **Vox-caster:** If a friendly **OFFICER** is within 3" of a unit with a vox-caster when using their Voice of Command ability, you may extend the range of the order to 18" if the target unit also contains a vox-caster.

FACTION KEYWORDS	**IMPERIUM, ASTRA MILITARUM, MILITARUM TEMPESTUS**
KEYWORDS	**INFANTRY, TEMPESTUS COMMAND SQUAD**

MINISTORUM PRIEST

NAME	M	WS	BS	S	T	W	A	Ld	Sv
Ministorum Priest	6"	4+	4+	3	3	4	3	7	6+

A Ministorum Priest is a single model armed with a laspistol, frag grenades and krak grenades.

WEAPON	RANGE	TYPE	S	AP	D	ABILITIES
Autogun	24"	Rapid Fire 1	3	0	1	-
Laspistol	12"	Pistol 1	3	0	1	-
Chainsword	Melee	Melee	User	0	1	Each time the bearer fights, it can make 1 additional attack with this weapon.
Frag grenade	6"	Grenade D6	3	0	1	-
Krak grenade	6"	Grenade 1	6	-1	D3	-

WARGEAR OPTIONS	• This model may take an autogun. • This model may take a chainsword.

ABILITIES	**Zealot:** You can re-roll failed hit rolls for this unit in a turn in which it charged, made a heroic intervention, or was charged by an enemy unit. **Rosarius:** This model has a 4+ invulnerable save.	**War Hymns:** You can add 1 to the Attacks characteristic of all models in **ADEPTUS MINISTORUM INFANTRY** and **ASTRA MILITARUM INFANTRY** units that are within 6" of any friendly **MINISTORUM PRIESTS**.

FACTION KEYWORDS	IMPERIUM, ASTRA MILITARUM, ADEPTUS MINISTORUM
KEYWORDS	CHARACTER, INFANTRY, MINISTORUM PRIEST

CRUSADERS

NAME	M	WS	BS	S	T	W	A	Ld	Sv
Crusader	6"	3+	4+	3	3	1	2	7	4+

This unit contains 2 Crusaders. It may contain up to 2 additional Crusaders (**Power Rating +1**), up to 4 additional Crusaders (**Power Rating +2**), up to 6 additional Crusaders (**Power Rating +3**) or up to 8 additional Crusaders (**Power Rating +4**). Each Crusader is armed with a power sword.

WEAPON	RANGE	TYPE	S	AP	D	ABILITIES
Power sword	Melee	Melee	User	-3	1	-

ABILITIES	**Acts of Faith:** Roll a D6 at the start of each of your turns. On a roll of 2+, one unit from your army with this ability can perform an Act of Faith chosen from the following list. *Hand of the Emperor:* The unit can immediately move as if it were the Movement phase. *Divine Guidance:* The unit can immediately shoot as if it were the Shooting phase. *The Passion:* The unit can, if it is within 1" of an enemy unit, immediately pile in and attack as if it were the Fight phase. *Spirit of the Martyr:* One model in the unit recovers D3 lost wounds, or you can return a single slain model to the unit with 1 wound remaining.	**Shield of Faith:** Models in this unit have a 6+ invulnerable save. In addition, this unit can attempt to deny one psychic power in each enemy Psychic phase in the same manner as a **PSYKER**. However, if it does so, instead of rolling 2D6, only roll a single D6; the psychic power is resisted if the roll is greater than the result of the Psychic test that manifested the power. When attempting to deny a psychic power, first select a model in the unit – measure range, visibility etc. from this model. **Zealot:** You can re-roll failed hit rolls for a unit with this ability in a turn in which it charged, made a heroic intervention, or was charged by an enemy unit. **Storm Shield:** Models in this unit have a 3+ invulnerable save.

FACTION KEYWORDS	IMPERIUM, ASTRA MILITARUM, ADEPTUS MINISTORUM
KEYWORDS	INFANTRY, CRUSADERS

TECH-PRIEST ENGINSEER

NAME	M	WS	BS	S	T	W	A	Ld	Sv
Tech-Priest Enginseer	6"	4+	4+	4	4	4	2	8	3+

A Tech-Priest Enginseer is a single model armed with an Omnissian axe, a laspistol and a servo-arm.

WEAPON	RANGE	TYPE	S	AP	D	ABILITIES
Laspistol	12"	Pistol 1	3	0	1	-
Omnissian axe	Melee	Melee	+1	-2	2	-
Servo-arm	Melee	Melee	x2	-2	3	Each servo-arm can only be used to make one attack each time this model fights. When a model attacks with this weapon, you must subtract 1 from the hit roll.

ABILITIES	
	Bionics: This model has a 6+ invulnerable save.
	Master of Machines: At the end of your Movement phase this model can repair a single friendly **<Forge World>** **Vehicle**, **Astra Militarum Vehicle** or **Questor Mechanicus** model within 3". If the model being repaired is a **<Forge World>** or **Astra Militarum** model, it regains D3 lost wounds; if it is a **Questor Mechanicus** model, it regains 1 lost wound. A model may not be the target of the Master of Machines ability more than once per turn.
	Designer's Note: *When selecting this unit for your army, choose which forge world it will be from. This replaces the* **<Forge World>** *keyword in all instances on this datasheet.*
FACTION KEYWORDS	**Imperium, Astra Militarum, Cult Mechanicus, <Forge World>**
KEYWORDS	**Character, Infantry, Tech-Priest, Enginseer**

SERVITORS

NAME	M	WS	BS	S	T	W	A	Ld	Sv
Servitor	5"	5+	5+	3	3	1	1	6	4+

This unit contains 4 Servitors. Each Servitor is armed with a servo-arm.

WEAPON	RANGE	TYPE	S	AP	D	ABILITIES
Heavy bolter	36"	Heavy 3	5	-1	1	-
Multi-melta	24"	Heavy 1	8	-4	D6	If the target is within half range of this weapon, roll two dice when inflicting damage with it and discard the lowest result.
Plasma cannon	When attacking with this weapon, choose one of the profiles below.					
- Standard	36"	Heavy D3	7	-3	1	-
- Supercharge	36"	Heavy D3	8	-3	2	On a hit roll of 1, the bearer is slain after all of this weapon's shots have been resolved.
Servo-arm	Melee	Melee	x2	-2	3	Each servo-arm can only be used to make one attack each time this model fights. When a model attacks with this weapon, you must subtract 1 from the hit roll.

WARGEAR OPTIONS	
	• Up to two models may replace their servo-arm with a heavy bolter, plasma cannon or multi-melta.

ABILITIES	
	Mindlock: Servitors improve both their Weapon Skill and Ballistic Skill to 4+, and their Leadership to 9, whilst they are within 6" of any friendly **Tech-Priests**.
	Designer's Note: *When selecting this unit for your army, choose which forge world it will be from. This replaces the* **<Forge World>** *keyword in all instances on this datasheet.*
FACTION KEYWORDS	**Imperium, Astra Militarum, Adeptus Mechanicus, <Forge World>**
KEYWORDS	**Infantry, Servitors**

COMMISSAR

NAME	M	WS	BS	S	T	W	A	Ld	Sv
Commissar	6"	3+	3+	3	3	3	3	8	5+

A Commissar is a single model armed with a bolt pistol.

WEAPON	RANGE	TYPE	S	AP	D	ABILITIES
Bolt pistol	12"	Pistol 1	4	0	1	-

WARGEAR OPTIONS	• This model may take up to two items from the *Melee Weapons* list. • This model may replace their bolt pistol with an item from the *Ranged Weapons* list.

ABILITIES	**Aura of Discipline:** **ASTRA MILITARUM** units within 6" of a friendly **COMMISSAR** can use the Commissar's Leadership instead of their own.	**Summary Execution:** **ASTRA MILITARUM** units within 6" of a friendly **COMMISSAR** can never lose more than one model as the result of any single failed Morale test.

FACTION KEYWORDS	**IMPERIUM, ASTRA MILITARUM, OFFICIO PREFECTUS**
KEYWORDS	**CHARACTER, INFANTRY, COMMISSAR**

OFFICER OF THE FLEET

NAME	M	WS	BS	S	T	W	A	Ld	Sv
Officer of the Fleet	6"	4+	3+	3	3	3	2	6	5+

An Officer of the Fleet is a single model armed with a laspistol.

WEAPON	RANGE	TYPE	S	AP	D	ABILITIES
Laspistol	12"	Pistol 1	3	0	1	-

ABILITIES	**Air Raid Requested:** Once per battle, in your Shooting phase, you can pick an enemy unit, other than a **CHARACTER**, that is visible to this model anywhere on the battlefield, and then roll a D6. On a roll of 1-3, nothing happens. On a roll of 4-5 the target unit suffers D3 mortal wounds. On a roll of 6, the target unit suffers 3 mortal wounds. You may only call in one air raid per turn, regardless of the number of Officers of the Fleet. **Strafing Coordinates:** At the start of the Shooting phase, pick an enemy unit, other than one which can **FLY**, within 18" of this model. For the duration of the phase, you can re-roll hit rolls of 1 for any friendly **AERONAUTICA IMPERIALIS** units that can **FLY** that target the unit you picked.

FACTION KEYWORDS	**IMPERIUM, ASTRA MILITARUM, AERONAUTICA IMPERIALIS**
KEYWORDS	**CHARACTER, INFANTRY, OFFICER, OFFICER OF THE FLEET**

WYRDVANE PSYKERS

NAME	M	WS	BS	S	T	W	A	Ld	Sv
Wyrdvane Psyker	6"	5+	4+	3	3	1	1	7	6+

This unit contains 3 Wyrdvane Psykers. It may contain up to 3 additional Wyrdvane Psykers (**Power Rating +1**) or up to 6 additional Wyrdvane Psykers (**Power Rating +2**). Each model is armed with a laspistol and a Wyrdvane stave.

WEAPON	RANGE	TYPE	S	AP	D	ABILITIES
Laspistol	12"	Pistol 1	3	0	1	-
Wyrdvane stave	Melee	Melee	+1	0	1	-

ABILITIES	**Choir of Minds:** Each time you take a Psychic test or Deny the Witch test for this unit, roll 1D6 instead of 2D6. You can add 1 to Psychic tests you make for this unit if it has 3 or more models, or 2 to tests if it has 6 or more models.

PSYKER	This unit can attempt to manifest one psychic power in each friendly Psychic phase, and attempt to deny one psychic power in each enemy Psychic phase. It knows the *Smite* power and one power from the Psykana discipline (pg 137). When manifesting or denying a psychic power, first select a model in the unit – measure range, visibility etc. from this model. If this unit suffers Perils of the Warp, it suffers D3 mortal wounds as described in the core rules, but units within 6" will only suffer damage if the Perils of the Warp causes the last model in the manifesting unit to be slain.

FACTION KEYWORDS	**IMPERIUM, ASTRA MILITARUM, ASTRA TELEPATHICA, SCHOLASTICA PSYKANA**
KEYWORDS	**INFANTRY, PSYKER, WYRDVANE PSYKERS**

ASTROPATH

1 POWER

NAME	M	WS	BS	S	T	W	A	Ld	Sv
Astropath	6"	5+	6+	3	3	3	1	6	6+

An Astropath is a single model armed with a Telepathica stave.

WEAPON	RANGE	TYPE	S	AP	D	ABILITIES
Laspistol	12"	Pistol 1	3	0	1	-
Telepathica stave	Melee	Melee	+1	0	D3	-

WARGEAR OPTIONS	• This model may replace its Telepathica stave with a laspistol.

ABILITIES	**Astral Divination:** At the start of your Shooting phase, pick an enemy unit within 18" of this model. For the duration of the phase, the unit you picked gains no bonus to their saving throws for being in cover when it is targeted by attacks made by friendly **Astra Militarum** units within 6" of this model. **Telepathic Assault:** Each time you take a Psychic test for this unit when it attempts to manifest *Smite*, roll 1D6 instead of 2D6.

PSYKER	This model can attempt to manifest one psychic power in each friendly Psychic phase, and attempt to deny one psychic power in each enemy Psychic phase. It knows the *Smite* power and one power from the Psykana discipline (pg 137).

FACTION KEYWORDS	**IMPERIUM, ASTRA MILITARUM, ASTRA TELEPATHICA, SCHOLASTICA PSYKANA**
KEYWORDS	**CHARACTER, INFANTRY, PSYKER, ASTROPATH**

OGRYN BODYGUARD

4 POWER

NAME	M	WS	BS	S	T	W	A	Ld	Sv
Ogryn Bodyguard	6"	3+	4+	5	5	6	4	8	5+

An Ogryn Bodyguard is a single model armed with a ripper gun, a huge knife and frag bombs.

WEAPON	RANGE	TYPE	S	AP	D	ABILITIES
Grenadier gauntlet	12"	Assault D6	4	0	1	-
Ripper gun (shooting)	12"	Assault 3	5	0	1	-
Bullgryn maul	Melee	Melee	+2	-1	2	-
Huge knife	Melee	Melee	User	-1	2	-
Ripper gun (melee)	Melee	Melee	User	-1	1	-
Frag bomb	6"	Grenade D6	4	0	1	-

WARGEAR OPTIONS	• This model may replace its ripper gun with a grenadier gauntlet or Bullgryn maul. • This model may replace its huge knife with a slabshield or brute shield. • This model may take Bullgryn plate.

ABILITIES	**Avalanche of Muscle:** You can add 1 to the Attacks characteristic of this model in the Fight phase on any turn in which it made a successful charge. This ability may only be used the first time this model fights each turn. **Brute Shield:** A model equipped with a brute shield has a 4+ invulnerable save. **Bullgryn Plate:** A model in Bullgryn plate has a Save characteristic of 4+.	**Bodyguard:** Roll a D6 each time a friendly **ASTRA MILITARUM CHARACTER** loses a wound whilst they are within 3" of this model; on a 3+ the Astra Militarum character does not lose a wound but this model suffers a mortal wound. In addition, this model may not be selected as your Warlord, and may not be given a Warlord Trait. **Slabshield:** Add 2 to any save rolls for a model equipped with a slabshield.

FACTION KEYWORDS	**IMPERIUM, ASTRA MILITARUM, MILITARUM AUXILLA**
KEYWORDS	**CHARACTER, INFANTRY, OGRYN, OGRYN BODYGUARD**

OGRYNS

NAME	M	WS	BS	S	T	W	A	Ld	Sv
Ogryn	6"	3+	4+	5	5	3	3	7	5+
Ogryn Bone 'ead	6"	3+	4+	5	5	3	4	8	5+

This unit contains 1 Ogryn Bone 'ead and 2 Ogryns. It may contain up to 3 additional Ogryns (**Power Rating +4**) or up to 6 additional Ogryns (**Power Rating +8**). Each model is armed with a ripper gun and frag bombs.

WEAPON	RANGE	TYPE	S	AP	D	ABILITIES
Ripper gun (shooting)	12"	Assault 3	5	0	1	-
Ripper gun (melee)	Melee	Melee	User	-1	1	-
Frag bomb	6"	Grenade D6	4	0	1	-

ABILITIES	**Avalanche of Muscle:** You can add 1 to the Attacks characteristic of this unit in the Fight phase on any turn in which it made a successful charge. This ability may only be used the first time this unit fights each turn.
FACTION KEYWORDS	IMPERIUM, ASTRA MILITARUM, MILITARUM AUXILLA
KEYWORDS	INFANTRY, OGRYN

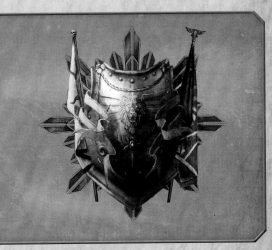

'IN ANY ARMY BALANCE IS THE KEY TO SUCCESS. A COMMANDER WHO PUTS HIS FAITH IN HEAVY WEAPONRY ALONE WILL BE OUTMANOEUVRED. A COMMANDER WHO RELIES ON CLOSE COMBAT WITHOUT SUPPORT WILL LOSE HIS FORCE TO ENEMY FIRE. EACH ELEMENT MUST WORK IN HARMONY, SO THAT THE EFFECTIVENESS OF THE ARMY IS GREATER THAN THE SUM OF ITS PARTS.'

- The Tactica Imperium

BULLGRYNS

NAME	M	WS	BS	S	T	W	A	Ld	Sv
Bullgryn	6"	3+	4+	5	5	3	3	7	4+
Bullgryn Bone 'ead	6"	3+	4+	5	5	3	4	8	4+

This unit contains 1 Bullgryn Bone 'ead and 2 Bullgryns. It may contain up to 3 additional Bullgryns (**Power Rating +6**) or up to 6 additional Bullgryns (**Power Rating +12**). Each model is armed with a grenadier gauntlet and frag bombs and equipped with a slabshield.

WEAPON	RANGE	TYPE	S	AP	D	ABILITIES
Grenadier gauntlet	12"	Assault D6	4	0	1	-
Bullgryn maul	Melee	Melee	+2	-1	2	-
Frag bomb	6"	Grenade D6	4	0	1	-

WARGEAR OPTIONS	• Any model may replace its grenadier gauntlet with a Bullgryn maul. • Any model may replace its slabshield with a brute shield.
ABILITIES	**Brute Shield:** Models equipped with a brute shield have a 4+ invulnerable save. **Slabshield:** Add 2 to the save rolls of any models equipped with a slabshield.	**Avalanche of Muscle:** You can add 1 to the Attacks characteristic of this unit in the Fight phase on any turn in which it made a successful charge. This ability may only be used the first time this unit fights each turn.
FACTION KEYWORDS	IMPERIUM, ASTRA MILITARUM, MILITARUM AUXILLA
KEYWORDS	INFANTRY, OGRYN, BULLGRYNS

NORK DEDDOG

NAME	M	WS	BS	S	T	W	A	Ld	Sv
Nork Deddog	6"	3+	4+	5	5	6	4	8	4+

Nork Deddog is a single model armed with a ripper gun, a huge knife and frag bombs. He can also deliver a thunderous headbutt. Only one of this model may be included in your army.

WEAPON	RANGE	TYPE	S	AP	D	ABILITIES
Ripper gun (shooting)	12"	Assault 3	5	0	1	-
Huge knife	Melee	Melee	User	-1	2	-
Ripper gun (melee)	Melee	Melee	User	-1	1	-
Thunderous headbutt	Melee	Melee	+3	-2	D3	Nork can only make a single thunderous headbutt attack each time he fights.
Frag bomb	6"	Grenade D6	4	0	1	-

ABILITIES	**Avalanche of Muscle:** You can add 1 to the Attacks characteristic of this model in the Fight phase on any turn in which it made a successful charge. This ability may only be used the first time this model fights each turn. **Heroic Sacrifice:** If Nork Deddog is slain in the Fight phase, you can immediately fight with him before removing his model as a casualty, even if he has already been chosen to fight during that phase.	**Loyal to the End:** Roll a D6 each time a friendly **ASTRA MILITARUM CHARACTER** loses a wound whilst he is within 3" of Nork Deddog; on a 2+ the Astra Militarum character does not lose a wound but Nork Deddog suffers a mortal wound. In addition, Nork Deddog may not be selected as your Warlord, and may not be given a Warlord Trait.
FACTION KEYWORDS	IMPERIUM, ASTRA MILITARUM, MILITARUM AUXILLA	
KEYWORDS	CHARACTER, INFANTRY, OGRYN, NORK DEDDOG	

RATLINGS

NAME	M	WS	BS	S	T	W	A	Ld	Sv
Ratling	5"	5+	3+	2	2	1	1	5	6+

This unit contains 5 Ratlings. It may contain up to 5 additional Ratlings (**Power Rating +1**). Each model is armed with a sniper rifle.

WEAPON	RANGE	TYPE	S	AP	D	ABILITIES
Sniper rifle	36"	Heavy 1	4	0	1	A model firing a sniper weapon can target an enemy **CHARACTER** even if they are not the closest enemy unit. If you roll a wound roll of 6+ for this weapon, it inflicts a mortal wound in addition to its normal damage.

ABILITIES	**Find the Best Spot:** Instead of deploying normally, this unit may wait until both armies are fully deployed and then be placed anywhere on the board that is more than 18" from any enemy models. **Shoot Sharp and Scarper:** Immediately after making a Shooting attack (other than firing Overwatch), this unit can move as if it were the Movement phase (though it cannot Advance as part of this move). **Naturally Stealthy:** Models in this unit receive a +2 bonus to their saving throw when they receive the benefits of cover instead of only +1.
FACTION KEYWORDS	IMPERIUM, ASTRA MILITARUM, MILITARUM AUXILLA
KEYWORDS	INFANTRY, RATLINGS

HELLHOUNDS

6 POWER

NAME	M	WS	BS	S	T	W	A	Ld	Sv
Hellhound	*	6+	*	6	7	11	*	7	3+
Devil Dog	*	6+	*	6	7	11	*	7	3+
Bane Wolf	*	6+	*	6	7	11	*	7	3+

DAMAGE

Some of this model's characteristics change as it suffers damage, as shown below:

REMAINING W	M	BS	A
6-11+	12"	4+	3
3-5	8"	5+	D3
1-2	4"	6+	1

This unit contains 1 Hellhound, Devil Dog or Bane Wolf. It can include 1 additional Hellhound, Devil Dog or Bane Wolf (**Power Rating +6**) or 2 additional Hellhounds, Devil Dogs and/or Bane Wolves in any combination (**Power Rating +12**).
- Each Hellhound is equipped with a heavy bolter and an inferno cannon.
- Each Devil Dog is equipped with a heavy bolter and a melta cannon.
- Each Bane Wolf is equipped with a heavy bolter and a chem cannon.

WEAPON	RANGE	TYPE	S	AP	D	ABILITIES
Chem cannon	8"	Heavy D6	*	-3	1	This weapon automatically hits its target. In addition, it wounds on a 2+, unless it is targeting a **Vehicle**, in which case it wounds on a 6+.
Heavy bolter	36"	Heavy 3	5	-1	1	-
Heavy flamer	8"	Heavy D6	5	-1	1	This weapon automatically hits its target.
Inferno cannon	16"	Heavy 2D6	6	-1	1	This weapon automatically hits its target.
Melta cannon	24"	Assault D3	8	-4	D6	If the target is within half range of this weapon, roll two dice when inflicting damage with it and discard the lowest result.
Multi-melta	24"	Heavy 1	8	-4	D6	If the target is within half range of this weapon, roll two dice when inflicting damage with it and discard the lowest result.

WARGEAR OPTIONS	- Any model may replace its heavy bolter with a heavy flamer or a multi-melta. - Any model may take items from the *Vehicle Equipment* list.
ABILITIES	**Explodes:** If a Hellhound, Devil Dog or Bane Wolf is reduced to 0 wounds, roll a D6 (adding 2 to the result in the case of a Hellhound) before removing it from the battlefield. On a 6+ it explodes, and each unit within 6" suffers D3 mortal wounds. **Smoke Launchers:** Once per game, instead of shooting any weapons in the Shooting phase, a Hellhound, Devil Dog or Bane Wolf can use its smoke launchers; until your next Shooting phase your opponent must subtract 1 from all hit rolls for ranged weapons that target it. **Vehicle Squadron:** The first time this unit is set up, all models in this unit must be placed within 6" of each other. From that point onwards, each operates independently and is treated as a separate unit for all rules purposes.
FACTION KEYWORDS	**Imperium, Astra Militarum, \<Regiment>**
KEYWORDS	**Vehicle, Hellhounds**

SCOUT SENTINELS

NAME	M	WS	BS	S	T	W	A	Ld	Sv
Scout Sentinel	9"	4+	4+	5	5	6	1	7	4+

This unit contains 1 Scout Sentinel. It can include 1 additional Scout Sentinel (**Power Rating +3**) or 2 additional Scout Sentinels (**Power Rating +5**). Each model is equipped with a multi-laser.

WEAPON	RANGE	TYPE	S	AP	D	ABILITIES
Autocannon	48"	Heavy 2	7	-1	2	-
Heavy flamer	8"	Heavy D6	5	-1	1	This weapon automatically hits its target.
Hunter-killer missile	48"	Heavy 1	8	-2	D6	Each hunter-killer missile can only be fired once per battle.
Lascannon	48"	Heavy 1	9	-3	D6	-
Missile launcher	When attacking with this weapon, choose one of the profiles below.					
- Frag missile	48"	Heavy D6	4	0	1	-
- Krak missile	48"	Heavy 1	8	-2	D6	-
Multi-laser	36"	Heavy 3	6	0	1	-
Sentinel chainsaw	Melee	Melee	User	-1	1	-

WARGEAR OPTIONS	• Any model may replace its multi-laser with a heavy flamer, autocannon, missile launcher or lascannon. • Any model may take a Sentinel chainsaw. • Any model may take a hunter-killer missile.
ABILITIES	**Explodes:** If a model in this unit is reduced to 0 wounds, roll a D6 before removing the model from the battlefield. On a 6 it explodes, and each unit within 3" suffers 1 mortal wound. **Scout Vehicle:** At the start of the first battle round but before the first turn begins, you can move this unit up to 9". It cannot end this move within 9" of any enemy models. **Smoke Launchers:** Once per game, instead of shooting any weapons in the Shooting phase, this unit can use its smoke launchers; until your next Shooting phase your opponent must subtract 1 from all hit rolls for ranged weapons that target it.
FACTION KEYWORDS	IMPERIUM, ASTRA MILITARUM, <REGIMENT>
KEYWORDS	VEHICLE, SCOUT SENTINELS

Sentinel squadrons stride effortlessly across the scrap-strewn battlefield to provide heavy fire support to infantry formations.

ARMOURED SENTINELS

NAME	M	WS	BS	S	T	W	A	Ld	Sv
Armoured Sentinel	8"	4+	4+	5	6	6	1	7	3+

This unit contains 1 Armoured Sentinel. It can include 1 additional Armoured Sentinel (**Power Rating +3**) or 2 additional Armoured Sentinels (**Power Rating +6**). Each model is equipped with a multi-laser.

WEAPON	RANGE	TYPE	S	AP	D	ABILITIES
Autocannon	48"	Heavy 2	7	-1	2	-
Heavy flamer	8"	Heavy D6	5	-1	1	This weapon automatically hits its target.
Hunter-killer missile	48"	Heavy 1	8	-2	D6	Each hunter-killer missile can only be fired once per battle.
Lascannon	48"	Heavy 1	9	-3	D6	-
Missile launcher	When attacking with this weapon, choose one of the profiles below.					
- Frag missile	48"	Heavy D6	4	0	1	-
- Krak missile	48"	Heavy 1	8	-2	D6	-
Multi-laser	36"	Heavy 3	6	0	1	-
Plasma cannon	When attacking with this weapon, choose one of the profiles below.					
- Standard	36"	Heavy D3	7	-3	1	-
- Supercharge	36"	Heavy D3	8	-3	2	On a hit roll of 1, the bearer is slain after all of this weapon's shots have been resolved.
Sentinel chainsaw	Melee	Melee	User	-1	1	-

WARGEAR OPTIONS	• Any model may replace its multi-laser with a heavy flamer, autocannon, missile launcher, lascannon or plasma cannon. • Any model may take a Sentinel chainsaw. • Any model may take a hunter-killer missile.
ABILITIES	**Explodes:** If a model in this unit is reduced to 0 wounds, roll a D6 before removing the model from the battlefield. On a 6 it explodes, and each unit within 3" suffers 1 mortal wound. **Smoke Launchers:** Once per game, instead of shooting any weapons in the Shooting phase, this unit can use its smoke launchers; until your next Shooting phase your opponent must subtract 1 from all hit rolls for ranged weapons that target it.
FACTION KEYWORDS	IMPERIUM, ASTRA MILITARUM, <REGIMENT>
KEYWORDS	VEHICLE, ARMOURED SENTINELS

HEAVY WEAPONS SQUAD

NAME	M	WS	BS	S	T	W	A	Ld	Sv
Heavy Weapons Team	6"	4+	4+	3	3	2	2	6	5+

This unit contains 3 Heavy Weapons Teams. Each model is armed with a lasgun and frag grenades.

WEAPON	RANGE	TYPE	S	AP	D	ABILITIES
Lasgun	24"	Rapid Fire 1	3	0	1	-
Frag grenade	6"	Grenade D6	3	0	1	-

WARGEAR OPTIONS	• Each model must take an item from the *Heavy Weapons* list.

FACTION KEYWORDS	IMPERIUM, ASTRA MILITARUM, <REGIMENT>

KEYWORDS	INFANTRY, HEAVY WEAPONS SQUAD

BASILISKS

DAMAGE

Some of this model's characteristics change as it suffers damage, as shown below:

REMAINING W	M	BS	A
6-11+	12"	4+	3
3-5	8"	5+	D3
1-2	4"	6+	1

NAME	M	WS	BS	S	T	W	A	Ld	Sv
Basilisk	*	6+	*	6	6	11	*	7	3+

This unit contains 1 Basilisk. It can include 1 additional Basilisk (**Power Rating +6**) or 2 additional Basilisks (**Power Rating +12**). Each model is equipped with an earthshaker cannon and a heavy bolter.

WEAPON	RANGE	TYPE	S	AP	D	ABILITIES
Earthshaker cannon	240"	Heavy D6	9	-3	D3	Roll two dice for the number of attacks when firing this weapon and discard the lowest result. This weapon can target units that are not visible to the bearer.
Heavy bolter	36"	Heavy 3	5	-1	1	-
Heavy flamer	8"	Heavy D6	5	-1	1	This weapon automatically hits its target.

WARGEAR OPTIONS	• Any model may replace its heavy bolter with a heavy flamer. • Any model may take items from the *Vehicle Equipment* list.

ABILITIES	**Vehicle Squadron:** The first time this unit is set up, all models in this unit must be placed within 6" of each other. From that point onwards, each operates independently and is treated as a separate unit for all rules purposes. **Explodes:** If this model is reduced to 0 wounds, roll a D6 before removing it from the battlefield. On a 6 it explodes, and each unit within 6" suffers D3 mortal wounds. **Smoke Launchers:** Once per game, instead of shooting any weapons in the Shooting phase, this model can use its smoke launchers; until your next Shooting phase your opponent must subtract 1 from all hit rolls for ranged weapons that target this vehicle.

FACTION KEYWORDS	IMPERIUM, ASTRA MILITARUM, <REGIMENT>

KEYWORDS	VEHICLE, BASILISKS

A Wyvern blankets the enemy lines in stormshard mortar shells, softening them up before troop transports are sent to the front.

WYVERNS

6 POWER

NAME	M	WS	BS	S	T	W	A	Ld	Sv
Wyvern	*	6+	*	6	6	11	*	7	3+

This unit contains 1 Wyvern. It can include 1 additional Wyvern (**Power Rating +6**) or 2 additional Wyverns (**Power Rating +12**). Each model is equipped with a Wyvern quad stormshard mortar and a heavy bolter.

DAMAGE

Some of this model's characteristics change as it suffers damage, as shown below:

REMAINING W	M	BS	A
6-11+	12"	4+	3
3-5	8"	5+	D3
1-2	4"	6+	1

WEAPON	RANGE	TYPE	S	AP	D	ABILITIES
Heavy bolter	36"	Heavy 3	5	-1	1	-
Heavy flamer	8"	Heavy D6	5	-1	1	This weapon automatically hits its target.
Wyvern quad stormshard mortar	48"	Heavy 4D6	4	0	1	This weapon can target units that are not visible to the bearer. You can re-roll failed wound rolls for this weapon.

WARGEAR OPTIONS	• Any model may replace its heavy bolter with a heavy flamer. • Any model may take items from the *Vehicle Equipment* list.
ABILITIES	**Explodes:** If this model is reduced to 0 wounds, roll a D6 before removing it from the battlefield. On a 6 it explodes, and each unit within 6" suffers D3 mortal wounds. **Smoke Launchers:** Once per game, instead of shooting any weapons in the Shooting phase, this model can use its smoke launchers; until your next Shooting phase your opponent must subtract 1 from all hit rolls for ranged weapons that target this vehicle. **Vehicle Squadron:** The first time this unit is set up, all models in this unit must be placed within 6" of each other. From that point onwards, each operates independently and is treated as a separate unit for all rules purposes.
FACTION KEYWORDS	**IMPERIUM, ASTRA MILITARUM, <REGIMENT>**
KEYWORDS	**VEHICLE, WYVERNS**

HYDRAS

DAMAGE
Some of this model's characteristics change as it suffers damage, as shown below:

REMAINING W	M	BS	A
6-11+	12"	4+	3
3-5	8"	5+	D3
1-2	4"	6+	1

NAME	M	WS	BS	S	T	W	A	Ld	Sv
Hydra	*	6+	*	6	6	11	*	7	3+

This unit contains 1 Hydra. It can include 1 additional Hydra (**Power Rating +6**) or 2 additional Hydras (**Power Rating +12**). Each model is equipped with a Hydra quad autocannon and a heavy bolter.

WEAPON	RANGE	TYPE	S	AP	D	ABILITIES
Heavy bolter	36"	Heavy 3	5	-1	1	-
Heavy flamer	8"	Heavy D6	5	-1	1	This weapon automatically hits its target.
Hydra quad autocannon	72"	Heavy 8	7	-1	2	Add 1 to all hit rolls made for this weapon against targets that can **FLY**. Subtract 1 from the hit rolls made for this weapon against all other targets.

WARGEAR OPTIONS	• Any model may replace its heavy bolter with a heavy flamer. • Any model may take items from the *Vehicle Equipment* list.
ABILITIES	**Explodes:** If this model is reduced to 0 wounds, roll a D6 before removing it from the battlefield. On a 6 it explodes, and each unit within 6" suffers D3 mortal wounds. **Smoke Launchers:** Once per game, instead of shooting any weapons in the Shooting phase, this model can use its smoke launchers; until your next Shooting phase your opponent must subtract 1 from all hit rolls for ranged weapons that target this vehicle. **Vehicle Squadron:** The first time this unit is set up, all models in this unit must be placed within 6" of each other. From that point onwards, each operates independently and is treated as a separate unit for all rules purposes.
FACTION KEYWORDS	**IMPERIUM, ASTRA MILITARUM, <REGIMENT>**
KEYWORDS	**VEHICLE, HYDRAS**

Hydra quad autocannons keep the skies clear, allowing a Tech-Priest Enginseer to shepherd other armoured units to battle.

Manticore

NAME	M	WS	BS	S	T	W	A	Ld	Sv
Manticore	*	6+	*	6	7	11	*	7	3+

DAMAGE

Some of this model's characteristics change as it suffers damage, as shown below:

REMAINING W	M	BS	A
6-11+	12"	4+	3
3-5	8"	5+	D3
1-2	4"	6+	1

A Manticore is a single model equipped with four storm eagle rockets and a heavy bolter.

WEAPON	RANGE	TYPE	S	AP	D	ABILITIES
Heavy bolter	36"	Heavy 3	5	-1	1	-
Heavy flamer	8"	Heavy D6	5	-1	1	This weapon automatically hits its target.
Storm eagle rocket	120"	Heavy 2D6	10	-2	D3	This weapon can target units that are not visible to the bearer. A model can only fire a single storm eagle rocket per turn. Each storm eagle rocket can only be fired once per battle.

WARGEAR OPTIONS	• This model may replace its heavy bolter with a heavy flamer. • This model may take items from the *Vehicle Equipment* list.
ABILITIES	**Explodes:** If this model is reduced to 0 wounds, roll a D6 before removing it from the battlefield. On a 6 it explodes, and each unit within 6" suffers D3 mortal wounds. **Smoke Launchers:** Once per game, instead of shooting any weapons in the Shooting phase, this model can use its smoke launchers; until your next Shooting phase your opponent must subtract 1 from all hit rolls for ranged weapons that target this vehicle.
FACTION KEYWORDS	IMPERIUM, ASTRA MILITARUM, <REGIMENT>
KEYWORDS	VEHICLE, MANTICORE

A Manticore from the Cadian 190th Armoured Regiment prepares to launch a storm eagle rocket.

9 POWER	

DEATHSTRIKE

DAMAGE
Some of this model's characteristics change as it suffers damage, as shown below:

REMAINING W	M	BS	A
6-11+	12"	4+	3
3-5	8"	5+	D3
1-2	4"	6+	1

NAME	M	WS	BS	S	T	W	A	Ld	Sv
Deathstrike	*	6+	*	6	7	11	*	7	3+

A Deathstrike is a single model equipped with a Deathstrike missile and a heavy bolter.

WEAPON	RANGE	TYPE	S	AP	D	ABILITIES
Deathstrike missile	200"	Heavy 3D6	*	*	*	This weapon can only be fired once per battle. This weapon can target units that are not visible to the bearer. Each time you hit the target with this weapon it suffers a mortal wound. After resolving all damage on the unit, roll a D6 for every other unit within 6" of the target unit – on a 4+ that unit also suffers D3 mortal wounds.
Heavy bolter	36"	Heavy 3	5	-1	1	-
Heavy flamer	8"	Heavy D6	5	-1	1	This weapon automatically hits its target.

WARGEAR OPTIONS	• This model may replace its heavy bolter with a heavy flamer. • This model may take items from the *Vehicle Equipment* list.

ABILITIES	**Explodes:** If this model is reduced to 0 wounds, roll a D6 before removing it from the battlefield. On a 6 it explodes, and each unit within 6" suffers D6 mortal wounds. **Smoke Launchers:** Once per game, instead of shooting any weapons in the Shooting phase, this model can use its smoke launchers; until your next Shooting phase your opponent must subtract 1 from all hit rolls for ranged weapons that target this vehicle.	**The Hour is Nigh:** The Deathstrike missile cannot be fired normally in the Shooting phase or during Overwatch. In one of your Shooting phases, if you wish to fire the Deathstrike missile, roll a D6 and add the battle round number. If the result is 8 or more, you can fire the Deathstrike missile during this Shooting phase. For example, in the third battle round, a roll of 5+ would be needed to fire the Deathstrike missile.

FACTION KEYWORDS	IMPERIUM, ASTRA MILITARUM, <REGIMENT>
KEYWORDS	VEHICLE, DEATHSTRIKE

'I have at my command an entire battle group of the Imperial Guard. Fifty regiments, including specialized drop troops, stealthers, mechanised formations, armoured companies and mobile artillery. Over half a million fighting men and thirty thousand tanks and artillery pieces are mine to command. Emperor show mercy to the fool who stands before me, for I shall not.'

- *Warmaster Demetrius, Salonika Crusade*

LEMAN RUSS BATTLE TANKS

DAMAGE

Some of this model's characteristics change as it suffers damage, as shown below:

REMAINING W	M	BS	A
7-12+	10"	4+	3
4-6	7"	5+	D3
1-3	4"	6+	1

NAME	M	WS	BS	S	T	W	A	Ld	Sv
Leman Russ Battle Tank	*	6+	*	7	8	12	*	7	3+

This unit contains 1 Leman Russ Battle Tank. It can include 1 additional Leman Russ Battle Tank (**Power Rating +10**) or 2 additional Leman Russ Battle Tanks (**Power Rating +20**). Each model is equipped with a battle cannon and a heavy bolter.

WEAPON	RANGE	TYPE	S	AP	D	ABILITIES
Battle cannon	72"	Heavy D6	8	-2	D3	-
Demolisher cannon	24"	Heavy D3	10	-3	D6	When attacking units with 5 or more models, change this weapon's Type to Heavy D6.
Eradicator nova cannon	36"	Heavy D6	6	-2	D3	Units attacked by this weapon do not gain any bonus to their saving throws for being in cover.
Executioner plasma cannon	When attacking with this weapon, choose one of the profiles below.					
- Standard	36"	Heavy D6	7	-3	1	-
- Supercharge	36"	Heavy D6	8	-3	2	For each hit roll of 1, the bearer suffers 1 mortal wound after all of this weapon's shots have been resolved.
Exterminator autocannon	48"	Heavy 4	7	-1	2	-
Heavy bolter	36"	Heavy 3	5	-1	1	-
Heavy flamer	8"	Heavy D6	5	-1	1	This weapon automatically hits its target.
Lascannon	48"	Heavy 1	9	-3	D6	-
Multi-melta	24"	Heavy 1	8	-4	D6	If the target is within half range of this weapon, roll two dice when inflicting damage with it and discard the lowest result.
Plasma cannon	When attacking with this weapon, choose one of the profiles below.					
- Standard	36"	Heavy D3	7	-3	1	-
- Supercharge	36"	Heavy D3	8	-3	2	On a hit roll of 1, the bearer is slain after all of this weapon's shots have been resolved.
Punisher gatling cannon	24"	Heavy 20	5	0	1	-
Vanquisher battle cannon	72"	Heavy 1	8	-3	D6	Roll two dice when inflicting damage with this weapon and discard the lowest result.

WARGEAR OPTIONS	
	• Any model may replace its battle cannon with an eradicator nova cannon, exterminator autocannon, vanquisher battle cannon, demolisher cannon, executioner plasma cannon or punisher gatling cannon. • Any model may replace its heavy bolter with a heavy flamer or a lascannon. • Any model may take two heavy bolters, two heavy flamers, two multi-meltas or two plasma cannons. • Any model may take items from the *Vehicle Equipment* list.

ABILITIES	
	Grinding Advance (pg 86) **Vehicle Squadron:** The first time this unit is set up, all models in this unit must be placed within 6" of each other. From that point onwards, each operates independently and is treated as a separate unit for all rules purposes. **Explodes:** If this model is reduced to 0 wounds, roll a D6 before removing it from the battlefield. On a 6 it explodes, and each unit within 6" suffers D3 mortal wounds. **Smoke Launchers:** Once per game, instead of shooting any weapons in the Shooting phase, this model can use its smoke launchers; until your next Shooting phase your opponent must subtract 1 from all hit rolls for ranged weapons that target this vehicle. **Emergency Plasma Vents:** If this model fires a supercharged plasma cannon, and you roll one or more hit rolls of 1, it is not automatically destroyed. Instead, for each hit roll of 1, the bearer suffers 1 mortal wound after all of this weapon's shots have been resolved.

FACTION KEYWORDS	**IMPERIUM, ASTRA MILITARUM, <REGIMENT>**
KEYWORDS	**VEHICLE, LEMAN RUSS, LEMAN RUSS BATTLE TANK**

CHIMERA

6 POWER

NAME	M	WS	BS	S	T	W	A	Ld	Sv
Chimera	*	6+	*	6	7	10	*	7	3+

DAMAGE
Some of this model's characteristics change as it suffers damage, as shown below:

REMAINING W	M	BS	A
6-10+	12"	4+	3
3-5	8"	5+	D3
1-2	4"	6+	1

A Chimera is a single model equipped with a multi-laser, a heavy bolter and two lasgun arrays.

WEAPON	RANGE	TYPE	S	AP	D	ABILITIES
Heavy bolter	36"	Heavy 3	5	-1	1	-
Heavy flamer	8"	Heavy D6	5	-1	1	This weapon automatically hits its target.
Lasgun array	24"	Rapid Fire 3	3	0	1	This weapon can only be fired if a unit is embarked upon the vehicle equipped with it.
Multi-laser	36"	Heavy 3	6	0	1	-

WARGEAR OPTIONS	• This model may replace its heavy bolter with a heavy flamer. • This model may replace its multi-laser with a heavy flamer or a heavy bolter. • This model may take items from the *Vehicle Equipment* list.
ABILITIES	**Explodes:** If this model is reduced to 0 wounds, roll a D6 before removing it from the battlefield and before any embarked models disembark. On a 6 it explodes, and each unit within 6" suffers D3 mortal wounds. **Smoke Launchers:** Once per game, instead of shooting any weapons in the Shooting phase, this model can use its smoke launchers; until your next Shooting phase your opponent must subtract 1 from all hit rolls for ranged weapons that target this vehicle.
TRANSPORT	This model can transport 12 **Astra Militarum Infantry** models. Each Heavy Weapons Team or Veteran Heavy Weapons Team takes the space of two other models and each **Ogryn** takes the space of three other models.
FACTION KEYWORDS	**Imperium, Astra Militarum, <Regiment>**
KEYWORDS	**Vehicle, Transport, Chimera**

TAUROX

4 POWER

NAME	M	WS	BS	S	T	W	A	Ld	Sv
Taurox	*	6+	*	6	6	10	*	7	3+

DAMAGE
Some of this model's characteristics change as it suffers damage, as shown below:

REMAINING W	M	BS	A
6-10+	14"	4+	3
3-5	10"	5+	D3
1-2	6"	6+	1

A Taurox is a single model equipped with two autocannons.

WEAPON	RANGE	TYPE	S	AP	D	ABILITIES
Autocannon	48"	Heavy 2	7	-1	2	-
Heavy stubber	36"	Heavy 3	4	0	1	-
Storm bolter	24"	Rapid Fire 2	4	0	1	-

WARGEAR OPTIONS	• This model may take a storm bolter or heavy stubber.
ABILITIES	**Explodes:** If this model is reduced to 0 wounds, roll a D6 before removing it from the battlefield and before any embarked models disembark. On a 6 it explodes, and each unit within 6" suffers D3 mortal wounds.
TRANSPORT	This model can transport 10 **Astra Militarum Infantry** models. Each Heavy Weapons Team or Veteran Heavy Weapons Team takes the space of two other models and each **Ogryn** takes the space of three other models.
FACTION KEYWORDS	**Imperium, Astra Militarum, <Regiment>**
KEYWORDS	**Vehicle, Transport, Taurox**

With its passengers unloaded, the Taurox Prime prepares to fire its missile launcher at the enemy.

6 POWER

TAUROX PRIME

DAMAGE			
Some of this model's characteristics change as it suffers damage, as shown below:			
REMAINING W	M	BS	A
6-10+	14"	3+	3
3-5	10"	4+	D3
1-2	6"	5+	1

NAME	M	WS	BS	S	T	W	A	Ld	Sv
Taurox Prime	*	6+	*	6	6	10	*	7	3+

A Taurox Prime is a single model equipped with a Taurox battle cannon and two hot-shot volley guns.

WEAPON	RANGE	TYPE	S	AP	D	ABILITIES
Autocannon	48"	Heavy 2	7	-1	2	-
Heavy stubber	36"	Heavy 3	4	0	1	-
Hot-shot volley gun	24"	Heavy 4	4	-2	1	-
Storm bolter	24"	Rapid Fire 2	4	0	1	-
Taurox battle cannon	48"	Heavy D6	7	-1	D3	-
Taurox gatling cannon	24"	Heavy 20	4	0	1	-
Taurox missile launcher	When attacking with this weapon, choose one of the profiles below.					
- Frag missile	48"	Heavy 2D6	4	0	1	-
- Krak missile	48"	Heavy 2	8	-2	D6	-

WARGEAR OPTIONS	• This model may replace its Taurox battle cannon with a Taurox gatling cannon or a Taurox missile launcher. • This model may replace its two hot-shot volley guns with two autocannons. • This model may take a storm bolter or a heavy stubber.
ABILITIES	**Explodes:** If this model is reduced to 0 wounds, roll a D6 before removing it from the battlefield and before any embarked models disembark. On a 6 it explodes, and each unit within 6" suffers D3 mortal wounds.
TRANSPORT	This model can transport 10 **MILITARUM TEMPESTUS** or **OFFICIO PREFECTUS INFANTRY** models.
FACTION KEYWORDS	**IMPERIUM, ASTRA MILITARUM, MILITARUM TEMPESTUS**
KEYWORDS	**VEHICLE, TRANSPORT, TAUROX PRIME**

8 POWER

VALKYRIES

NAME	M	WS	BS	S	T	W	A	Ld	Sv
Valkyrie	*	6+	*	7	7	14	3	7	3+

DAMAGE
Some of this model's characteristics change as it suffers damage, as shown below:

REMAINING W	M	BS
8-14+	20-45"	4+
4-7	20-30"	5+
1-3	20"	6+

This unit contains 1 Valkyrie. It can include 1 additional Valkyrie (**Power Rating +8**) or 2 additional Valkyries (**Power Rating +15**). Each model is equipped with a multi-laser and hellstrike missiles.

WEAPON	RANGE	TYPE	S	AP	D	ABILITIES
Heavy bolter	36"	Heavy 3	5	-1	1	-
Hellstrike missiles	72"	Heavy 1	8	-2	D6	Roll two dice when inflicting damage with this weapon and discard the lowest result.
Lascannon	48"	Heavy 1	9	-3	D6	-
Multi-laser	36"	Heavy 3	6	0	1	-
Multiple rocket pod	36"	Assault D6	5	-1	1	-

WARGEAR OPTIONS	• Any model may replace its multi-laser with a lascannon. • Any model may replace its hellstrike missiles with two multiple rocket pods. • Any model may take two heavy bolters.

ABILITIES

Vehicle Squadron: The first time this unit is set up, all models in this unit must be placed within 6" of each other. From that point onwards, each operates independently and is treated as a separate unit for all rules purposes.

Grav-chute Insertion: Models may disembark from this vehicle at any point during its move, but if the Valkyrie moves more than 20", you must roll a D6 for each model disembarking. On a 1, that model is slain. Models that disembark in this manner must be set up more than 9" from any enemy models.

Hover Jet: Before this model moves in your Movement phase, you can declare it will hover. Its Move characteristic becomes 20" until the end of the phase, and it loses the Airborne, Hard to Hit and Supersonic abilities until the beginning of your next Movement phase.

Roving Gunship: If this model hovers in its Movement phase, add 1 to all hit rolls made for it in the following Shooting phase.

Airborne: This model cannot charge, can only be charged by units that can **FLY**, and can only attack or be attacked in the Fight phase by units that can **FLY**.

Hard to Hit: Your opponent must subtract 1 from hit rolls for attacks that target this model in the Shooting phase.

Supersonic: Each time this model moves, first pivot it on the spot up to 90° (this does not contribute to how far the model moves), and then move the model straight forwards. Note that it cannot pivot again after the initial pivot. When this model Advances, increase its Move characteristic by 20" until the end of the phase – do not roll a dice.

Crash and Burn: If this model is reduced to 0 wounds, roll a D6 before removing it from the battlefield and before any embarked models disembark. On a 6 it crashes in a fiery explosion and each unit within 6" suffers D3 mortal wounds.

TRANSPORT	This model can transport 12 **ASTRA MILITARUM INFANTRY** models. Each Heavy Weapons Team or Veteran Heavy Weapons Team takes the space of two other models and each **OGRYN** takes the space of three other models.
FACTION KEYWORDS	**IMPERIUM, ASTRA MILITARUM, AERONAUTICA IMPERIALIS**
KEYWORDS	**VEHICLE, TRANSPORT, FLY, VALKYRIES**

BANEBLADE

NAME	M	WS	BS	S	T	W	A	Ld	Sv
Baneblade	*	5+	*	9	8	26	*	8	3+

DAMAGE
Some of this model's characteristics change as it suffers damage, as shown below:

REMAINING W	M	BS	A
14-26+	10"	4+	9
7-13	7"	5+	6
1-6	4"	6+	3

A Baneblade is a single model equipped with an autocannon, a Baneblade cannon, a demolisher cannon, a twin heavy bolter and adamantium tracks.

WEAPON	RANGE	TYPE	S	AP	D	ABILITIES
Autocannon	48"	Heavy 2	7	-1	2	-
Baneblade cannon	72"	Heavy 3D6	9	-3	3	-
Demolisher cannon	24"	Heavy D3	10	-3	D6	When attacking units with 5 or more models, change this weapon's Type to Heavy D6.
Heavy stubber	36"	Heavy 3	4	0	1	-
Hunter-killer missile	48"	Heavy 1	8	-2	D6	Each hunter-killer missile can only be fired once per battle.
Lascannon	48"	Heavy 1	9	-3	D6	-
Storm bolter	24"	Rapid Fire 2	4	0	1	-
Twin heavy bolter	36"	Heavy 6	5	-1	1	-
Twin heavy flamer	8"	Heavy 2D6	5	-1	1	This weapon automatically hits its target.
Adamantium tracks	Melee	Melee	User	-2	D3	-

WARGEAR OPTIONS	
	• This model may take a hunter-killer missile.
	• This model may take a storm bolter or a heavy stubber.
	• This model may take either two sponsons, or four sponsons; each sponson is equipped with a lascannon and either a twin heavy bolter or twin heavy flamer.

ABILITIES	
	Explodes: If this model is reduced to 0 wounds, roll a D6 before removing it from the battlefield. On a 6 it explodes, and each unit within 2D6" suffers D6 mortal wounds. **Smoke Launchers:** Once per game, instead of shooting any weapons in the Shooting phase, this model can use its smoke launchers; until your next Shooting phase your opponent must subtract 1 from all hit rolls for ranged weapons that target this vehicle.	**Steel Behemoth:** This model does not suffer the penalty to hit rolls for moving and firing Heavy weapons. This model can Fall Back in the Movement phase and still shoot and/or charge during its turn. It can also still fire its weapons if enemy units are within 1" of it (but only its twin heavy bolter or twin heavy flamer can target units that are within 1" of it – its other guns must target other units). In addition this model only gains a bonus to its save in cover if at least half of the model is obscured from the firer.

FACTION KEYWORDS	IMPERIUM, ASTRA MILITARUM, <REGIMENT>
KEYWORDS	**VEHICLE, TITANIC, BANEBLADE**

Few foes can withstand the devastation unleashed by *Ancients' Wrath*, Baneblade of the Vostroyan 191st Super-heavy Regiment.

BANEHAMMER

NAME	M	WS	BS	S	T	W	A	Ld	Sv
Banehammer	*	5+	*	9	8	26	*	8	3+

A Banehammer is a single model equipped with a tremor cannon, a twin heavy bolter and adamantium tracks.

DAMAGE

Some of this model's characteristics change as it suffers damage, as shown below:

REMAINING W	M	BS	A
14-26+	10"	4+	9
7-13	7"	5+	6
1-6	4"	6+	3

WEAPON	RANGE	TYPE	S	AP	D	ABILITIES
Heavy stubber	36"	Heavy 3	4	0	1	-
Hunter-killer missile	48"	Heavy 1	8	-2	D6	Each hunter-killer missile can only be fired once per battle.
Lascannon	48"	Heavy 1	9	-3	D6	-
Storm bolter	24"	Rapid Fire 2	4	0	1	-
Tremor cannon	60"	Heavy 3D6	8	-2	3	If a unit is hit by this weapon, in their following Movement phase they must halve their Move characteristic and cannot Advance.
Twin heavy bolter	36"	Heavy 6	5	-1	1	-
Twin heavy flamer	8"	Heavy 2D6	5	-1	1	This weapon automatically hits its target.
Adamantium tracks	Melee	Melee	User	-2	D3	-

WARGEAR OPTIONS
- This model may take a hunter-killer missile.
- This model may take a storm bolter or a heavy stubber.
- This model may take either two sponsons, or four sponsons; each sponson is equipped with a lascannon and either a twin heavy bolter or twin heavy flamer.

ABILITIES

Explodes: If this model is reduced to 0 wounds, roll a D6 before removing it from the battlefield and before any embarked models disembark. On a 6 it explodes, and each unit within 2D6" suffers D6 mortal wounds.

Firing Deck: Up to 10 models being transported by a Banehammer can shoot in their Shooting phase, measuring and drawing line of sight from any point on the vehicle. Units that shoot in this manner count as having moved if they or the Banehammer moved in the preceding Movement phase.

Smoke Launchers: Once per game, instead of shooting any weapons in the Shooting phase, this model can use its smoke launchers; until your next Shooting phase your opponent must subtract 1 from all hit rolls for ranged weapons that target this vehicle.

Steel Behemoth: This model does not suffer the penalty to hit rolls for moving and firing Heavy weapons. This model can Fall Back in the Movement phase and still shoot and/or charge during its turn. It can also still fire its weapons if enemy units are within 1" of it (but only its twin heavy bolter or twin heavy flamer can target units that are within 1" of it – its other guns must target other units). In addition this model only gains a bonus to its save in cover if at least half of the model is obscured from the firer.

TRANSPORT

This model can transport 25 **Astra Militarum Infantry** models. Each Heavy Weapons Team or Veteran Heavy Weapons Team takes the space of two other models and each **Ogryn** takes the space of three other models.

FACTION KEYWORDS

Imperium, Astra Militarum, <Regiment>

KEYWORDS

Vehicle, Titanic, Transport, Banehammer

'IDENTIFY YOUR TARGET. CONCENTRATE YOUR FIRE ON IT TO THE EXCLUSION OF ALL ELSE. WHEN IT IS DESTROYED CHOOSE ANOTHER TARGET. THAT IS THE WAY TO SECURE VICTORY!'

- *The Tactica Imperium*

BANESWORD

NAME	M	WS	BS	S	T	W	A	Ld	Sv
Banesword	*	5+	*	9	8	26	*	8	3+

DAMAGE

Some of this model's characteristics change as it suffers damage, as shown below:

REMAINING W	M	BS	A
14-26+	10"	4+	9
7-13	7"	5+	6
1-6	4"	6+	3

A Banesword is a single model equipped with a quake cannon, a twin heavy bolter and adamantium tracks.

WEAPON	RANGE	TYPE	S	AP	D	ABILITIES
Heavy stubber	36"	Heavy 3	4	0	1	-
Hunter-killer missile	48"	Heavy 1	8	-2	D6	Each hunter-killer missile can only be fired once per battle.
Lascannon	48"	Heavy 1	9	-3	D6	-
Quake cannon	140"	Heavy 2D6	14	-4	D6	When rolling for this weapon's damage, treat any rolls of 1 or 2 as 3 instead.
Storm bolter	24"	Rapid Fire 2	4	0	1	-
Twin heavy bolter	36"	Heavy 6	5	-1	1	-
Twin heavy flamer	8"	Heavy 2D6	5	-1	1	This weapon automatically hits its target.
Adamantium tracks	Melee	Melee	User	-2	D3	-

WARGEAR OPTIONS	• This model may take a hunter-killer missile. • This model may take a storm bolter or a heavy stubber. • This model may take either two sponsons, or four sponsons; each sponson is equipped with a lascannon and either a twin heavy bolter or twin heavy flamer.

ABILITIES

Explodes: If this model is reduced to 0 wounds, roll a D6 before removing it from the battlefield. On a 6 it explodes, and each unit within 2D6" suffers D6 mortal wounds.

Smoke Launchers: Once per game, instead of shooting any weapons in the Shooting phase, this model can use its smoke launchers; until your next Shooting phase your opponent must subtract 1 from all hit rolls for ranged weapons that target this vehicle.

Steel Behemoth: This model does not suffer the penalty to hit rolls for moving and firing Heavy weapons. This model can Fall Back in the Movement phase and still shoot and/or charge during its turn. It can also still fire its weapons if enemy units are within 1" of it (but only its twin heavy bolter or twin heavy flamer can target units that are within 1" of it – its other guns must target other units). In addition this model only gains a bonus to its save in cover if at least half of the model is obscured from the firer.

FACTION KEYWORDS	IMPERIUM, ASTRA MILITARUM, <REGIMENT>
KEYWORDS	VEHICLE, TITANIC, BANESWORD

Positioned far behind the front line, this Banesword is able to sunder the enemy's formations with its quake cannon.

DOOMHAMMER

NAME	M	WS	BS	S	T	W	A	Ld	Sv
Doomhammer	*	5+	*	9	8	26	*	8	3+

DAMAGE

Some of this model's characteristics change as it suffers damage, as shown below:

REMAINING W	M	BS	A
14-26+	10"	4+	9
7-13	7"	5+	6
1-6	4"	6+	3

A Doomhammer is a single model equipped with a magma cannon, a twin heavy bolter and adamantium tracks.

WEAPON	RANGE	TYPE	S	AP	D	ABILITIES
Heavy stubber	36"	Heavy 3	4	0	1	-
Hunter-killer missile	48"	Heavy 1	8	-2	D6	Each hunter-killer missile can only be fired once per battle.
Lascannon	48"	Heavy 1	9	-3	D6	-
Magma cannon	60"	Heavy 2D6	10	-5	D6	If the target is within half range of this weapon, roll two dice when inflicting damage with it and discard the lowest result.
Storm bolter	24"	Rapid Fire 2	4	0	1	-
Twin heavy bolter	36"	Heavy 6	5	-1	1	-
Twin heavy flamer	8"	Heavy 2D6	5	-1	1	This weapon automatically hits its target.
Adamantium tracks	Melee	Melee	User	-2	D3	-

WARGEAR OPTIONS	• This model may take a hunter-killer missile. • This model may take a storm bolter or a heavy stubber. • This model may take either two sponsons, or four sponsons; each sponson is equipped with a lascannon and either a twin heavy bolter or twin heavy flamer.
ABILITIES	**Explodes:** If this model is reduced to 0 wounds, roll a D6 before removing it from the battlefield and before any embarked models disembark. On a 6 it explodes, and each unit within 2D6" suffers D6 mortal wounds. **Firing Deck:** Up to 10 models being transported by a Doomhammer can shoot in their Shooting phase, measuring and drawing line of sight from any point on the vehicle. Units that shoot in this manner count as having moved if they or the Doomhammer moved in the preceding Movement phase. **Smoke Launchers:** Once per game, instead of shooting any weapons in the Shooting phase, this model can use its smoke launchers; until your next Shooting phase your opponent must subtract 1 from all hit rolls for ranged weapons that target this vehicle. **Steel Behemoth:** This model does not suffer the penalty to hit rolls for moving and firing Heavy weapons. This model can Fall Back in the Movement phase and still shoot and/or charge during its turn. It can also still fire its weapons if enemy units are within 1" of it (but only its twin heavy bolter or twin heavy flamer can target units that are within 1" of it – its other guns must target other units). In addition this model only gains a bonus to its save in cover if at least half of the model is obscured from the firer.
TRANSPORT	This model can transport 25 **ASTRA MILITARUM INFANTRY** models. Each Heavy Weapons Team or Veteran Heavy Weapons Team takes the space of two other models and each **OGRYN** takes the space of three other models.
FACTION KEYWORDS	**IMPERIUM, ASTRA MILITARUM, <REGIMENT>**
KEYWORDS	**VEHICLE, TITANIC, TRANSPORT, DOOMHAMMER**

The Armageddon Hellhammer, *Ghost of Hades*, prowls the shattered streets and crumbling ruins of a besieged city.

HELLHAMMER

30 POWER

NAME	M	WS	BS	S	T	W	A	Ld	Sv
Hellhammer	*	5+	*	9	8	26	*	8	3+

A Hellhammer is a single model equipped with an autocannon, a demolisher cannon, a Hellhammer cannon, a twin heavy bolter, a lasgun and adamantium tracks.

DAMAGE

Some of this model's characteristics change as it suffers damage, as shown below:

REMAINING W	M	BS	A
14-26+	10"	4+	9
7-13	7"	5+	6
1-6	4"	6+	3

WEAPON	RANGE	TYPE	S	AP	D	ABILITIES
Autocannon	48"	Heavy 2	7	-1	2	-
Demolisher cannon	24"	Heavy D3	10	-3	D6	When attacking units with 5 or more models, change this weapon's Type to Heavy D6.
Heavy stubber	36"	Heavy 3	4	0	1	-
Hellhammer cannon	36"	Heavy 3D6	10	-4	3	Units attacked by this weapon do not gain any bonus to their saving throws for being in cover.
Hunter-killer missile	48"	Heavy 1	8	-2	D6	Each hunter-killer missile can only be fired once per battle.
Lascannon	48"	Heavy 1	9	-3	D6	-
Lasgun	24"	Rapid Fire 1	3	0	1	-
Storm bolter	24"	Rapid Fire 2	4	0	1	-
Twin heavy bolter	36"	Heavy 6	5	-1	1	-
Twin heavy flamer	8"	Heavy 2D6	5	-1	1	This weapon automatically hits its target.
Adamantium tracks	Melee	Melee	User	-2	D3	-

WARGEAR OPTIONS	
	• This model may take a hunter-killer missile. • This model may take a storm bolter or a heavy stubber. • This model may take either two sponsons, or four sponsons; each sponson is equipped with a lascannon and either a twin heavy bolter or twin heavy flamer.

ABILITIES		
	Explodes: If this model is reduced to 0 wounds, roll a D6 before removing it from the battlefield. On a 6 it explodes, and each unit within 2D6" suffers D6 mortal wounds. **Smoke Launchers:** Once per game, instead of shooting any weapons in the Shooting phase, this model can use its smoke launchers; until your next Shooting phase your opponent must subtract 1 from all hit rolls for ranged weapons that target this vehicle.	**Steel Behemoth:** This model does not suffer the penalty to hit rolls for moving and firing Heavy weapons. This model can Fall Back in the Movement phase and still shoot and/or charge during its turn. It can also still fire its weapons if enemy units are within 1" of it (but only its twin heavy bolter or twin heavy flamer can target units that are within 1" of it – its other guns must target other units). In addition this model only gains a bonus to its save in cover if at least half of the model is obscured from the firer.

FACTION KEYWORDS	IMPERIUM, ASTRA MILITARUM, <REGIMENT>
KEYWORDS	VEHICLE, TITANIC, HELLHAMMER

| 26 POWER | SHADOWSWORD |

DAMAGE

Some of this model's characteristics change as it suffers damage, as shown below:

REMAINING W	M	BS	A
14-26+	10"	4+	9
7-13	7"	5+	6
1-6	4"	6+	3

NAME	M	WS	BS	S	T	W	A	Ld	Sv
Shadowsword	*	5+	*	9	8	26	*	8	3+

A Shadowsword is a single model equipped with a volcano cannon, a twin heavy bolter and adamantium tracks.

WEAPON	RANGE	TYPE	S	AP	D	ABILITIES
Heavy stubber	36"	Heavy 3	4	0	1	-
Hunter-killer missile	48"	Heavy 1	8	-2	D6	Each hunter-killer missile can only be fired once per battle.
Lascannon	48"	Heavy 1	9	-3	D6	-
Storm bolter	24"	Rapid Fire 2	4	0	1	-
Twin heavy bolter	36"	Heavy 6	5	-1	1	-
Twin heavy flamer	8"	Heavy 2D6	5	-1	1	This weapon automatically hits its target.
Volcano cannon	120"	Heavy 3D3	16	-5	2D6	You can re-roll failed wound rolls when targeting **TITANIC** units with this weapon.
Adamantium tracks	Melee	Melee	User	-2	D3	-

WARGEAR OPTIONS	• This model may take a hunter-killer missile. • This model may take a storm bolter or a heavy stubber. • This model may take either two sponsons, or four sponsons; each sponson is equipped with a lascannon and either a twin heavy bolter or twin heavy flamer.
ABILITIES	**Explodes:** If this model is reduced to 0 wounds, roll a D6 before removing it from the battlefield. On a 6 it explodes, and each unit within 2D6" suffers D6 mortal wounds. **Smoke Launchers:** Once per game, instead of shooting any weapons in the Shooting phase, this model can use its smoke launchers; until your next Shooting phase your opponent must subtract 1 from all hit rolls for ranged weapons that target this vehicle. **Steel Behemoth:** This model does not suffer the penalty to hit rolls for moving and firing Heavy weapons. This model can Fall Back in the Movement phase and still shoot and/or charge during its turn. It can also still fire its weapons if enemy units are within 1" of it (but only its twin heavy bolter or twin heavy flamer can target units that are within 1" of it – its other guns must target other units). In addition this model only gains a bonus to its save in cover if at least half of the model is obscured from the firer. **Shadowsword Targeters:** Add 1 to any hit rolls you make for this model for shooting attacks that target **TITANIC** units.
FACTION KEYWORDS	**IMPERIUM, ASTRA MILITARUM, <REGIMENT>**
KEYWORDS	**VEHICLE, TITANIC, SHADOWSWORD**

A Shadowsword swivels amongst the debris of battle, bringing its volcano cannon to bear on a fresh target.

26
POWER

STORMLORD

NAME	M	WS	BS	S	T	W	A	Ld	Sv
Stormlord	*	5+	*	9	8	26	*	8	3+

DAMAGE
Some of this model's characteristics change as it suffers damage, as shown below:

REMAINING W	M	BS	A
14-26+	10"	4+	9
7-13	7"	5+	6
1-6	4"	6+	3

A Stormlord is a single model equipped with two heavy stubbers, a twin heavy bolter, a vulcan mega-bolter and adamantium tracks.

WEAPON	RANGE	TYPE	S	AP	D	ABILITIES
Heavy stubber	36"	Heavy 3	4	0	1	-
Hunter-killer missile	48"	Heavy 1	8	-2	D6	Each hunter-killer missile can only be fired once per battle.
Lascannon	48"	Heavy 1	9	-3	D6	-
Storm bolter	24"	Rapid Fire 2	4	0	1	-
Twin heavy bolter	36"	Heavy 6	5	-1	1	-
Twin heavy flamer	8"	Heavy 2D6	5	-1	1	This weapon automatically hits its target.
Vulcan mega-bolter	60"	Heavy 20	6	-2	2	-
Adamantium tracks	Melee	Melee	User	-2	D3	-

WARGEAR OPTIONS
- This model may take a hunter-killer missile.
- This model may take a storm bolter or an additional heavy stubber.
- This model may take either two sponsons, or four sponsons; each sponson is equipped with a lascannon and either a twin heavy bolter or twin heavy flamer.

ABILITIES

Explodes: If this model is reduced to 0 wounds, roll a D6 before removing it from the battlefield and before any embarked models disembark. On a 6 it explodes, and each unit within 2D6" suffers D6 mortal wounds.

Extended Firing Deck: Up to 20 models being transported by a Stormlord can shoot in their Shooting phase, measuring and drawing line of sight from any point on the vehicle. Units that shoot in this manner count as having moved if they or the Stormlord moved in the preceding Movement phase.

Smoke Launchers: Once per game, instead of shooting any weapons in the Shooting phase, this model can use its smoke launchers; until your next Shooting phase your opponent must subtract 1 from all hit rolls for ranged weapons that target this vehicle.

Steel Behemoth: This model does not suffer the penalty to hit rolls for moving and firing Heavy weapons. This model can Fall Back in the Movement phase and still shoot and/or charge during its turn. It can also still fire its weapons if enemy units are within 1" of it (but only its twin heavy bolter or twin heavy flamer can target units that are within 1" of it – its other guns must target other units). In addition this model only gains a bonus to its save in cover if at least half of the model is obscured from the firer.

TRANSPORT
This model can transport 40 **ASTRA MILITARUM INFANTRY** models. Each Heavy Weapons Team or Veteran Heavy Weapons Team takes the space of two other models and each **OGRYN** takes the space of three other models.

FACTION KEYWORDS
IMPERIUM, ASTRA MILITARUM, <REGIMENT>

KEYWORDS
VEHICLE, TITANIC, TRANSPORT, STORMLORD

Bristling with various bolter-pattern armaments, the Stormlord ploughs across the battlefield to unload its cargo of infantry.

Infantry Squads move along the flanks of a Stormsword to charge the breach just blown in the enemy's defences.

STORMSWORD

26 POWER

NAME	M	WS	BS	S	T	W	A	Ld	Sv
Stormsword	∗	5+	∗	9	8	26	∗	8	3+

A Stormsword is a single model equipped with a Stormsword siege cannon, a twin heavy bolter and adamantium tracks.

DAMAGE
Some of this model's characteristics change as it suffers damage, as shown below:

REMAINING W	M	BS	A
14-26+	10"	4+	9
7-13	7"	5+	6
1-6	4"	6+	3

WEAPON	RANGE	TYPE	S	AP	D	ABILITIES
Heavy stubber	36"	Heavy 3	4	0	1	-
Hunter-killer missile	48"	Heavy 1	8	-2	D6	Each hunter-killer missile can only be fired once per battle.
Lascannon	48"	Heavy 1	9	-3	D6	-
Storm bolter	24"	Rapid Fire 2	4	0	1	-
Stormsword siege cannon	36"	Heavy 2D6	10	-4	D6	Units attacked by this weapon do not gain any bonus to their saving throws for being in cover. Re-roll damage rolls of 1 for this weapon.
Twin heavy bolter	36"	Heavy 6	5	-1	1	-
Twin heavy flamer	8"	Heavy 2D6	5	-1	1	This weapon automatically hits its target.
Adamantium tracks	Melee	Melee	User	-2	D3	-

WARGEAR OPTIONS	• This model may take a hunter-killer missile. • This model may take a storm bolter or a heavy stubber. • This model may take either two sponsons, or four sponsons; each sponson is equipped with a lascannon and either a twin heavy bolter or twin heavy flamer.
ABILITIES	**Explodes:** If this model is reduced to 0 wounds, roll a D6 before removing it from the battlefield. On a 6 it explodes, and each unit within 2D6" suffers D6 mortal wounds. **Smoke Launchers:** Once per game, instead of shooting any weapons in the Shooting phase, this model can use its smoke launchers; until your next Shooting phase your opponent must subtract 1 from all hit rolls for ranged weapons that target this vehicle. **Steel Behemoth:** This model does not suffer the penalty to hit rolls for moving and firing Heavy weapons. This model can Fall Back in the Movement phase and still shoot and/or charge during its turn. It can also still fire its weapons if enemy units are within 1" of it (but only its twin heavy bolter or twin heavy flamer can target units that are within 1" of it – its other guns must target other units). In addition this model only gains a bonus to its save in cover if at least half of the model is obscured from the firer.
FACTION KEYWORDS	**IMPERIUM, ASTRA MILITARUM, <REGIMENT>**
KEYWORDS	**VEHICLE, TITANIC, STORMSWORD**

ARMOURY OF THE IMPERIUM

The Astra Militarum is a vast organisation with access to a massive array of weaponry, from the standard-issue lasgun to the apocalyptic Deathstrike missile. Whatever the mission, the men and women of the Imperial Guard have the right tools for the job. The profiles for their weapons of war are detailed below.

RANGED WEAPONS

WEAPON	RANGE	TYPE	S	AP	D	ABILITIES
Artillery barrage	100"	Heavy D6	8	-2	D3	This weapon can only be fired once per battle, and cannot be used if the bearer moves. This weapon can target units that are not visible to the bearer (when doing so, subtract 1 from the hit rolls). You may only use one artillery barrage per turn, regardless of how many Masters of Ordnance you have in your army.
Autocannon	48"	Heavy 2	7	-1	2	-
Autogun	24"	Rapid Fire 1	3	0	1	-
Bale Eye	6"	Pistol 1	3	-2	1	-
Baneblade cannon	72"	Heavy 3D6	9	-3	3	-
Battle cannon	72"	Heavy D6	8	-2	D3	-
Bolt pistol	12"	Pistol 1	4	0	1	-
Boltgun	24"	Rapid Fire 1	4	0	1	-
Chem cannon	8"	Heavy D6	*	-3	1	This weapon automatically hits its target. In addition, it wounds on a 2+, unless it is targeting a VEHICLE, in which case it wounds on a 6+.
Deathstrike missile	200"	Heavy 3D6	*	*	*	This weapon can only be fired once per battle. This weapon can target units that are not visible to the bearer. Each time you hit the target with this weapon it suffers a mortal wound. After resolving all damage on the unit, roll a D6 for every other unit within 6" of the target unit – on a 4+ that unit also suffers D3 mortal wounds.
Demolisher cannon	24"	Heavy D3	10	-3	D6	When attacking units with 5 or more models, change this weapon's Type to Heavy D6.
Earthshaker cannon	240"	Heavy D6	9	-3	D3	Roll two dice for the number of attacks when firing this weapon and discard the lowest result. This weapon can target units that are not visible to the bearer.
Eradicator nova cannon	36"	Heavy D6	6	-2	D3	Units attacked by this weapon do not gain any bonus to their saving throws for being in cover.
Executioner plasma cannon	When attacking with this weapon, choose one of the profiles below.					
- Standard	36"	Heavy D6	7	-3	1	-
- Supercharge	36"	Heavy D6	8	-3	2	For each hit roll of 1, the bearer suffers 1 mortal wound after all of this weapon's shots have been resolved.
Exterminator autocannon	48"	Heavy 4	7	-1	2	-
Flamer	8"	Assault D6	4	0	1	This weapon automatically hits its target.
Frag bomb	6"	Grenade D6	4	0	1	-
Frag grenade	6"	Grenade D6	3	0	1	-
Grenade launcher	When attacking with this weapon, choose one of the profiles below.					
- Frag grenade	24"	Assault D6	3	0	1	-
- Krak grenade	24"	Assault 1	6	-1	D3	-
Grenadier gauntlet	12"	Assault D6	4	0	1	-
Heavy bolter	36"	Heavy 3	5	-1	1	-
Heavy flamer	8"	Heavy D6	5	-1	1	This weapon automatically hits its target.
Heavy stubber	36"	Heavy 3	4	0	1	-
Hellhammer cannon	36"	Heavy 3D6	10	-4	3	Units attacked by this weapon do not gain any bonus to their saving throws for being in cover.
Hellstrike missiles	72"	Heavy 1	8	-2	D6	Roll two dice when inflicting damage with this weapon and discard the lowest result.
Hot-shot lasgun	18"	Rapid Fire 1	3	-2	1	-
Hot-shot laspistol	6"	Pistol 1	3	-2	1	-
Hot-shot volley gun	24"	Heavy 4	4	-2	1	-
Hunter-killer missile	48"	Heavy 1	8	-2	D6	Each hunter-killer missile can only be fired once per battle.

RANGED WEAPONS

WEAPON	RANGE	TYPE	S	AP	D	ABILITIES
Hydra quad autocannon	72"	Heavy 8	7	-1	2	Add 1 to all hit rolls made for this weapon against targets that can **FLY**. Subtract 1 from the hit rolls made for this weapon against all other targets.
Inferno cannon	16"	Heavy 2D6	6	-1	1	This weapon automatically hits its target.
Krak grenade	6"	Grenade 1	6	-1	D3	-
Lascannon	48"	Heavy 1	9	-3	D6	-
Lasgun	24"	Rapid Fire 1	3	0	1	-
Lasgun array	24"	Rapid Fire 3	3	0	1	This weapon can only be fired if a unit is embarked upon the vehicle equipped with it.
Laspistol	12"	Pistol 1	3	0	1	-
Magma cannon	60"	Heavy 2D6	10	-5	D6	If the target is within half range of this weapon, roll two dice when inflicting damage with it and discard the lowest result.
Melta cannon	24"	Assault D3	8	-4	D6	If the target is within half range of this weapon, roll two dice when inflicting damage with it and discard the lowest result.
Meltagun	12"	Assault 1	8	-4	D6	If the target is within half range of this weapon, roll two dice when inflicting damage with it and discard the lowest result.
Missile launcher	When attacking with this weapon, choose one of the profiles below.					
- Frag missile	48"	Heavy D6	4	0	1	-
- Krak missile	48"	Heavy 1	8	-2	D6	-
Mortar	48"	Heavy D6	4	0	1	This weapon can target units that are not visible to the bearer.
Multi-laser	36"	Heavy 3	6	0	1	-
Multi-melta	24"	Heavy 1	8	-4	D6	If the target is within half range of this weapon, roll two dice when inflicting damage with it and discard the lowest result.
Multiple rocket pod	36"	Assault D6	5	-1	1	-
Payback	36"	Assault 3	5	-2	1	-
Plasma cannon	When attacking with this weapon, choose one of the profiles below.					
- Standard	36"	Heavy D3	7	-3	1	-
- Supercharge	36"	Heavy D3	8	-3	2	On a hit roll of 1, the bearer is slain after all of this weapon's shots have been resolved.
Plasma gun	When attacking with this weapon, choose one of the profiles below.					
- Standard	24"	Rapid Fire 1	7	-3	1	-
- Supercharge	24"	Rapid Fire 1	8	-3	2	On a hit roll of 1, the bearer is slain after all of this weapon's shots have been resolved.
Plasma pistol	When attacking with this weapon, choose one of the profiles below.					
- Standard	12"	Pistol 1	7	-3	1	-
- Supercharge	12"	Pistol 1	8	-3	2	On a hit roll of 1, the bearer is slain.
Punisher gatling cannon	24"	Heavy 20	5	0	1	-
Quake cannon	140"	Heavy 2D6	14	-4	D6	When rolling for this weapon's damage, treat any rolls of 1 or 2 as 3 instead.
Ripper gun (shooting)	12"	Assault 3	5	0	1	-

RANGED WEAPONS

WEAPON	RANGE	TYPE	S	AP	D	ABILITIES
Shotgun	12"	Assault 2	3	0	1	If the target is within half range, add 1 to this weapon's Strength.
Sniper rifle	36"	Heavy 1	4	0	1	A model firing a sniper weapon can target an enemy **CHARACTER** even if they are not the closest enemy unit. If you roll a wound roll of 6+ for this weapon, it inflicts a mortal wound in addition to its normal damage.
Storm bolter	24"	Rapid Fire 2	4	0	1	-
Storm eagle rocket	120"	Heavy 2D6	10	-2	D3	This weapon can target units that are not visible to the bearer. A model can only fire a single storm eagle rocket per turn. Each storm eagle rocket can only be fired once per battle.
Stormsword siege cannon	36"	Heavy 2D6	10	-4	D6	Units attacked by this weapon do not gain any bonus to their saving throws for being in cover. Re-roll damage rolls of 1 for this weapon.
Taurox battle cannon	48"	Heavy D6	7	-1	D3	-
Taurox gatling cannon	24"	Heavy 20	4	0	1	-
Taurox missile launcher		When attacking with this weapon, choose one of the profiles below.				
- Frag missile	48"	Heavy 2D6	4	0	1	-
- Krak missile	48"	Heavy 2	8	-2	D6	-
Tremor cannon	60"	Heavy 3D6	8	-2	3	If a unit is hit by this weapon, in their following Movement phase they must halve their Move characteristic and cannot Advance.
Twin heavy bolter	36"	Heavy 6	5	-1	1	-
Twin heavy flamer	8"	Heavy 2D6	5	-1	1	This weapon automatically hits its target.
Vanquisher battle cannon	72"	Heavy 1	8	-3	D6	Roll two dice when inflicting damage with this weapon and discard the lowest result.
Volcano cannon	120"	Heavy 3D3	16	-5	2D6	You can re-roll failed wound rolls when targeting **TITANIC** units with this weapon.
Vulcan mega-bolter	60"	Heavy 20	6	-2	2	-
Wyvern quad stormshard mortar	48"	Heavy 4D6	4	0	1	This weapon can target units that are not visible to the bearer. You can re-roll failed wound rolls for this weapon.

MELEE WEAPONS

WEAPON	RANGE	TYPE	S	AP	D	ABILITIES
Adamantium tracks	Melee	Melee	User	-2	D3	-
Bionic arm with devil's claw	Melee	Melee	User	-1	2	-
Bullgryn maul	Melee	Melee	+2	-1	2	-
Chainsword	Melee	Melee	User	0	1	Each time the bearer fights, it can make 1 additional attack with this weapon.
Force stave	Melee	Melee	+2	-1	D3	-
Huge knife	Melee	Melee	User	-1	2	-
Omnissian axe	Melee	Melee	+1	-2	2	-
Power fist	Melee	Melee	x2	-3	D3	When attacking with this weapon, you must subtract 1 from the hit roll.
Power klaw	Melee	Melee	x2	-3	D3	When attacking with this weapon, you must subtract 1 from the hit roll.
Power sword	Melee	Melee	User	-3	1	-
Ripper gun (melee)	Melee	Melee	User	-1	1	-
Sentinel chainsaw	Melee	Melee	User	-1	1	-
Servo-arm	Melee	Melee	x2	-2	3	Each servo-arm can only be used to make one attack each time this model fights. When a model attacks with this weapon, you must subtract 1 from the hit roll.
Telepathica stave	Melee	Melee	+1	0	D3	-
Thunderous headbutt	Melee	Melee	+3	-2	D3	Nork can only make a single thunderous headbutt attack each time he fights.
Wyrdvane stave	Melee	Melee	+1	0	1	-

OTHER WARGEAR

VEHICLE EQUIPMENT

Augur array	Once per battle, in the Shooting phase, you can re-roll a single failed hit roll for a vehicle with an augur array.
Dozer blade	If a vehicle with a dozer blade charges in the Charge phase, add 1 to hit rolls made for it until the end of the ensuing Fight phase.
Track Guards	A vehicle with track guards always counts as having its starting number of Wounds when determining its Move characteristic (i.e. its Move characteristic does not decrease as it suffers wounds).

BULWARK OF HUMANITY

In this section you will find rules for Battle-forged armies that include Astra Militarum Detachments – that is, any Detachment which includes only Astra Militarum units. These rules include the abilities below and a series of Stratagems that can only be used by the Astra Militarum. This section also contains the unique Warlord Traits, Relics and Tactical Objectives of the Imperial Guard. Together, these rules reflect the character and fighting style of the many varied regiments of the Astra Militarum in your games of Warhammer 40,000.

DEFENDERS OF HUMANITY

The Astra Militarum is the shield of Mankind. Only by its sacrifice and heroism are the worlds of the Imperium kept safe.

If your army is Battle-forged, all Troops units in Astra Militarum Detachments and all Leman Russ units in Spearhead Detachments gain this ability. Such a unit that is within range of an objective marker (as specified in the mission) controls the objective marker even if there are more enemy models within range of it. If an enemy unit within range of the same objective marker has a similar ability, then the objective marker is controlled by the player who has the most models within range of it as normal.

REGIMENTAL DOCTRINES

Each Astra Militarum regiment has its own distinct traditions, training regimes, tactics and methods of waging war.

If your army is Battle-forged, all <Regiment> units in an Astra Militarum Detachment (excluding those in Super-heavy Auxiliary Detachments) gain a Regimental Doctrine, so long as every unit in that Detachment (apart from the exceptions noted opposite) is drawn from the same regiment. The Regimental Doctrine gained depends upon the regiment they are drawn from, as shown opposite. For example, a Cadian unit with the Regimental Doctrines ability gains the Born Soldiers doctrine.

If your chosen regiment does not have an associated Regimental Doctrine, you may pick the doctrine that you feel best represents your army. For example, as your army of Ventrillian Nobles does not have an associated Regimental Doctrine, you can decide that the Vostroyan Heirloom Weapons doctrine best suits these wealthy and well-equipped fighters.

Militarum Tempestus

Militarum Tempestus units can be included in an Astra Militarum Detachment without preventing other units in that Detachment from gaining a Regimental Doctrine. Note, however, that the Militarum Tempestus units do not themselves benefit from any Regimental Doctrine unless every unit in that Detachment is from the Militarum Tempestus (in which case they will gain the Storm Troopers doctrine).

Advisors and Auxilla

The units listed below can be included in an Astra Militarum Detachment without preventing other units in that Detachment from gaining a Regimental Doctrine. Note, however, that the units listed below can never themselves benefit from a Regimental Doctrine.

- Tech-Priest Enginseer
- Servitors
- Ministorum Priest
- Crusaders
- Aeronautica Imperialis units
- Militarum Auxilla units
- Officio Prefectus units
- Scholastica Psykana units

'They can kill our heroes, destroy our world, drive us back to the very gates of Terra themselves. None of it matters, for we still stand, and so long as even one of her sons and daughters draws breath, then Cadia stands with us.'

- Captain Tarn, Cadian 20th

MATCHED PLAY RULE: COMMAND SQUADS

If you are playing a matched play game, then in a Battle-forged army, you can include a maximum of one <Regiment> Command Squad (pg 96) in a Detachment for each <Regiment> Officer in that Detachment. Similarly, if you are playing a matched play game, then in a Battle-forged army, you can include a maximum of one Militarum Tempestus Command Squad (pg 98) in a Detachment for each Tempestor Prime (pg 91) in that Detachment.

REGIMENTAL DOCTRINES

CADIAN:
BORN SOLDIERS
Cadians are raised from birth to fight the Imperium's endless wars. Decades of rigorous firing drills have forged them into expert sharp-shooters.

Re-roll hit rolls of 1 in the Shooting phase for units with this doctrine if they did not move in the previous Movement phase. If an **INFANTRY** unit with this doctrine is issued the 'Take Aim!' order and it did not move in the previous Movement phase, re-roll all failed hit rolls for the unit until the end of the phase instead.

CATACHAN:
BRUTAL STRENGTH
In the deadly jungles of Catachan, only the strongest survive. The sons and daughters of this death world are ferocious warriors, taller and more powerful than typical humans.

INFANTRY units with this doctrine add 1 to their Strength characteristic. In addition, they can add 1 to their Leadership characteristic if they are within 6" of a friendly **CATACHAN OFFICER**. Each time a **VEHICLE** with this doctrine fires a ranged weapon that makes a random number of attacks (e.g. Heavy D6, Heavy 2D6 etc.) you can re-roll one of the dice used to determine the number of attacks made.

VALHALLAN:
GRIM DEMEANOUR
Possessed of a grim fatalism regarding the prospect of death, Valhallan Ice Warriors will march unflinchingly into the most hellish of firestorms.

INFANTRY units with this doctrine halve the number of models that flee, rounding up, if they fail a Morale test. **VEHICLES** with this doctrine that have a damage table double the number of Wounds they have remaining for the purposes of determining what their characteristics are.

VOSTROYAN:
HEIRLOOM WEAPONS
Each and every Vostroyan weapon is lovingly hand-crafted and engraved with intricate ornamental detail. These are no artisanal trinkets, however, as victims of their deadly accurate firepower will attest.

Units with this doctrine can add 6" to the maximum range of Heavy or Rapid Fire weapons they fire which would normally have a range of 24" or more.

ARMAGEDDON:
INDUSTRIAL EFFICIENCY
To the Steel Legions of Armageddon, the pitiless mathematics of industrialised slaughter have become a grim fact of life. One by one, their foes are butchered with dispassionate efficiency.

INFANTRY units with this doctrine may double the number of attacks they make with Rapid Fire weapons at a range of up to 18", rather than half the weapon's range as normal. **VEHICLES** with this doctrine treat attacks against them with an AP of -1 as having AP 0.

TALLARN:
SWIFT AS THE WIND
Masters of the lightning ambush, Tallarn warriors strike with overwhelming force before swiftly fading into the wilderness as if they were never there at all.

INFANTRY units with this doctrine can Advance and still shoot any weapon type (except Heavy weapons). When they do so, they do not suffer the usual penalties to hit rolls for Assault weapons. **VEHICLES** with this doctrine do not suffer the penalty to their hit rolls for moving and firing Heavy weapons. If a **TITANIC VEHICLE** with this doctrine Advances, it treats all Heavy weapons it is equipped with as Assault weapons until the end of the turn (e.g. a Heavy D6 weapon is treated as an Assault D6 weapon).

MILITARUM TEMPESTUS:
STORM TROOPERS
The warriors of the Militarum Tempestus are the best of the best, merciless killers trained to obliterate their foes in a pinpoint fusillade of hot-shot las rounds.

If a model with this doctrine is shooting a target at half range or less, it can make an extra shot with the same weapon, at the same target, for each hit roll of 6+ you make for that model. These extra shots do not themselves generate any more additional shots.

MORDIAN:
PARADE DRILL
Mordian regiments are proud, unyielding soldiers. They fight and die facing the enemy, standing tall in ordered ranks and unleashing a devastating fusillade of las-fire.

If the base of every model in an **INFANTRY** unit with this doctrine is touching the base of at least one other model from the same unit, the unit has +1 Leadership and you can add 1 to hit rolls made for models in that unit when firing Overwatch. You can add 1 to hit rolls made for **VEHICLES** with this doctrine when firing Overwatch if they are within 3" of one or more other friendly **MORDIAN VEHICLES**.

STRATAGEMS

If your army is Battle-forged and includes any Astra Militarum Detachments (excluding Auxiliary Support Detachments), you have access to the Stratagems shown below, meaning you can spend Command Points to activate them. These help to reflect the unique tactics and strategies used by the Imperial Guard on the battlefield.

VORTEX MISSILE

3CP

Astra Militarum Stratagem

Vortex Missiles are amongst the most lethal and horrific warheads available to the Astra Militarum. Upon impact, these weapons tear a hole in the very fabric of reality, draining everything within a wide blast radius into the warp.

Use this Stratagem before you fire a Deathstrike missile. You can re-roll failed hit rolls for this shot. In addition, add 1 to the roll made to determine whether other units within 6" are hit. If a model is wounded but not slain by the attack, roll another dice; on a 6, the model suffers a further D6 mortal wounds.

FIRE ON MY POSITION

3CP

Astra Militarum Stratagem

Even as they are overwhelmed, brave soldiers of the Astra Militarum may carry out one last act of vengeful defiance, calling in a creeping bombardment on their own position.

Use this Stratagem when the last model is slain from an **Astra Militarum** unit from your army equipped with a vox-caster. Before removing the model, roll a D6 for each unit within 3" of it. On a 4+ that unit suffers D3 mortal wounds.

CRUSH THEM!

1CP

Astra Militarum Stratagem

Should the enemy be too close to engage with heavy cannons, Imperial armour will simply rumble forward to crush them beneath their grinding treads.

Use this Stratagem at the start of the Charge phase. Select an **Astra Militarum Vehicle** unit from your army. This unit can charge even if it Advanced this turn. In the following Fight phase, attacks made by this unit hit on a 2+.

AERIAL SPOTTER

2CP

Astra Militarum Stratagem

Aeronautica Imperialis recon planes send back pinpoint coordinates to artillery positions, allowing them to unleash a punishingly accurate salvo.

Use this Stratagem at the start of the Shooting phase. Select a Basilisk or Wyvern model from your army. You can re-roll failed hit rolls for this unit in this phase.

JURY RIGGING

1CP

Astra Militarum Stratagem

Imperial tank jockeys and Enginseers have devised a number of improvised mechanical techniques to get their damaged steeds back into the fight.

Use this Stratagem at the start of your turn. Select an **Astra Militarum Vehicle** from your army. It cannot move, charge or pile in this turn, but immediately heals 1 wound.

CONSOLIDATE SQUADS

1CP

Astra Militarum Stratagem

Astra Militarum officers must quickly learn to adapt in the thick of battle, forming ad hoc fire teams from the fragments of depleted infantry squads.

Use this Stratagem at the end of your Movement phase. Choose an Infantry Squad (pg 93) from your army that is within 2" of another of your Infantry Squads from the same **<Regiment>**. You can merge these squads into a single unit and they are treated as such for the rest of the battle.

IMPERIAL COMMANDER'S ARMOURY

1CP/3CP

Astra Militarum Stratagem

By leveraging their considerable influence upon the Departmento Munitorum, high-ranking Imperial commanders can secure vital resources for their military campaigns.

Use this Stratagem before the battle. Your army can have one extra relic from the Heirlooms of Conquest for 1 CP, or two extra relics for 3 CPs. All of the relics that you include must be different and be given to different **Astra Militarum Characters**. You can only use this Stratagem once per battle.

OFFICIO PREFECTUS COMMAND TANK

2CP

Astra Militarum Stratagem

Many regimental Commissars prefer to bellow threats and orders from the cupola of a Leman Russ battle tank.

Use this Stratagem at the start of the first battle round, before the first turn begins. Select a **Leman Russ** from your army. All friendly **Astra Militarum** units have a Leadership characteristic of 9 (unless it would otherwise be higher) whilst they are within 6" of this vehicle.

MOBILE COMMAND VEHICLE
1CP

Astra Militarum Stratagem

Command vehicles allow intrepid officers to lead from the front of the battle, racing across the lines, raising the spirits of their warriors and reacting with speed to any emerging threats.

Use this Stratagem at the start of any turn. Choose a Chimera from your army. Until the end of the turn, an **OFFICER** from your army with the Voice of Command ability may still issue orders whilst embarked within that Chimera (measuring ranges from any point on the vehicle), and is treated as being within 3" of a vox-caster.

PRELIMINARY BOMBARDMENT
2CP

Astra Militarum Stratagem

An Astra Militarum assault often begins with an initial bombardment of the enemy line, softening up the foe before the mass advance of infantry and armour.

Use this Stratagem after both sides have deployed, but before the first battle round begins. Roll a dice for each enemy unit on the battlefield. On a 6, that unit suffers 1 mortal wound. You can only use this Stratagem once per battle.

INSPIRED TACTICS
1CP

Astra Militarum Stratagem

A skilled officer can turn a battle on its head, throwing the enemy into confusion and inspiring their own soldiers to acts of remarkable heroism.

Use this Stratagem after an **OFFICER** from your army has issued an order or tank order. That officer may immediately issue an additional order.

DEFENSIVE GUNNERS
1CP

Astra Militarum Stratagem

As enemy anti-armour troops advance upon their vehicles, sponson and turret gunners unleash a devastating hail of fire.

Use this Stratagem when a charge is declared against one of your **ASTRA MILITARUM VEHICLE** units. When that unit fires Overwatch this phase, they successfully hit on a roll of 5 or 6, instead of only 6.

TAKE COVER!
1CP

Astra Militarum Stratagem

Sometimes the only possible response to overwhelming enemy fire is to hit the dirt and wait for the storm to pass, before springing up to unleash an answering volley.

Use this Stratagem in your opponent's Shooting phase when your opponent selects one of your units as a target. You can add 1 to saving throws you make for this unit until the end of the phase.

GRENADIERS
1CP

Astra Militarum Stratagem

Against packed formations of enemy infantry, a favoured tactic of Astra Militarum assault troops is to hurl an opening salvo of grenades en masse.

Use this Stratagem before an **ASTRA MILITARUM INFANTRY** unit from your army shoots or fires Overwatch. Up to ten models in the unit that are armed with grenades can throw a grenade this phase, instead of only one model being able to do so.

FIGHT TO THE DEATH
1CP

Astra Militarum Stratagem

They may be mere mortals in a galaxy of gods and monsters, but the soldiers of the Astra Militarum stand tall in the face of obliteration, lasguns blazing.

Use this Stratagem at the start of the Morale phase. Pick an **ASTRA MILITARUM INFANTRY** unit from your army that is required to take a Morale test. You can roll a D3 for the unit, rather than a D6, when taking this test.

GO! RECON!
1CP

Astra Militarum Stratagem

Scout Sentinels can sacrifice firepower for speed, darting across the battlefield in search of new threats.

Use this Stratagem at the start of your Shooting phase. Select a unit of Scout Sentinels from your army. This unit can immediately move 2D6" but cannot shoot or charge this turn.

VENGEANCE FOR CADIA!
1CP

Astra Militarum Stratagem

Soldiers of the Astra Militarum yearn to visit destruction upon those responsible for the fall of mighty Cadia.

Use this Stratagem when you select one of your **ASTRA MILITARUM** units to shoot or fire Overwatch. Re-roll failed hit and wound rolls for models in this unit that target **CHAOS** units until the end of the phase.

VOLLEY FIRE
Mordian Stratagem

Mordian troops are trained to hold their fire until the perfect moment, before unleashing a single, devastingly accurate volley that cuts the foe to pieces.

Use this Stratagem before a **MORDIAN INFANTRY** unit from your army shoots in the Shooting phase. Each time you make a hit roll of 6+ for a model in that unit, that model can immediately shoot again with the same weapon at the same target (these bonus attacks cannot themselves generate any further attacks).

1CP

SUPERIOR INTELLIGENCE
Militarum Tempestus Stratagem

Storm troopers of the Militarum Tempestus have access to the latest operational intelligence, and are ready to greet enemy reinforcements with a hail of hot-shot rounds.

Use this Stratagem immediately after your opponent sets up a unit that is arriving on the battlefield as reinforcements within 12" of one of your **MILITARUM TEMPESTUS INFANTRY** units. Your unit can immediately shoot at that enemy unit as if it were the Shooting phase, but you must subtract 1 from all the resulting hit rolls.

1CP

OVERLAPPING FIELDS OF FIRE
Cadian Stratagem

Cadian combat doctrine utilises the intense concentration of firepower, focused upon the most dangerous enemy targets.

Use this Stratagem after a **CADIAN** unit from your army has inflicted an unsaved wound on an enemy unit in the Shooting phase. You can add 1 to hit rolls for any other **CADIAN** units from your army that target the same enemy unit this phase.

2CP

AMBUSH
Tallarn Stratagem

The Tallarns launch their assault from multiple directions, fixing the enemy in a lethal crossfire and throwing them into terrified confusion.

Use this Stratagem during deployment. Choose up to three **TALLARN** units to set up in ambush instead of placing them on the battlefield. At the end of any of your Movement phases these units can strike from hiding – set each of them up wholly within 7" of any battlefield edge and more than 9" from any enemy models.

3CP

SEND IN THE NEXT WAVE!
Valhallan Stratagem

Valhallan regiments drown the enemy under sheer weight of numbers, wearing them down with endless infantry assaults.

Use this Stratagem at the end of your Movement phase. Select a **VALHALLAN INFANTRY** unit from your army (excluding **CHARACTERS** and Infantry Squads that have used the Combined Squads Stratagem) that was destroyed earlier in the battle. Set up this unit wholly within your deployment zone, within 6" of the edge of the battlefield and more than 9" from any enemy models.

2CP

ARMOURED FIST
Armageddon Stratagem

The Armageddon Steel Legions have perfected the art of the mechanised assault. Gas-masked troopers leap from their transports into the heart of the foe, lasguns blasting.

Use this Stratagem at the start of your Shooting phase. Select an **ARMAGEDDON INFANTRY** unit from your army that disembarked from an **ARMAGEDDON TRANSPORT VEHICLE** this turn. You can re-roll hit rolls of 1 for that unit until the end of the phase.

1CP

FIRSTBORN PRIDE
Vostroyan Stratagem

Driven to repay their home world's ancient debt, the Vostroyan Firstborn fight with prideful defiance, seeing each battle as a chance to reclaim their honour.

Use this Stratagem at the start of your Shooting phase. Select a **VOSTROYAN** unit from your army. You can add 1 to hit rolls made for this unit until the end of the phase.

1CP

VICIOUS TRAPS
Catachan Stratagem

Catachan Jungle Fighters lace the ground ahead of their defences with all manner of lethal devices, including snare mines, razor-shard tripwires and incendiary charges.

Use this Stratagem when an enemy unit finishes a charge move within 1" of a **CATACHAN** unit from your army that is wholly on or within a terrain feature. Roll a dice; on a 4+ that enemy unit suffers D3 mortal wounds.

1CP

PSYKANA DISCIPLINE

The psykers who accompany the soldiery of the Astra Militarum perform a variety of battlefield roles, but each one is a deadly tool of war. Whether channelling the energies of the warp to protect and embolden their allies, or to confound and destroy the foe, each commands powers capable of turning the tide of battle.

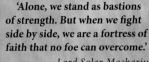

Before the battle, generate the psychic powers for **Psykers** that can use powers from the Psykana discipline using the table below. You can either roll a D6 to generate their powers randomly (re-roll any duplicate results), or you can select the psychic powers you wish the psyker to have.

1. TERRIFYING VISIONS

The psyker fills his enemies' minds with nightmarish images and visions of torment, seeking to send them fleeing in terror.

Terrifying Visions has a warp charge value of 7. If manifested, choose an enemy unit within 18" of the psyker. That unit subtracts 2 from its Leadership until the start of your next turn.

2. GAZE OF THE EMPEROR

The psyker cages the immense power of the immaterium within his physical form, and his eyes blaze with the Emperor's vengeful fury.

Gaze of the Emperor has a warp charge value of 6. If manifested, draw a straight line 2D6" long directly away from the psyker. Roll a dice for each model the centre of the line passes over. On a 4+ that model's unit suffers a mortal wound.

3. PSYCHIC BARRIER

The psyker weaves an aegis of pure psychic energy around his allies, against which enemy fire sparks and spatters harmlessly.

Psychic Barrier has a warp charge value of 6. If manifested, select a friendly **Astra Militarum** unit within 12" of the psyker. Until the start of your next Psychic phase, add 1 to that unit's saving throws.

4. NIGHTSHROUD

Calling upon the power of the empyrean, the psyker cloaks his allies in a flowing curtain of shadow, concealing them from the enemy.

Nightshroud has a warp charge value of 6. If manifested, choose a friendly **Astra Militarum** unit within 12" of the psyker. Until the start of your next turn, any enemy unit that targets the chosen unit with a ranged weapon suffers a -1 penalty to its hit rolls.

5. MENTAL FORTITUDE

Drawing on boundless reserves of inner strength, the psyker shields his allies' minds from mortal fears and the threat of sorcerous assault.

Mental Fortitude has a warp charge value of 4. If manifested, select a friendly **Astra Militarum** unit within 12" of the psyker. Until the start of your next Psychic phase, that unit automatically passes Morale tests.

6. PSYCHIC MAELSTROM

The psyker unleashes the full might of his mind, summoning a roiling psychic tempest that envelops his enemy, lifting them from the ground and wrenching them about like a rag doll.

Psychic Maelstrom has a warp charge value of 7. If manifested, select an enemy unit within 18" of the psyker. Roll a D6. On a 2+, that unit suffers a mortal wound. Unless this mortal wound is negated, you can then roll another dice. On a 3+ that enemy unit suffers another mortal wound. Continue this process, adding 1 to the dice roll required each time (so the next roll would need 4+, then 5+, etc.) until you fail to cause a mortal wound, or the enemy unit is destroyed.

HEIRLOOMS OF CONQUEST

Since the dawn of the Imperium, Humanity's greatest heroes have wielded weapons and equipment of extraordinary power. Some of these have been lost, whilst others are held in great shrines where pilgrims flock to see them. A few, however, are still in use, borne by those on the front lines of battle against the enemies of the Emperor.

If your army is led by an **ASTRA MILITARUM** Warlord, then before the battle you may give one of the following Heirlooms of Conquest to an **ASTRA MILITARUM CHARACTER**. Named characters such as Lord Castellan Creed already have one or more artefacts, and cannot be given any of the following relics.

Note that some weapons replace one of the character's existing weapons. Where this is the case, if you are playing a matched play game or are otherwise using points values, you must still pay the cost of the weapon that is being replaced. Write down any Heirlooms of Conquest your characters may have on your army roster.

THE EMPEROR'S BENEDICTION

Wielded by a succession of brutal, uncompromising Commissars, this masterwork bolt pistol is feared by all. Its elementary but bloodthirsty machine spirit has been blamed for a series of unfortunate 'accidents' on the field of battle. In spite of this, the Officio Prefectus view the Emperor's Benediction as an artefact of some distinction – some say that it can taste cowardice even before the reprehensible act has been committed.

COMMISSAR or **LORD COMMISSAR** with a bolt pistol only. The Emperor's Benediction replaces the model's bolt pistol and has the following profile:

WEAPON	RANGE	TYPE	S	AP	D
The Emperor's Benediction	12"	Pistol 3	4	-1	2

Abilities: This weapon can target a **CHARACTER** even if it is not the closest enemy unit, unless the bearer is within 1" of an enemy unit.

THE LAURELS OF COMMAND

The Laurels of Command are a callous and controversial means to ensure obedience. Concealed within their peerless artistry is a band of empathic-impulsion circuitry which allows the wearer limited control over the minds of indoctrinated individuals via subliminal suggestion. Under their effects even cowards fight to the last, while orders are executed in perfect synchronisation.

OFFICER with Voice of Command ability only. Roll a dice each time the bearer issues an order to a friendly **<REGIMENT>** unit within 6" of them. On a 4+ the bearer can immediately issue another order to the same unit. This does not count towards the maximum number of orders this model may issue each turn.

THE DEATHMASK OF OLLANIUS

Ollanius the Pious is the epitome of Imperial sainthood, believed martyred at the hands of Horus himself. In the millennia since his passing, Ollanius' deathmask has been revered as a holy relic; whosoever wears this ancient artefact is granted the determination and endurance of the famous martyr himself. The mask is a terrifying piece of craftsmanship, depicting in obsidian and void- fired bronze the agonised visage of a tortured angel. It is said that, in the presence of traitors, the Deathmask will weep tears of blood.

INFANTRY model only. The bearer of this item has a 4+ invulnerable save. In addition, once per game, at the start of any of your turns, the bearer may immediately heal D3 wounds.

THE DAGGER OF TU'SAKH

Tu'Sakh Khan of the 2nd Attilan Rough Riders was known as a particularly cunning and bold commander, with an almost preternatural ability to find the perfect time and place to strike. On his death bed, he dictated that his ornate dagger be gifted to an ally as a gesture of respect. Over the decades since, this gifting has become tradition, each owner presenting the dagger to a fellow commander upon arrival at a new war zone. Many an owner has found themselves inspired by the rash spirit of Tu'Sakh, leading their men in daring raids deep in the heart of the enemy's territory.

During deployment, you can set up the bearer and one **INFANTRY** unit from your army behind enemy lines instead of placing them on the battlefield. The infantry unit must have the same **<REGIMENT>** keyword as the bearer if the bearer has one. At the end of any of your Movement phases these units can launch their daring attack – set them up within 3" of each other, anywhere on the battlefield that is wholly within 6" of any battlefield edge and more than 9" away from any enemy models.

KUROV'S AQUILA

General Kurov was one of the most gifted officers in Imperial history. Upon retirement, he recorded dozens of tactical treatises that were translated into vox-ghosts and uploaded into a two-headed avian servitor referred to as 'Kurov's Aquila'. An officer who possesses this prestigious tool can turn to it for tactical guidance. In response, the servitor's blindfolded head will vocalise the most relevant vox-ghost in Kurov's stentorian tones. The other head's eyes glow above its bound-shut beak as they project a hololithic display of Kurov himself, his image flickering as it reveals the secrets of the foe.

OFFICERS only. Each time your opponent uses a Stratagem, roll a D6. On a 5+ you gain 1 Command Point.

THE BLADE OF CONQUEST

The greatest Imperial Guard commander ever to bestride the stars, Warmaster Solar Macharius reclaimed a thousand worlds for the Emperor. Upon his death he was enshrined as a saint; the six ornate blades of his subordinate generals laid upon the altar to his glory. Only one of these weapons has been reclaimed to active service. Any man who wields this sword can light a righteous fire in the hearts of his men, for they fight in the shadow of Saint Solar himself.

Model with power sword only. The Blade of Conquest replaces the model's power sword and has the following profile:

WEAPON	RANGE	TYPE	S	AP	D
Blade of Conquest	Melee	Melee	+2	-4	D3

RELIC OF LOST CADIA

Though Cadia was destroyed by the Thirteenth Black Crusade, its most sacred artefacts live on. The most meaningful amongst the medals and skulls of fallen heroes resonates with energies of defiance and inspires those around them to acts of retribution.

CADIAN model only. The bearer can unveil this relic at the start of any turn. Until the end of that turn, you can re-roll hit and wound rolls of 1 for all CADIAN units within 12" of the bearer. You can instead re-roll all failed hit and wound rolls for these units until the end of the turn if they are targeting a CHAOS unit.

MAMORPH TUSKBLADE

This viciously sharp blade was quenched in the blood of a Shambling Mamorph. It is said by the Jungle Fighters that the strength of that great beast – a mass of muscle and hair that can eviscerate an Ogryn with a single sweep of its oversized tusks – lives in the sword's edge.

CATACHAN model with power sword only. The Mamorph Tuskblade replaces the model's power sword and has the following profile:

WEAPON	RANGE	TYPE	S	AP	D
Mamorph Tuskblade	Melee	Melee	+2	-3	2

PIETROV'S MK 45

Commander Wladislaw Pietrov was well-known for the bulky Valhallan Mk 45 bolt pistol with which he dispensed rough justice – he who wields it is both inspiring and daunting to all Valhallans.

VALHALLAN model with bolt pistol only. Pietrov's Mk 45 replaces the model's bolt pistol and has the following profile:

WEAPON	RANGE	TYPE	S	AP	D
Pietrov's Mk 45	12"	Pistol	4	-1	2

Abilities: Friendly VALHALLAN units within 6" of the bearer can never lose more than one model as the result of any single failed Morale test.

THE ARMOUR OF GRAF TOSCHENKO

Toschenko, famous throughout the Firstborn for his indomitability against the T'au during the Nimbosa crusade, wore ornate augmetic armour that has since been passed to a dozen spiritual descendants.

VOSTROYAN INFANTRY model only. Increase the model's Toughness characteristic to 4 and Save characteristic to 2+.

SKULL MASK OF ACHERON

Possessing an almost totemic quality, the Skull Mask has been worn by a succession of Steel Legion commanders – he who dons it puts aside his identity, but carries a fell reputation as a killer of xenos.

ARMAGEDDON CHARACTER only. Enemy units within 3" of the bearer suffer a -1 penalty to their Leadership. ORK units suffer a -2 penalty instead.

CLAW OF THE DESERT TIGERS

Famously used by Captain Al'rahem of the Tallarn 3rd to take the head of the Aeldari Autarch Kaliell, this power sword was crafted by master artisans and embellished with emblems of the desert.

TALLARN model with power sword only. Claw of the Desert Tigers replaces the model's power sword and has the following profile:

WEAPON	RANGE	TYPE	S	AP	D
Claw of the Desert Tigers	Melee	Melee	User	-3	2

Abilities: Each time the bearer fights, it can make 2 additional attacks with this weapon.

THE TACTICAL AUTO-RELIQUARY OF TYBERIUS

Built into the gold-chased skull of Lord Commander Lucellin Tyberius himself, this device contains a web of psycho-circuitry containing Tyberius' memory engrams and tactical acumen – and with it, his curmudgeonly and overbearing personality. Borne aloft by its own gravitic motors, the device observes and evaluates an officer's decisions. The moment it considers an order poorly chosen, the skull cuts into the vox and loudly overrides its exasperated owner.

MILITARUM TEMPESTUS model only. When using the Voice of Command ability, this model can issue one additional order per turn. Roll a dice before issuing this additional order. On a roll of 1, the Reliquary issues contradictory nonsense and nothing happens.

ORDER OF THE IRON STAR OF MORDIAN

The Mordians are resolute and tenacious, and none more so than one who has earned the Order of the Iron Star. This impressive medallion is said to carry a fraction of the Emperor's protective grace.

MORDIAN INFANTRY model only. Each time the bearer suffers a wound or mortal wound, roll a dice; on a 4+ the wound is negated and has no effect.

WARLORD TRAITS

The generals of the Astra Militarum come from a variety of backgrounds, either born into their rank, schooled in an academy, or from climbing the ranks through personal achievement. Some are great strategists whilst others are inspirational fighters.

If a <REGIMENT>, MILITARUM TEMPESTUS or OFFICIO PREFECTUS CHARACTER is your Warlord, they can generate a Warlord Trait from the following table instead of the one in the *Warhammer 40,000* rulebook. You can either roll on the table below to randomly generate a Warlord Trait, or you can select the one that best suits your general's temperament and preferred style of waging war.

D6 RESULT

1 GRAND STRATEGIST
This Warlord is capable of precisely anticipating the ebb and flow of war.

Whilst your Warlord is alive, you can re-roll a single hit roll, wound roll or saving throw per battle. In addition, if your army is Battle-forged and this Warlord is on the battlefield, roll a dice for each Command Point spent when using Stratagems. On a 5+ that Command Point is immediately refunded.

2 OLD GRUDGES
The Warlord has learned his nemesis' weakness, and will exploit it ruthlessly.

After deployment, but before the first battle round begins, choose a unit in your opponent's army. You can re-roll failed wound rolls for ASTRA MILITARUM units from your army that target the unit you chose whilst they are within 6" of your Warlord.

3 IMPLACABLE DETERMINATION
The Warlord is known for leading swift and inexorable advances.

When your Warlord and a single friendly unit within 3" of them Advances, they may both add 6" to their Move characteristic for that Movement phase instead of rolling a dice.

4 DRACONIAN DISCIPLINARIAN
The Warlord believes that to spare the lash is to spoil the soldier, and is never hesitant in dealing out despotic punishments. His men fear his wrath more than any mortal foe.

You can re-roll failed Morale tests for friendly ASTRA MILITARUM INFANTRY units within 6" of your Warlord in the Morale phase.

5 BELLOWING VOICE
Every order given by this Warlord is bellowed to his men with perfect clarity and at ear-splitting volume, ensuring those under his command know his will and act on it without hesitation.

Add 3" to the range of any abilities on your Warlord's datasheet (such as Aura of Discipline or Voice of Command).

6 MASTER OF COMMAND
This Warlord commands his forces with a masterful knowledge of their abilities and even individual personalities, ensuring he gets the best from the men around him.

Your Warlord gains the Voice of Command ability. If your Warlord already has the Voice of Command or Tank Orders ability, they may instead issue one additional order per turn.

NAMED CHARACTERS AND WARLORD TRAITS
If a named character with a specific regiment keyword is your Warlord, they must be given the associated Warlord Trait. For example, Colonel 'Iron Hand' Straken must take the Catachan 'Lead From the Front' Warlord Trait (see opposite) as he has the CATACHAN keyword.

If Commissar Yarrick is your Warlord, he must have the Master of Command Warlord Trait (above).

'I've seen Orks the size of Sentinels, that could punch a man's head clean off. Seen them Tyranids swarming over the ridge at Shatterpeak, all blades and fangs and spittin' acid that turned tanks to metal sludge. I was right in the middle of Kalda City when the firestorm came down, and went toe-to-toe with Chaos worshippers so crazed with their false religion that they'd keep fighting a man even as they burned up like rations on a cookfire. Through all that I learned one thing that always holds true. Don't matter how big, or crazed, or unnatural your enemy is, he can't kill you if you saw his damn head off with your Catachan fang.'

- Corporal 'Razorback' Mahoney, Catachan XLI

REGIMENTAL WARLORD TRAITS

If you wish, you can pick a Regimental Warlord Trait from the list below instead of from the Astra Militarum Warlord Traits, but only if your Warlord is from the appropriate regiment.

REGIMENT	WARLORD TRAIT
Cadian	**Superior Tactical Training:** *Cadian officers are known for their strategic excellence, as are those they command. Their long training and curt, well-established battle cant allows them to issue the right order at the right time with consummate speed and efficiency.* Roll a dice each time your Warlord issues an order or tank order. On a 4+ that order can affect an additional CADIAN unit of the same type as the original target (INFANTRY or LEMAN RUSS) within 6" of the Warlord.
Catachan	**Lead From the Front:** *Catachan officers dive into the thick of the fray without hesitation, their blades and their teeth bared – mortal enemies hold little fear for those who have fought the mega-fauna of a death world jungle and survived.* This Warlord can perform a Heroic Intervention if, after the enemy has completed all their charge moves, they are within 6" of any enemy units. This Warlord can move up to 6" when performing a Heroic Intervention, so long as they end the move closer to the nearest enemy model. In addition, if your Warlord charged, was charged or performed a Heroic Intervention, then until the end of the turn you can re-roll failed hit rolls made for them.
Valhallan	**Tenacious:** *Valhallan officers are famously merciless, and freely sacrifice the lives of their men in order to carry the day – yet they are not afraid of danger, and will fight on even when sustaining deep wounds, the better to inspire obedience in their men.* Roll a dice each time your Warlord suffers a wound or mortal wound. On a 5+, the wound is ignored. If your Warlord has the VEHICLE keyword, the wound is ignored on a roll of a 6+ instead.
Vostroyan	**Honoured Duellist:** *The sword-forms of the Vostroyan aristocracy are steeped in tradition, yet at their heart is a deadly efficacy of movement – those trained in such honour duels make formidable opponents at close quarters.* Re-roll failed hit and wound rolls in the Fight phase for attacks made by your Warlord.
Armageddon	**Ex-gang Leader:** *It is common amongst the regiments of Armageddon to recruit from the underhive gangs of the planet's towering metropoli – those who once led gangs in urban warfare fight dirty even on the field of open war.* Add 1 to this Warlord's Attacks characteristic. In addition, add 1 to any wound rolls made for your Warlord in the Fight phase.
Tallarn	**Swift Attacker:** *The Tallarn way of war is to ebb and flow, to fall back and to sprint forward at a single barked command from their leaders. To fight them is to fight a hurricane of blades, bolts and las blasts that can change direction in a heartbeat.* Your Warlord and all friendly TALLARN units within 6" of them can charge even if they Fell Back that turn.
Militarum Tempestus	**Faithful Servant of the Throne:** *The Scions of the Militarum Tempestus, raised by the punitively strict Schola Progenia, are possessed of an iron mental fortitude. The strongest amongst them have a faith that can turn aside hostile psychic emanations.* Your Warlord can attempt to deny one psychic power in each enemy Psychic phase in the same manner as a Psyker.
Mordian	**Iron Discipline:** *The steel in the soul of Mordian's officers is further hardened by a lifetime of oppression and conflict – those who fight under their stern gaze are inspired to battle on even against impossible odds.* Roll a dice for each model that flees from any friendly MORDIAN units within 6" of your Warlord in the Morale phase. On a 4+, that model does not flee.

POINTS VALUES

If you are playing a matched play game, or a game that uses a points limit, you can use the following lists to determine the total points cost of your army. Simply add together the points costs of all your models and the wargear they are equipped with to determine your army's total points value.

UNITS

UNIT	MODELS PER UNIT	POINTS PER MODEL (Does not include wargear)
Armoured Sentinels	1-3	40
Astropath	1	15
Baneblade	1	390
Banehammer	1	390
Banesword	1	390
Basilisks	1-3	100
Bullgryns	3-9	35
Chimera	1	75
Command Squad *	4	6
Commissar	1	30
Company Commander	1	30
Conscripts	20-30	3
Crusaders	2-10	11
Deathstrike	1	155
Doomhammer	1	420
Heavy Weapons Squad	3	6
Hellhammer	1	410
Hellhounds	1-3	73
Hydras	1-3	100
Infantry Squad *	10	4
Knight Commander Pask	1	177
Leman Russ Battle Tanks	1-3	122
Lord Commissar	1	50
Manticore	1	125
Master of Ordnance	1	30
Militarum Tempestus Command Squad	4	9
Militarum Tempestus Scions	5-10	9
Ministorum Priest	1	35
Officer of the Fleet	1	25
Ogryn Bodyguard	1	55
Ogryns	3-9	30
Platoon Commander	1	20
Primaris Psyker	1	28
Ratlings	5-10	5
Scout Sentinels	1-3	35
Servitors	4	2
Shadowsword	1	390
Special Weapons Squad	6	4
Stormlord	1	430
Stormsword	1	390
Tank Commander	1	167
Taurox	1	40
Taurox Prime	1	65
Tech-Priest Enginseer	1	30
Tempestor Prime	1	40

UNITS

UNIT	MODELS PER UNIT	POINTS PER MODEL (Does not include wargear)
Valkyries	1-3	110
Veterans *	10	6
Wyrdvane Psykers	3-9	8
Wyverns	1-3	85

* If models in these units form Heavy Weapons Teams, there is no additional points cost.

NAMED CHARACTERS

UNIT	MODELS PER UNIT	POINTS PER MODEL (Including wargear)
Colonel 'Iron Hand' Straken	1	75
Colour Sergeant Kell	1	50
Commissar Yarrick	1	130
Lord Castellan Creed	1	70
Nork Deddog	1	80
Sergeant Harker	1	50

OTHER WARGEAR

WARGEAR	POINTS PER ITEM
Augur array	10
Brute shield	0
Bullgryn plate	5
Dozer blade	5
Medi-pack	10
Platoon standard	5
Regimental standard	5
Slabshield	0
Tempestus command rod	0
Track guards	10
Vox-caster	5

MELEE WEAPONS

WEAPON	POINTS PER WEAPON
Adamantium tracks	0
Bullgryn maul	7
Chainsword	0
Force stave	12
Huge knife	0
Omnissian axe	0
Power fist	10
Power sword	4
Sentinel chainsaw	2
Telepathica stave	6
Servo-arm	12
Wyrdvane stave	0

RANGED WEAPONS

WEAPON	POINTS PER WEAPON
Artillery barrage	0
Autocannon	15
Autogun	0
Baneblade cannon	0
Battle cannon	22
Bolt pistol	1
Boltgun	1
Chem cannon	15
Deathstrike missile	0
Demolisher cannon	40
Earthshaker cannon	0
Eradicator nova cannon	25
Executioner plasma cannon	20
Exterminator autocannon	25
Flamer	7
Frag bomb	0
Frag grenades	0
Grenade launcher	5
Grenadier gauntlet	10
Heavy bolter	8
Heavy flamer	17
Heavy stubber	4
Hellhammer cannon	0
Hellstrike missiles	20
Hot-shot lasgun	1
Hot-shot laspistol	1
Hot-shot volley gun	6
Hunter-killer missile	6
Hydra quad autocannon	0
Inferno cannon	20
Krak grenades	0
Lascannon	20
Lasgun	0

RANGED WEAPONS

WEAPON	POINTS PER WEAPON
Lasgun array	0
Laspistol	0
Magma cannon	0
Melta cannon	20
Meltagun	12
Missile launcher	20
Mortar	5
Multi-laser	10
Multi-melta	20
Multiple rocket pod	11
Plasma cannon	15
Plasma gun (model with a Ballistic Skill of 4+)	7
Plasma gun (other models)	13
Plasma pistol	5
Punisher gatling cannon	20
Quake cannon	0
Ripper gun	0
Shotgun	0
Sniper rifle	2
Storm bolter	2
Storm eagle rockets	0
Stormsword siege cannon	0
Taurox battle cannon	28
Taurox gatling cannon	18
Taurox missile launcher	50
Tremor cannon	0
Twin heavy bolter	14
Twin heavy flamer	30
Vanquisher battle cannon	25
Volcano cannon	0
Vulcan mega-bolter	0
Wyvern quad stormshard mortar	0

> 'We've run into scorpions the size of battle tanks. Three men died from Eyerot last week and I've sweated enough to fill a lake. Emperor help me, I love this place – it's just like home!'
>
> *- Captain Rock of the Catachan III 'Green Devils' commenting on Varestus Prime*

TACTICAL OBJECTIVES

The Astra Militarum is made up of a wide array of regiments, able to turn its hand to the completion of almost any objective with the correct application of the vast resources it has available.

If your army is led by an **ASTRA MILITARUM** Warlord, these Tactical Objectives replace the Capture and Control Tactical Objectives (numbers 11-16) in the *Warhammer 40,000* rulebook. If a mission uses Tactical Objectives, players use the normal rules for using Tactical Objectives with the following exception: when an Astra Militarum player generates a Capture and Control objective (numbers 11-16), they instead generate the corresponding Astra Militarum Tactical Objective, as shown below. Other Tactical Objectives (numbers 21-66) are generated normally.

D66	TACTICAL OBJECTIVE
11	Overkill
12	Regimental Pride
13	Chain of Command
14	Troops on the Ground
15	Hammer of the Emperor
16	Death from Afar

---

11 — OVERKILL — *Astra Militarum*

The tanks of the Imperial Guard are thunderous in their wrath. Their every kill is a statement of superior firepower.

Score 1 victory point if an **ASTRA MILITARUM VEHICLE** unit from your army destroyed an enemy unit during this turn. If an **ASTRA MILITARUM TITANIC VEHICLE** unit from your army destroyed an enemy unit during this turn, score D3 victory points instead.

---

12 — REGIMENTAL PRIDE — *Astra Militarum*

Each regiment has a long and storied history of battle lore – those added to the annals of fame due to exceptional acts of valour are counted amongst the finest of heroes.

Score 1 victory point if an enemy **CHARACTER** was slain as a result of an attack made by one of your **<REGIMENT> CHARACTERS** during this turn.

---

13 — CHAIN OF COMMAND — *Astra Militarum*

The central nervous system of the Astra Militarum is its command structure – those who efficiently coordinate their platoons through decisive and well-timed commands can clinch a lasting victory.

Score 1 victory point if you issued 3-5 different orders or tank orders this turn. If you issued 6 or more different orders or tank orders this turn, score D3 victory points instead.

---

14 — TROOPS ON THE GROUND — *Astra Militarum*

The endless ranks of the Astra Militarum come into their own when deployed en masse – when several platoons march forth to claim the field as one, there are few foes that can wrest it from their grip.

Score D3 victory points if you control 3-5 objective markers with **INFANTRY** units. If you control all 6 objective markers with **INFANTRY** units, score D3+3 victory points instead.

---

15 — HAMMER OF THE EMPEROR — *Astra Militarum*

The sledgehammer force of an Imperial Guard assault can blast an enemy from a defended position in the matter of a few heartbeats. Those that witness such brute force cannot help but be in awe.

Score 1 victory point if you destroyed an enemy unit that was controlling an objective marker at the start of the turn.

---

16 — DEATH FROM AFAR — *Astra Militarum*

Many a battle has been won from extreme range; those foes that lurk out of the reach of the rank-and-file are brought to a violent end by heavy weapons, turret guns and mobile artillery.

Score 1 victory point if an enemy unit that was wholly within their deployment zone at the start of the turn was destroyed by a unit wholly within your deployment zone during this turn.